"This book is a simply great idea."
--Santa Cruz Sentinel

"The guide presents an opportunity for families to explore some of the state's little-known towns."
--Los Angeles Times

"The final word on celebrations in our state is California Festivals."
--The Montclarion

". . . delivers some slightly wacky information in a highly useful way."
--National Motorist

". . . the book is a godsend for those of us who enjoy weekend car trips, and a great holiday gift for anyone who's a lover of offbeat travel."
--KCET Magazine, Southern California Public Television Station

"Connoisseurs of California take note . . ."
--Bon Appétit

Third Edition

Carl and Katie Landau
with Kathy Kincade

Your Guided Tour to Over 300 California Festivals

Landau Communications • San Francisco, California

Third Edition

Your Guided Tour to Over 300 California Festivals

Published by Landau Communications
1032 Irving Street
Suite 604
San Francisco, California 94122
(415) 564-5689

Copyright © 1992 by Carl and Katie Landau

All rights reserved. No part of this book may be reproduced or transmitted in any form or by any means electronic or mechanical, including photocopying, recording, or by any information storage and retrieval system without written permission from the author, except for the inclusion of brief quotations in a review.

The information in this book was supplied in large part by the festivals themselves, and is therefore subject to change without notice. We strongly recommend that you call ahead and always verify the information in this book before making your plans. We cannot be held responsible in the event that any information listed here is incorrect.

Editor: Kathy Kincade
Associate Editor: Alan Byers
Researcher: Len Fecko
Cover Design and Illustration: Linda Byrne, Steve Rank Inc. Concord, California
Production: Kristen Avery
Back cover photography credits: Sherrie Fearis (pumpkin patch), Chris Irwin (La Mesa Oktoberfest), Santa Cruz Beach Boardwalk (Brussels Sprout Harvest Festival), Ashton Graham (Old Spanish Days), Francis Clement (Carnaval San Francisco), Mary Lou Johnson (Balloons).
Publishers: Carl Landau and Steve Rank

Library of Congress Cataloging-in-Publication Data

Landau, Carl, 1956-
   California festivals: your guided tour to over 300 California festivals / Carl and Katie Landau with Kathy Kincade. -- 3rd ed.
     p. cm.
   ISBN 0-929881-13-3: $11.95

   1. Festivals--California--Guide-books. 2. California--Social life and customs--Guide-books. 3. California--Description and travel--1981--Guide-books. I. Landau, Katie, 1960-. II. Kincade, Kathy, 1960-. III. Title
   GT4810. C2L36 1991
   394.2'09794--dc20   91-21299
                                                           CIP

Printed in the United States of America   Third Edition

California Festivals

Acknowledgments

Trying to cover over 300 festivals in a state the size of California is not an easy task. But thanks to the help and goodwill of the following people, we managed to pull it off. Many thanks to our distinguished Editorial Board of Directors, our dedicated California Festivals Reporters, and to everyone else for putting up with us: Odilia Araujo, Gail Berkley, Bruce Bostrom, Brian Chabowski, Erin Colin, Charlie Cunningham, Tom Dorsaneo, Ellen Faustine, Jonathan Faustine, Donald Fearis, Sherrie Fearis, The Firm, Sandy Fletcher, David Hamamoto, J.D. Hildebrand, Kelly Keller, Leonel Martinez, Kristina Maguire, Susan McDonald, Andy Mickus, Miller Freeman Publications, Nancy Priewe, Dan Poynter, Petek Rank, Vince Ridley, Joe Stevens, Gary Warth, Mark Larson, Michael Wilbert, Sol Morrison and all those thankless festival volunteers who make the festivals possible.

Special thanks to...
Steve Rank, for persistently nagging us about doing this project, Linda Byrne for designing a fabulous cover, and Kristen Avery for her wizardry on the MacIntosh.

Kim Johnson, for her enthusiasm and willingness to do anything (even eat slugs).

Regina Starr Ridley, for doing all the thankless jobs with kindness.

Liz Swain, a great writer and one of the nicest people in the world, who superbly covered much of Southern California for us.

Mary Lou and Doug Johnson, our star reporters, who started covering festivals for us before we had a clue about how to put this book together.

Alan Byers, for his dedication in updating the book and being an all-around good guy.

Finally, thanks to two people who are as equally responsible for producing this book as we are. Len Fecko, a great friend who went way beyond the call of duty talking to festival directors on the phone for months and attending many festivals. And Kathy Kincade, who edited the entire book, wrote much of it, and held our hand. She's a very talented writer and a loyal friend.

California Festivals

For Our Parents

California Festivals

Contents

What is a festival? i

Festivals in this Book 11

Calendar of Festivals 19
   Information Key 19
    January 21
    February 23
    March 31
    April 43
    May 59
    June 95
    July 119
    August 137
    September 163
    October 199
    November 229
    December 233

Map of Festival Regions 240

Festivals by Region 241
   Central Coast, Central Valley, Deserts, Gold Country, High Sierra, Inland Empire, Greater Los Angles Area, North Coast, Orange County, San Diego County, San Francisco Bay Area, Shasta-Cascade

Festivals by Theme 257
   Agriculture, Arts & Crafts, Community, Ethnic Events, Film & Theatre, Food & Wine, Historical, Hot-Air Balloons, Marine & Aquatic, Music & Dance, Western Gold Rush

Yearly Calenders 266

California Festivals

California Festivals

What is a festival?

What is a festival? Ever since we started working on this book, we've tried to come up with a clear, concise definition of what constitutes a festival and what does not. Our first editorial directors' meeting practically turned into a riot. No one could agree on the criteria for festivals. The only thing we could agree on is that the definition of a festival is totally subjective.

Once we realized that even a group of 10 well-educated and normally civilized human beings could not agree on the criteria, we decided democracy was not the way to go and came up with the Landau Rule of Festivals. In this scheme, the key ingredient to a good festival is a central theme, which usually is followed through with the festival's music, food, and entertainment.

An example of a great festival is the Banana Slug Derby in Orick. The day begins with a parade, followed by the crowning of the Banana Slug Queen and the singing of the Banana Slug anthem. You can bring your own slug or rent one at the park for anyone who wishes to participate in the "sticky" competition. Competitors are grouped into three categories: adults, children and government agencies, and the slugs go head to head in a race for the coveted "Top Banana" award. After the derby even the fastest slug is returned to its home in the forest so it can continue to munch on plants and return nutrients to the soil. Now that's a festival!

What is not a festival? Merchants getting together with the primary intent of selling stuff and making money. Also, fairs are not festivals. If you see a kid buying a ticket to a ride that turns him upside down, you're not at a festival. Of course, you'll find countless examples all through this book of festivals that contradict the Landau Rule of Festivals. Hey, it's our book, and we made up the rules!

If you find that one of your favorite festivals is missing, just drop us a note. We've done an incredible amount of research to come up with these 300+ festivals, but California is a huge state and we're sure a few good ones are missing. Plus, new festivals are starting up all the time. Just contact us at Landau Communications and we will try to include your suggestions in our next edition.

California Festivals

Tips on using California Festivals

We've tried our best to make this book easy and useful to use. Note that the book is cross-referenced alphabetically, chronologically, and geographically and by themes. The main section of the book is the "Calendar of Festivals." In this section, all festivals are listed by the month they are held. Within each month the festivals are listed alphabetically. Is this confusing enough?

We've included the annual date or approximate time of month the festivals are held each year. About 90% of the time the festivals will keep to these dates. But we recommend that you call ahead before making your plans. Heed and be warned: festival dates have been known to change, so be sure to doublecheck dates before packing the car.

Have fun

Eleven million people will be attending California festivals this year. The rich traditions and diversity of California are reflected in the variety of festivals covered in this book. The important thing is to get out there and explore this beautiful state and its people.

And have fun!

—**Carl and Katie Landau**

California Festivals

Festivals Covered in this Book

Festival	City	PageNo.
A la carte, a la park	San Francisco	163
Adobe Tour	Monterey	43
African Cultural Festival	Oakland	31
Almond Blossom Festival	Ripon	23
Alpenfest	Mount Shasta	24
Anderson Marsh Blackberry Festival	Lower Lake	137
Annual Italian Benevolent Society Picnic and Parade	Sutter Creek	95
Annie & Mary Day Fair	Blue Lake	138
Apple Blossom Festival	Sebastopol	43
Apple Festival	Templeton	164
Apple Valley Days	Apple Valley	199
Arcata's Fourth of July Celebration	Arcata	119
Art & Wine Festival	Walnut Creek	95
Arvin Wildflower Festival	Arvin	44
Atwater Fall Festival	Atwater	164
Auburn Craft & Christmas Marketplace	Auburn	229
Balloons Over the Valley Hot Air Balloon Festival	Modesto	165
Banana Slug Derby	Orick	139
Bay-to-Burgers	San Francisco	166
Bay Area Cajun & Zydeco Festival	San Rafael	166
Beach Street Revival	Santa Cruz	199
Berryessa Art & Wine Festival	San Jose	59
Bidwell Bar Day	Oroville	59
Big Bear Lake Oktoberfest	Big Bear Lake	167
Big Time Indian Days	Pine Grove	168
Bigfoot Daze	Willow Creek	168
Bodega Bay Fisherman's Festival	Bodega Bay	45
Bok Kai Festival	Marysville	32
Brawley Cattle Call	Brawley	229
Brownsville Mountain Fair	Brownsville	168
Brussels Sprout and Italian Heritage Festival	Santa Cruz	200
Butter and Egg Day Parade	Petaluma	46
Cajun Crawfish Festival	Fairfield	60
Calico Days	Barstow	201
Calico Fine Arts Festival	Barstow	230
Calico Hullabaloo	Barstow	32
Calico Spring Festival	Barstow	61
California Avocado Festival	Carpinteria	201
California Dry Bean Festival	Tracy	140
California Festival of Beers	San Luis Obispo	61
California Prune Festival	Yuba City	169

11

California Festivals

California Rodeo Salinas	Salinas	119
California Strawberry Festival	Oxnard	62
California Wine Exposition	Redondo Beach	62
Calistoga Beer & Sausage Fest	Calistoga	202
Campbell Highland Games	Campbell	203
Capitola Art and Wine Festial	Capitola	170
Capitola National Begonia Festival	Capitola	170
Carlsbad Village Faire	Carlsbad	63,230
Carmel Bach Festival	Carmel	120
Carnaval San Francisco	San Francisco	96
Castroville Artichoke Festival	Castroville	171
Ceres Western Art Show & Sale	Ceres	205
Cherries Jubilee	Placerville	97
Cherry Blossom Festival	San Francisco	46
Cherry Festival	Linden	97
Cherry Festival Beaumont	Beaumont	97
Chinese New Year Food and Cultural Faire	Del Mar	25
Chocolate Lovers Fantasy Faire	S. Lake Tahoe	63
Christmas on the Prado	San Diego	233
Christmas Walk	Corona del Mar	234
Cinco de Mayo	Borrego Springs	64
Cinco de Mayo Fiesta and Art Fair	El Monte	64
Cinco de Mayo Kermesse	Lamont	65
Cinco de Mayo— San Diego	San Diego	66
Clam Chowder Cook-Off and Chowder Chase	Santa Cruz	24
Clam Festival	Pismo Beach	203
Cloverdale Citrus Fair	Cloverdale	26
Coalinga Horned Toad Derby	Coalinga	66
Colony Days Celebration	Atascadero	204
Columbia Diggin's	Columbia	98
Columbus Day Celebration	San Francisco	204
Concord Fall Fest	Concord	171
Cotati Indian Festival	Cotati	205
Cotton Harvest Festival	Buttonwillow	172
Coulterville Coyote Howling	Coulterville	67
Currier and Ives Christmas Open House	Sutter Creek	234
Danish Days	Solvang	172
Davis Street Faire	Davis	98
Delicato Charity Grape Stomp	Manteca	172
Denver Dan's Apple Bake Off	Camino	174
Desert Festival	Borrego Springs	206
Dinuba Raisin Festival	Dinuba	174
Dixieland Monterey	Monterey	33
Dixon Lambtown Festival	Dixon	141
Dolbeer Steam Donkey Days	Eureka	47
East Palo Alto Juneteenth Festival	East Palo Alto	99
Easter in July Lily Festival	Smith River	120
Eastfield Ming Quong Strawberry Festival	Los Gotos	99

California Festivals

Festival	Location	Page
East West Orchid Show	Los Angeles	206
Egyptian Festival	Hayward	175
Encinitas Flower Festival	Encinitas	100
Escondido Harvest Festival	Escondido	207
Exeter Fall Festival	Exeter	208
Fall Festival	Desert Hot Springs	208
Fall Festival	Castro Valley	175
Fall Festival of Wines	Gardena Valley	208
Fall Fun Fest	Seaside	209
Feather River Railroad Days	Portola	141
Festival Red Bluff	Red Bluff	100
Festival at the Lake	Oakland	101
Festival of Cultures	Merced	210
Festival of Greece	Oakland	67
Festival of the Springs	Desert Hot Springs	48
Field and Fair Day	Lodi	176
Fiesta de las Artes	Hermosa Beach	68, 176
Fiesta del Sol	Solana Beach	68
Fiesta Italiana	Santa Barbara	209
Fiesta La Ballona	Culver City	69
Fiestas Patrias Celebrations	San Jose	70, 177
Fishermen's Fiesta	San Pedro	210
For Our Children Food & Wine Festival	Redondo Beach	26
Fort Bragg Beer Fest	Fort Bragg	33
Fort Ross VFD Summer Music Festival	Fort Ross	101
Fourth of July—Exeter	Exeter	121
Fourth of July	Bridgeport	121
Fourth of July Celebration	Crescent City	122
Fourth of July Festival	Martinez	122
Frontier Christmas	Oroville	235
Frontier Days	Canyon Country	211
Frontier Days—Lake Elsinore Valley	Lake Elsinore Valley	70
Gasquet Raft Races	Crescent City	122
Gilroy Garlic Festival	Gilroy	123
Gilroy Hispanic Culture Festival	Gilroy	142
Gladiola Festival	Union City	143
Gold Nugget Days	Paradise	48
Goleta Valley Days	Goleta	211
Gourmet Food and Wine Tasting Festival	Torrance	143
Grape Bowl Festival	Sanger	177
Grape Harvest Festival	Rancho Cucamonga	212
Gravenstein Apple Fair	Sebastopol	144
Great Halloween and Pumpkin Festival	San Francisco	212
Great Monterey Squid Festival	Monterey	71
Great Potato Harvest Festival	Somerset	162
Great Sutter Creek Duck Race	Sutter Creek	49
Greek Festival	Cardiff	178

California Festivals

Festival	Location	Page
Greek Food Festival	Modesto	179
Greenfield Broccoli Festival	Greenfield	179
Grubstake Days	Yucca Valley	72
Gunfighter's Rendevous	Coulterville	180
Half Moon Bay Art & Pumpkin Festival	Half Moon Bay	212
Hangtown Dixieland Jazz Jubilee	Placerville	213
Harbor Days	Oceanside	214
Harvest Craft Faire	Rocklin	214
Harvest Festival	Carmel	215
Hayward Art and Wine Festival	Hayward	144
Hayward Zucchini Festival	Hayward	145
Health & Harmony Music and Arts Festival	Santa Rosa	102
Heritage Festival	San Juan Capistrano	34
Hilmar Dairy Festival	Hilmar	103
Holtville Annual Carrot Festival	Holtville	21
Hometown Festival	Greater Ukiah	72
Huck Finn Jubilee	Victorville	104
Hughson Fruit & Nut Festival	Hughson	73
Humboldt Folklife Festival	Arcata	104
Imperial Sweet Onion Festival	Imperial City	74
I Madonnari Italian St. Painting Festival	Santa Barbara	73
International Beer and Food Festival	San Francisco	124
International Calamari Festival	Santa Cruz	146
International Percussion Explosion	Oakland	147
Isleton Crawdad Festival	Isleton	105
Italian American Cultural Festival	San Jose	215
Jackass Mail Run	Porterville	50
Jazz And All That Art On Fillmore	San Francisco	125
Jazz on the Lake	Garberville	106
Jazz on the Waterfront	Stockton	180
Jazzaffair	Three Rivers	50
Johnny Appleseed Day	Paradise	215
Julian Fall Apple Harvest Festival	Julian	216
July 4th Celebration	Lemoore	125
July 4th Independence Celebration	Modesto	126
Jumping Frog Jubilee	Angels Camp	74
Juneteenth	Berkeley	106
KQED Wine and Food Festival	San Francisco	51
Kingsburg Swedish Festival	Kingsburg	75
Klamath Salmon Festival	Klamath	107
Konocti Winery Harvest Festival	Kelseyville	217
La Fiesta de San Luis Obispo	San Luis Obispo	76
La Habra Corn Festival	La Habra	148
La Jolla Festival of the Arts	La Jolla	107
La Mesa Oktoberfest	La Mesa	217
La Quinta Arts Festival	La Quinta	35
Lakeport Revival on Clear Lake	Lakeport	108
Lake Tahoe Kokanee Salmon Festival	S. Lake Tahoe	218
Lake Tahoe Starlight Jazz Festival	S. Lake Tahoe	148

California Festivals

Lakeside Chili Cook-Off	Lakeside	181
Lamb Derby Festival	Willows	76
Lemon Grove Old Time Days	Lemon Grove	77
Lilac Festival	Palmdale	52
Linda Vista Multicultural Fair	San Diego	181
Living History Days	Petaluma	77
Living History Days	San Jose	108
Lodi Grape Festival & National Wine Show	Lodi	182
Lompoc Valley Flower Festival	Lompoc	109
Long Beach Lesbian and Gay Pride Celebration	Long Beach	78
Los Angeles Classic Jazz Festival	Los Angeles	182
Mariposa County Storytelling Festival	Mariposa	35
Manteca Pumpkin Fair	Manteca	218
May Festival	Fillmore	78
Mendocino Christmas Festival	Mendocino	235
Mendocino Music Festival	Mendocino	126
Mendocino Whale Festival	Mendocino	36
Millbrae Art & Wine Festival	Millbrae	183
Mission Christmas Faire	Oceanside	236
Monrovia Days	Monrovia	79
Monterey Jazz Festival	Monterey	183
Morgan Hill Mushroom Mardi Gras	Morgan Hill	79
Morro Bay Harbor Festival	Morro Bay	219
Mother Lode Dixieland Jazz Benefit	Jackson	52
Motherlode Scots Festival of Lights	Volcano	236
Mountain View Art and Wine Festival	Mountain View	184
Mozart Festival	San Luis Obispo	127
Mule Days Celebration	Bishop	80
Music at Sand Harbor	Tahoe City	128
Nation's Christmas Tree Festival	Sanger	237
Newark Days Celebration	Newark	186
New York Landing Seafood Festival	Pittsburg	186
Newman Fall Festival	Newman	185
Newport Beach Salute to the Arts	Newport Beach	81
Nisei Week Japanese Festival	Los Angeles	149
North Beach Fair	San Francisco	110
North Lake Tahoe Chocolate Festival	Northstar	184
North Monterey County Strawberry Festival	Watsonville	110
Novato Art and Wine Festival	Novato	111
Nut Tree Pumpkin Patch & Scarecrow Contest	Vacaville	219
Oakland Chinatown Street Festival	Oakland	150
Ojai Music Festival	Ojai	111
Oktoberfest	Montrose	220

California Festivals

Old Adobe Fiesta	Petaluma	150
Old-Fashioned Ice Cream Social & Tasting	San Francisco	187
Old Miner's Days	Big Bear Lake	128
Old Spanish Days Fiesta	Santa Barbara	151
Orange County Fiesta Days	Fountain Valley	129
Pacific Beach Block Party	San Diego	81
Pacific Coast Collegiate Jazz Festival	Berkeley	53
Pacific Coast Fog Fest	Pacifica	188
Pacific States Craft Fair	San Francisco	152
Palo Alto Celebrates the Arts	Palo Alto	153
Pan American Festival	Lakewood	82
Parade of Lights	Oxnard	237
Park Street Art and Wine Faire	Alameda	153
Patterson Apricot Fiesta	Patterson	82
Peach Festival and Annual Rickshaw Race	Willow Creek	188
Pear Fair	Courtland	130
Petaluma River Festival	Petaluma	154
Picnic Day	Davis	53
Pilgrim Festival	Claremont	231
Pioneer Days	Artesia	220
Pioneer Days	Tweny-nine Palms	221
Poway Days	Poway	189
Prunefestival Wine and Arts	Campbell	83
Railroad Days	Dunsmuir	112
Raisin Festival	Selma	83
Rancho California Balloon & Wine Festival	Temecula	84
Red Suspenders Days	Gridley	85
Reedley Fiesta	Reedley	222
Reggae on the River	Garberville	155
Renaissance of Kings Cultural Arts Faire	Hanford	222
Renaissance Pleasure Faire	Novato	156
Rhododendron Festival	Eureka	54
Riverbank's Cheese and Wine Exposition	Riverbank	223
Riverside County Fair and National Date Festival	Indio	27
Rocklin Jubilee	Rocklin	112
Round Valley Blackberry Festival	Covelo	157
Russian River Jazz Festival	Guerneville	189
Russian River Wine Festival	Healdsburg	85
Sacramento Camellia Festival	Sacramento	36
Sacramento Dixieland Jubilee	Sacramento	86
Salsa Tasting & Music Festival	Fresno	158
San Anselmo Art and Wine Festival	San Anselmo	113
San Diego St. Patrick's Day Annual Parade	San Diego	37
San Dimas Festival of Western Art	San Dimas	54

California Festivals

San Fernando Fiesta	San Fernando	87
San Francisco Examiner Bay to Breakers—Footstock	San Francisco	87
San Francisco International Film Festival	San Francisco	38
San Luis Obispo Mardi Gras	San Luis Obispo	28
San Marcos Chili Cook-Off	San Marcos	113
Sandcastle Days	Imperial Beach	130
Santa Barbara Arts Festival	Santa Barbara	55
Santa Barbara International Film Festival	Santa Barbara	39
Santa Clara Art & Wine Festival	Santa Clara	190
Santa Cruz Spring Fair	Santa Cruz	88
Santa Lucia Festival of Lights	Kingsburg	238
Santa Rosalia Festival	Monterey	190
Saratoga Blossom Festival	Saratoga	114
Sausalito Art Festival	Sausalito	191
Sawdust Festival	Laguna Beach	131
Scandinavian Festival	Thousand Oaks	56
Scandinavian Midsummer Festival	Ferndale	114
Seafood Festival	Crescent City	191
Secession Day	Rough & Ready	115
Semana Nautica	Santa Barbara	132
Serbian Festival	San Diego	192
Shafter Potato 'n Cotton Festival	Shafter	89
Shakespeare at Sand Harbor	North Tahoe	158
Shasta Dixieland Jazz Festival	Redding	39
Sierra Madre Art Fair	Sierra Madre	89
Sierra Showcase of Wine	Plymouth	90
Silverado Days	Buena Park	223
Sixteenth of September Fiesta	Calexico	193
Snowfest Winter Carnival	Tahoe City	40
Somethin's Brewing: A Fine Beer Tasting	Santa Rosa	159
Sonoma's "Salute to the Arts"	Sonoma	133
Sonoma Summer Arts Festival	Sonoma	160
Sonora Celtic Celebration	Sonora	41
Sonora Christmas Festival	Sonora	231
Spirit of Christmas Crafts Faire & Celebration	Santa Rosa	238
Spring Wine Festival	Gilroy	90
Springville Apple Festival	Springville	224
Stagecoach Days	Banning	224
Stockton Asparagus Festival	Stockton	57
Strawberry Festival	Arroyo Grande	91
Strawberry Festival	Garden Grove	91
Summer Arts Festival	Garberville	116
Sunnyvale Art and Wine Festival	Sunnyvale	117
Sunset Junction Street Faire	Los Angeles	160
Swedish Crayfish Festival	Kingsburg	161
Tapestry In Talent	San Jose	134
Taste of San Mateo	San Mateo	193

17

California Festivals

Festival	City	Page
Tehachapi Mountain Festival	Tehachapi	161
Tet Vietnamese New Year Festival	San Jose	22
Tuolumne County Wild West Film Fest	Sonora	194
Twenty Mule Team Days	Boron	225
Union Street Spring Festival Arts and Crafts Fair	San Francisco	117
Vacaville Fiesta Days	Vacaville	92
Vacaville Onion Festival	Vacaville	194
Valley of the Moon	Sonoma	195
Village Venture Street Faire	Claremont	225
Walnut Festival	Walnut Creek	195
Wasco Festival of Roses	Wasco	196
Waterford Western Heritage Day	Waterford	226
Weaverville Fourth of July	Weaverville	134
Weed Carnevale	Weed	118
Weihnachtsmarkt	Carmel	239
Western Days	San Dimas	226
Whaleboat Regatta	Vallejo	227
Whole Earth Festival	Davis	92
Whiskey Flat Days	Kernville	29
Wild Game Barbecue	San Luis Obispo	196
Wildwood Days	Rio Dell	162
Windsor Laff-Off	Windsor	93
Wine & Food Renaissance	Lakeport	118
WINESONG!	Fort Bragg	197
Winterfest	Laguna Beach	30
World Championship Crab Races	Crescent City	30
Ye Olde English Faire	San Marcos	227
Zucchini Festival	Angels Camp	198

California Festivals

Calendar of Festivals

The main section of this book, the Calendar of Festivals, is broken out month by month. For easy reference, each month is in alphabetical order by festival.

> NOTE: Festival dates have been known to change at the last minute. We recommend calling ahead to confirm dates, times, and directions.

Information Key

Festival name

Castroville Artichoke Festival

City — Castroville   (408) 633-2726 — *Festival phone no.*

Annual date — **Third weekend in September (Saturday and Sunday).** *Days held*   **50,000.** — *Attendance*

Years held — **32 years. Adults $2. Children free. Community Center. Hwy. 1 to Hwy. 183 to Castroville.**

Location   *Admission fee*   *Directions*

19

California Festivals   January

Holtville Annual Carrot Festival
Holtville   (619) 356-2923

Begins third Saturday in January (Nine days). 1,000. 45 years. Free (fee for some events). Holtville, 129 miles east of San Diego on I-8. 49 miles west of Yuma, Arizona.

So maybe you didn't like them much when you were a kid, but your mom made you eat 'em anyway. Now that you have such great eyesight, aren't you glad she did? Well, at least the folks in Holtville are, because carrots are how many of them make their living. Yes, carrots are big in the "Carrot Capital of the World"—more carrots are shipped from this area than anywhere else.

But there's a lot more than just carrots out there in the Imperial Valley, especially during the Carrot Festival. This week-long event features a horseshow and a 4-H and FFA livestock show the first weekend, plus a carnival that lasts all week lon, children's games and a petting zoo. After going on all those great rides, you can check out the carrot recipe contest (ever tried carrot ice cream?). The second weekend there's a 10K run, a parade, an art show, a tractor pull, and more of the carnival. And throughout the festival, you can support local churches and organizations by visiting the many food booths (Mexican, hot dogs and hamburgers, etc.) scattered around the site.

With all those carrots around, you may even see a silly wabbit or two.

California Festivals   January

Tet Vietnamese New Year Festival
San Jose   (408) 295-9210, (408) 971-7861

Late January, early February. 50,000. 9 years. Adults $5, children $2. Santa Clara County Fairgrounds. From Hwy. 101 in San Jose, take Tully Rd. exit west. Go 1 mile. You'll see big signs all the way.

"Tet," as the Vietnamese call it, is the shortened form of Tet Nguyen Dan, meaning the Feast of the First Day. It is the most important and picturesque holiday in Vietnam, like our Thanksgiving, Christmas, and New Year's combined. For the Vietnamese, the holiday celebrates the new year, the birth of Spring, and the promise of the future, which they honor as gifts from Heaven and Earth. Traditionally the celebration begins on the first day of the first month of the lunar year and continues for several days. It is a festival of sounds, colors, and perfumes. The air is filled with the popping of firecrackers and the smell of incense, exotic foods, and sweet flowers. Many centuries-old traditions are respected and carried out.

During the San Jose Tet Festival, you can explore the Vietnamese culture through crafts, fine arts, photography, and community exhibitions. There is also an international table tennis tournament, martial arts open championships, cultural music shows, the Miss Tet pageant, the Freedom Torch Run, volleyball and soccer tournaments, a cultural quiz featuring poetry and sentence construction, a photography contest, a student variety show, a fashion show, and dances both Friday and Saturday nights.

Last but not least, this festival features food from 40 Vietnamese restaurants, including barbecued meats, noodle soups, salads, sandwiches, and rice dishes. (Don't hesitate to ask for an explanation of something on the the menu since it most likely won't be written in English.)

California Festivals — February

Almond Blossom Festival
Ripon   (209) 599-7519

Last week in February (Thursday-Saturday). 50,000. 30 years. Free. Community Center and downtown Ripon. 20 miles south of Stockton and 3 miles north of Modesto on Hwy. 99.

Though it may be primarily a local community event, some 50,000 people attended Ripon's Almond Blossom Festival —quite a crowd for a town where, when we asked for directions, we were told "you can't get lost in Ripon." This three-day festival not only pays tribute to the lovely almond blossom—at its most abundant and beautiful in late February and early March—but also honors local arts and crafts, industry, and city services and recognizes Ripon's namesake cities in England and Wisconsin.

One of the festival's biggest highlights is the founder and "Godmother of South County," Mrs. C.F. Mulholland. She's been running the show for the last 29 years, almost as long as she's been the Chamber of Commerce secretary. She organized the festival back in the early 60s when almonds first started becoming popular. At that time, they sold for 10 cents a pound!

You'll see a little bit of history and a lot of almonds at Ripon's Almond Blossom Festival. (Photo courtesy of the Ripon Chamber of Commerce)

California Festivals   February

Alpenfest
Mount Shasta   (916) 926-4865
                (800) 427-0909 (CA only)

First weekend in February (Friday-Sunday). 5,000. 8 years. Free. Various locations in the city. 60 miles north of Redding on I-5, 65 miles south of Oregon.

Situated at the foot of majestic Mt. Shasta, this festival takes advantage of natural settings and traditional winter activities to celebrate winter and the beloved teddy bear. Among the many events are a winter carnival, snow sculpturing, ski races, a torchlight parade, a teddy bear parade, a yodel-off, and a giant teddy bear giveaway.

In keeping with the Alpenfest tradition, the featured food is German and the music is provided by an oompah-pah band.

The area around Mt. Shasta and nearby Mt. Lassen is a winter sports lover's paradise, with many areas for both downhill and cross-country skiing, plus snowmobiling and ice skating. And for you camera buffs, the scenery this time of year is nothing short of breath taking.

Clam Chowder Cook-Off and Chowder Chase
Santa Cruz   (408) 423-5590

Third weekend in February (Saturday-Sunday). 10,000. 10 years. Free; chowder tasting kits are $4. Santa Cruz Beach Boardwalk. Hwy. 1 or 17 into Santa Cruz, then follow the signs to the main beach. Santa Cruz is located 35 miles south of San Jose, 40 miles north of Monterey.

On a cool winter day, what tastes better than a bowl of steaming hot chowder? How about 80 bowls? At the Clam Chowder Cook-Off, over 80 teams compete along the Santa Cruz Beach Boardwalk to see who has the best Boston or Manhattan clam chowder, so you can "chowder taste" to your heart's content. The grand prize winners are treated to two round-trip tickets to (where else?) Boston or New York, and prizes are also given for the best booth and the most tasted chowder.

But some of the best entertainment is the teams themselves—the members dress up in tuxedos, clam outfits, even scuba gear, in an attempt to attract the most crowd attention and support. You'll also be entertained by the sights and sounds of the Boardwalk itself (people-watching at its best!).

California Festivals   February

The next day begins with the Chowder Chase, a 4.5 mile run through Santa Cruz. Just what you'll need to work up an appetite for all that great chowder.

Chinese New Year Food and Cultural Faire
Del Mar   (619) 234-4447

Early February (in conjunction with Chinese New Year). 14,000. 9 years. Adults $3, children under 12 free. Del Mar Fairgrounds. From I-5, take Via de la Valle west to Jimmy Durante Blvd., turn left.

San Diego may not have a China Town, but the county loves to help the 50,000-member Chinese community ring in the New Year. Close to 14,000 residents turn out for the Chinese New Year Food and Cultural Faire.

True to its name, the fair offers Chinese cuisine and culture in the form of entertainment, art displays, and wares sold at commercial booths. The two-day fair is a fundraiser for the San Diego Chinese Center, a nonprofit organization. There are performances by the Chinese Choral Society, exhibitions of regional dances, and displays of ancient Chinese costumes. The martial arts demonstration always draws a crowd, as do the Lucky Lion dancers, an ensemble of young men who dance to the beat of a drum while holding a long dragon costume over their heads. It's quite a balancing act!

The Chinese items for sale include exotic soaps, toys, gems, and rice paper books. There are booths with information on traveling to China, the Taoist sanctuary, and the future through psychic readings. Food items include won ton soup, sponge cake and butterflies, five-spice chicken, dim sum, and lo mein. In addition, American beer, ice cream, and soft drinks are sold.

Food and entertainment are combined in cooking demonstrations by celebrity chefs such as San Diego Charger and local media personalities. The audience gets to sample the food, and the recipes are in the free souvenir program, which also lists Chinese phrases that can add authenticity when cooking Chinese food at home. If a guest asks "Womenwanshang-jidian-zhong chi fan?" ("When are we having dinner?"), the host or hostess should answer, "Liangwei-man zou" ("Don't be in a hurry to leave").

Gung Hay Fat Choy! (Happy New Year!)   --L.S.

California Festivals   February

Cloverdale Citrus Fair
Cloverdale   (707) 894-3992

Presidents' Day weekend (Friday-Monday). 25,000. 100 years. Adults $4, chldren 7 and under and seniors $3. Cloverdale Citrus Fairgrounds. Hwy 101 to Cloverdale, follow signs to fairgrounds.

It's a "Centennial Celebration" at the Cloverdale Citrus Fair. This event has been of interest to people all over Northern California since its inception in 1892. This four-day fair features some mind-boggling, three-dimensional citrus displays. Each year a particular scene or object is glorified in citrus; past models have included castles, a Statue of Liberty, a pirate ship, and missions of California—fashioned from up to 90 dozen pieces of fruit reaching up to 18 feet tall.

Saturday's big events are a parade with local bands and a square dance. In addition, there's a citrus queen pageant, a gourmet food and wine show (featuring wines from Sonoma, Lake and Mendocino counties), as well as food booths for American, Dutch, Mexican and Italian fare. Music includes Dixieland, cajun, country/western and jazz.

For Our Children Food & Wine Festival
Redondo Beach   (213) 540-1222

First Sunday in February. 500. 6 years. $65. Parking lot of Chez Melange, 1716 Pacific Coast Hwy. Take I-110, exit onto Pacific Coast Hwy. (north). Chez Melange is on the right side of the road between Prospect and Palos Verdes Blvd.

There's nothing quite like guilt-free indulgence, which is what this festival offers: the chance to taste a wide variety of gourmet food and wine and in the process benefit three children's charities in the Los Angeles area. This one-day event lets you sample such delicacies as duck ravioli, smoked sweetbreads, bressiola (a dried Italian beef), and a tableful of truffles and desserts, plus a variety of California wines, all for $65 (the fee allows you to eat and drink as much as you want). The goal of this event (in addition to raising as much money as possible for the charities) is to provide a wide diversity of food and wine from as many restaurants as they can, with nearly 50 wineries and 60 restaurants participating. There's also music to eat by, with combos playing reggae and swing.

California Festivals										February

Riverside County Fair and National Date Festival
Indio   (619) 342-8247

Begins President's Day weekend (10 days). 270,000. 46 years. Adults $5, seniors (62 & above) $4, children 5-11 $2, Parking $2 350 Arabia St. Exit I-10 to Monroe, right (west) on Monroe past Hwy. 111 to Dr. Carreon Blvd., left on Carreon to Date Festival parking lot on Arabia.

Looking for a date? How about 10? Twenty? A thousand? You'll find all the dates you could ever want at this festival, which celebrates the end of the date harvest in the country's largest date-producing area. It's 10 days in the sunshine of the southern California desert. (Why do you think they have it during the winter?)

The theme of this event is Arabian Nights, and an Arabian Nights Pageant—featuring a different colorful story about Scheherazade each year with elaborate costumes, lighting, and songs—is presented every evening at an outdoor stage designed as an Arabian Nights Village. There's also a county-wide Queen Scheherazade Pageant and an Arabian Nights street parade, with floats, equestrian units, bands, and marching groups.

In honor of the festival's namesake, you'll find exotic exhibits of dates, along with citrus and other farm crops found in Riverside County. Other exhibits include fine art, photography, wood carving, gems and minerals, home arts, and flowers and plants. There's also a junior fair and livestock show, where local youths display their talents in industrial arts, agricultural mechanics, home arts, community services, floriculture, handicrafts, and mineralogy. The livestock show features an auction of the winning animals.

Not to be missed are the camel and ostrich races, where winning isn't everything—in fact, it often isn't anything. But it's easy to pick the losing jockies: they're the ones who are dumped shortly after the beginning of a race. You may not want to bet on these

How do, you take your camel, one hump or two? (Photos courtesy of Riverside County Fair and National Date Festival)

races, but you can bet (via satellite) on horse races at Santa Anita and Los Alamitos.

The festival also features live music (country/western, Spanish, rock and roll, and easy listening), a midway carnival with rides and games, and food booths with Mexican, Italian, Thai, Japanese, Chinese, Greek, and American food, cotton candy, cinnamon rolls, date shakes, and, of course, just plain ol' dates.

Indio is a family-oriented community that finds visitors coming for a short visit and deciding to buy a home here in desert country, 30 minutes from Palm Springs and the relaxing stars, five minutes from the polo matches, and about an hour and a half from Los Angeles. For those concerned with enjoying life, look again at this sweet fruit of kings and warriors of old - - more protein than an apple, a few more carbohydrates, and more fiber.--S.R.

There's nothing like a puppet show to bring out the smiles.

San Luis Obispo Mardi Gras
San Luis Obispo   (805) 541-2183

Saturday before Fat Tuesday. 14 years. Parade & Street Fair is free. Downtown San Luis Obispo. Hwy. 101 to San Luis Obispo.

If you've always dreamed of going to Mardi Gras but just couldn't find an easy or inexpensive way to get to New Orleans, look no further: they celebrate this carnival of carnivals right here in sunny California, in the town of San Luis Obispo.

This popular California version of New Orlean's finest, founded by some homesick Louisiana expatriots, features a daytime street fair, Gumbo cookoff and masked revelers and mini-floats in an evening parade where, in the Mardi Gras tradition, parade participants toss mementos, trinkets, and commemorative doubloons to parade watchers. The parade is followed by the Maskers Ball, where you're treated to costumes galore, Cajun and Creole food. And the music? Jazz, of course.

One of the festival's odd requirements is that only members of the Mystic Krewe may attend the ball. However, since the Mystic Krewe only meets once a year at Mardi Gras, anyone can be a member, so anyone can attend!

Whiskey Flat Days
Kernville   (619) 376-2629

Presidents' weekend (Friday-Monday). 50,000. 37 years. Fees vary with events. Downtown Kernville. 50 miles east of Bakersfield on Hwy. 178.

The folks in Kernville—just a three-hour drive from Los Angeles—say they've got the friendliest little town in the southern Sierras, with a great river (the Kern), a beautiful lake (Isabella), wonderful fishing, perfect weather, and a lot of history from the gold rush days. They also say they exaggerate just a little—but a visit to their Whiskey Flat Days is still "the greatest weekend you and your family will ever spend!"

This four-day event is packed full of parades and parties, races and rodeos, games and galas—something for every member of the family—and you can camp out or rough it in a hotel. Saturday features some of the biggest events: the Whiskey Flat Grand Parade, with floats, bands, horses—the works; a frogjumping contest; the Rodeo; a greased pig contest; and a performance of The Melodrama. Sunday features a pancake breakfast, more frog races, an art show, a costume contest, a beard-growing ("Whiskerino") contest, a tour of some of Kernville's oldest homes, and another performance of The Melodrama.

Other events throughout the festival are a pet parade; tours of the Old Bull Run Mine area, the Historical Society Museum, Keysville, and the old town site; an epitaph contest; a political rally for mayoral candidates; and booths of food, games, and arts and crafts. The food booths sell Indian tacos, pastrami sandwiches, barbecued beef, and more. There's continuous music, too, mostly country/western and bluegrass.

Whiskey Flat Days is a chance for the people of this mountain community to turn back the clock and relive the gold rush days of the 1860s, when Kernville was known as Whiskey Flat and its first building was a saloon. Why the name change? Apparently some of the local ladies didn't appreciate the notoriety.

California Festivals　　　　　　　　　　　　　February

Winterfest
Laguna Beach　　(714) 494-1018

Presidents' weekend (Saturday-Monday). 7,500. 26 years. $2-$3. 650 Laguna Canyon Rd. (Festival of Arts Grounds). I-405 or I-5 to Hwy. 133 (Laguna Fwy.), south 8 miles to festival.

　Primarily an art festival, the three-day Winterfest gives approximately 125 artists a chance to show and sell their work. It's also an opportunity to visit this lovely beach town, located about half way between Los Angeles and San Diego, and catch a few rays over the three-day weekend.

　In addition to the art festival there's also an art auction, the body-building championships (where else but on the beaches of Southern California?), and a winefest where you can taste many locally produced California wines. Concession stands feature a variety of food and refreshments, and there's even live music—mostly rock and roll.

　If you're looking for an excuse to slip away to the beach for a day or two this winter, this low-key community festival might be just the ticket.

World Championship Crab Races
Crescent City　　(707) 464-3174

Sunday of Presidents' weekend. 2,500. 27 years. $1 at the door, $3 to race a crab. Del Norte County Fairgrounds. Take Hwy. 101 to Crescent City—fairgrounds are directly off the freeway.

　The local Chamber of Commerce heralds Crescent City as the place "where the redwoods meet the sea." It's a beautiful part of the Northern California coast, and the site of one of the more interesting sporting events you'll ever find: crab races.

　Why crabs? Because it's crabbing season in this coastal community, and those little critters already have running on their minds. The 9- to 11-inch Dungeness crabs claw their way down a four-foot plywood raceway, urged on by their coaches. Trophies are awarded, and the Grand Champion gets the best prize of all: a free trip back to the city's harbor, where it is ceremoniously set free. The races stem from an old fishing custom: after a day of crabbing, local fishermen would return to port and select their liveliest catch of the day to race within a chalked circle.

　If you've got a pet crab, bring him along. Anyone is eligible to enter, and drug testing is not mandatory. If your favorite crab has recently gone to that big crab pot in the sky, don't worry—crabs can be rented and entered the day of the race. Whether you participate or not, don't miss the huge crab feed at the end of the day, where you can claw your way through about 3,000 pounds of fresh cracked crab, plus cole slaw, garlic bread, and—for those not too seaworthy—hot dogs.

African Cultural Festival
Oakland (510) 763-3962

Last weekend in February/ early March. (Friday and Saturday). 1,900. 9 years. $12 in advance, $14 at the door, children under 12 and seniors $8. Henry J. Kaiser Convention Center. I-880 to Oak St. exit. Follow Oak St. to 10th St. Turn left to Fallon.

Northern California's African Cultural Festival, popularly known as "The Africans are Coming," is the largest professional African cultural event in the U.S. For many visitors it is their first exposure to professional African cultural arts theater. The thrills include a production staged by the Mandeleo Institute and executed by a cast of over 125 performers drawn from five renowned and culturally diverse sub-Saharan repertory companies.

The African Cultural Festival is sponsored by the Mandeleo Institute, an Oakland-based, nonprofit African Heritage Coalition dedicated to the preservation, education and promotion of African Cultural Arts. The Mandeleo Institute is also the largest multicultural presenter in California committed to a rediscovery of the ties between Africans born on the Continent and Africans born in the Americas.

This is your chance to see authentic sub-Saharan costumes and dancing. (Photo by Henry Wade)

Bok Kai Festival
Marysville   (916) 742-2787

Early March (Saturday and Sunday). 20,000. 1993 will be the 112th year. Free. Downtown Marysville between First St. and C St. Located 45 miles north of Sacramento on Hwy. 70 and Hwy. 65. And from the North State HWY 20 and 99

This cultural event is organized and celebrated by the entire community, not just the Chinese. The parade, featuring floats, marching bands, equestrian groups, and antique vehicles, flows through town, accompanied by the crackling of firecrackers. The grand finale is a weaving, undulating 150-foot dragon, manned by 75 enthusiastic dragon dancers.

In addition to the parade, there are cultural exhibits (past festivals have featured clever dragon sculptures by local students and charming watercolors by children from Taiwan), footraces, lion dancing, martial arts demonstrations kite flying in Riverfront Park, and a "wok a mile" event. The festival's exciting conclusion is the bomb firing. Roughly 100 bombs resembling huge firecrackers explode in the air, scattering rings to be retrieved for good luck.

The Bok Kai Festival is enjoyable for both children and adults. There's plenty of great food (Chinese and other) at the many restaurants in the area, plus shops and services. The beauty of the northern Sacramento Valley in early Spring is worth the trip alone. —D.J. and M.J.

Calico Hullabaloo
Barstow   (619) 254-2122

Palm Sunday weekend (Saturday and Sunday). 10,000. 16 years. Adults $5, juniors $2, children 5 and under free. Camping $9. Calico Ghost Town. Take I-15, go 10 miles north of Barstow, take the Ghost Town Rd. exit.

Get a taste of the Old West during these three days of stew cooking, flapjack racing, and horseshoe pitching, plus the World Tobacco Spitting Championships, reenacted gunfights, and campfire programs (camping is available for $9 per night).

You can join in or remain an innocent bystander, but don't miss the country and bluegrass concert or some of the fine country cooking, including miner's stew, chicken-fried steak, and ice cream. You can also visit some old-time saloons for a mug of beer or glass of wine. It's a chance to learn about silver mining in a real ghost town.

California Festivals — March

It's no-holds-barred at the World Tobacco Spitting Championships during the Calico Hullabaloo. (Photo courtesy of Barstow Area Chamber of Commerce)

Dixieland Monterey
Monterey   (408) 443-5260

First weekend in March (Friday-Sunday). 12 years. All-events badge: $35. Doubletree Inn. Downtown Monterey.

You can walk along Monterey's wharf and waterfront and hear some of the finest Dixieland bands from around the country play good ol' Dixieland jazz. Nearly 20 bands perform throughout the three days, and Saturday features a musical parade through old downtown Monterey, giving you a chance to view some of the city's historic buildings.

All cabaret music locations are within walking distance of one another, and performances by such bands as Uncle Yoke and Uncle Yoke's Black Dog Band, High Sierra, Night Blooming Jazz Men, Cat Yankee and Her Gentlemen of Jazz, Igore's, Climax, Blue Street Jazz Band, Market Street Jazz Band, Devil's Mountain, Professor Plum, Abalone Stompers and more are scheduled to allow plenty of time to get from one site to another. Several of the waterfront restaurants, bars, and cafes are open only to festival attendees, and many hotels offer special rates.

Fort Bragg Beer Fest
Fort Bragg   (707) 964-3153

Third Saturday in March. Sunday is the Whale Festival Run. 2,000. 9 years. Free. Fee for tasting mugs. Downtown Fort Bragg. 170 miles north of San Francisco on Hwy. 1.

California Festivals   March

This festival is a companion to one two weeks earlier in Mendocino, twelve miles south of Fort Bragg. Many of the events are located within a dozen or so downtown blocks. You will need a car, however, to get to the whale-watching sites or out to the Pt. Cabrillo lighthouse for a tour. Whale-watching cruises operate out of Noyo Harbor, one mile south of Fort Bragg; walking tours are at MacKerricher State Park, three miles north of the city.

The tenth annual Whale Festival will feature microbrewery products from throughout California. These breweries and beer pubs will offer flavorful, distinctive lagers, ales, stouts, porters, and pilsners. The "official tasting mug" is cheap at $10. You can also taste the chowder of more than a dozen local restaurants and cast your vote for your favorite; take in the baseball card, orchid, or gem and mineral shows—D.J. and M.J.

Heritage Festival
San Juan Capistrano   (714) 493-4700

Throughout the month of March. 30,000. 39 years. Free. C. Russell Cook Park. I-5 to Ortega Hwy. Go to Hwy. 74 East, then to Rancho Viejo Rd. Turn right. Go to Arroyo. Turn left to Park and Central.

The month of March is a busy one around San Juan Capistrano, as a multitude of activities and events honors the area's history and cultural diversity. It begins the first weekend with a 10K/3K run/walk, followed the same day by a community fair. The fair features food, games, and exhibit booths plus many arts and crafts booths and activities for the kids: pony rides, hayrides, clowns, face painting, and a children's train. Other entertainment includes bands, a Western stunt show, puppet and magic shows, and strolling entertainers. This fair is followed on Sunday by the Authors and Artists Fair, where works are displayed and sold.

Other events throughout the month include a city softball game, golf tournament, team penning competition (a type of rodeo), St. Patrick's Day celebration, St. Joseph's Day celebration (in conjunction with Swallows Day, honoring the annual arrival of the swallows), El Presidente Ball, pet parade, hat contest, town decoration day, hairiest man contest, and "Hoosegow Day." The month-long festivities culminate the last weekend in March with a pancake breakfast on Saturday morning, followed by the annual Fiesta de las Golondrinas (Swallows Day) parade and a two-day rodeo.

Throughout the month, a wide variety of food and music is available at the many events. The focus of most food dishes is on Spanish, Mexican, and American Indian foods, while the music ranges from jazz and reggae to Gaelic and country/western.

California Festivals   March

La Quinta Arts Festival
La Quinta   (619) 564-1244

Third weekend in March (Thursday through Sunday). 25,000. 10 years. $4. Take Highway 10 to Washington Street turnoff. Go south on Washington to Eisenhower. Take a right on Eisenhower to festival grounds.

The town of La Quinta is sometimes called the "Carmel of the Desert" and has become a mecca for artists who derive inspiration from the natural beauty of this tiny valley tucked into the Santa Rosa mountains. Art lovers can stroll through the community park—turned into an outdoor gallery for this event— and view works by over 180 artists who come from all over the U.S. Last year nearly $750,000 worth of artwork was sold. Live music helps to heighten the experience with such genres as bluegrass, jazz, classical and rock and roll represented. Musicians who have appeared include Frank Flynn, Joe Masters, Kevin Henry, Pickett Line, The Desert String Quartet and the International Chamber Orchestra.

Mariposa County Storytelling Festival
Mariposa   (209) 966-2456

Second weekend in March (Friday-Sunday). 3,000. 5 years. Full package $50, evening performances $5.50. Mariposa County Fairgrounds. Take Hwy 140 East from Hwy 99 (Merced) for 37 miles. Turn right onto Hwy 495 and go 1.5 miles. Fairgrounds are on the left.

This three-day festival will enchant and entertain you through the fine art of storytelling, brought to you by nationally acclaimed storytellers. There are gala performances Friday and Saturday evenings and Sunday mornings, plus special Saturday workshops, a children's story hour and a story swap. These stories will transport you back to your childhood and a time when there were no limits to your imagination. The festival has become so popular that it will be taped for PBS this year.

California Festivals   March

Mendocino Whale Festival
Mendocino   (707) 964-3153

First weekend in March (Saturday-Sunday). 2,000. 9 years. $5 chowder taste, $10 wine glass. Throughout the village of Mendocino. Hwy. 101 north of San Francisco, west on Hwy. 128 to Hwy. 1, north to Mendocino.

This festival is more for adults than children. If you want the youngsters to see migrating whales, take them some other time or some other place, or bring along a babysitter so you can enjoy wine and cioppino tasting, art gallery and boutique browsing, and the special charm and visual splendor of this unique village.

You can park your car and do most everything on foot. This town is small, perched on a Pacific headland just off of Highway 1, and you can see the spouts and sometimes the bodies of passing whales as you walk along the cliffs at town's edge (bring your binoculars!). If you want to stay overnight in Mendocino or any of the surrounding communities, reservations are a must for both hotels and bed and breakfasts.

Additional attractions include the Whale Bus from Oakland and Ranger talks at the Ford House, Mendocino Headlands State Park (on Main Street), charter flights to whale watch at Little River Airport (four miles south), and tours of Pt. Cabrillo lighthouse (four miles north) and Pt. Arena lighthouse (30 miles south). —D.J. and M.J.

Sacramento Camellia Festival
Sacramento   (916) 442-8166

March through April. 75,000. 38 years. Free (fee for some events). Community Center Exhibit Hall. From I-5, I-80, or Hwy. 50, follow signs to downtown.

Sacramento calls itself "The Camellia City," and with its ideal growing conditions it is no surprise that camellias--the official city flower--abound. For the last 35 years, the flower show has been part of a large festival put on by the Sacramento Camellia Festival Association, whose ambitious goal is to "enhance the cultural, recreational, and social lifestyle of Sacramento." There are now some 30 events over the course of 10 days.

If you are a lover of camellias or at least willing to flirt with them, the Camellia Show in the Exhibit Hall is the place to be. 7,000 blossoms await you, plus flower arrangements and competitions and colorful international exhibits representing Sacramento's diverse ethnic groups.

Other Camellia Festival events include the parade (over 200 floats, bands, marching units and special entries), ball (a formal event costing $60), jazz concert (with such artists as George Duke and Stanley Clarke), luncheon (prizes are awarded to guests wearing hats decorated with camellias), bicycle races, folk dance pageant, gymfest, classic car caravan, golf tournament, fun run, walkathon, and performances by the Camellia Symphony Orchestra and the Sacramento Chorale.

Not to worry: you won't be faced with the decision of whether or not to eat camellia chili, camellia ice cream or camellia stir-fry. There are as yet no theme foods at this festival. You needn't go hungry, though, because food from a concession stand or city restaurant is never more than a petal throw away! --M.J. and D.J.

San Diego St. Patrick's Day Annual Parade
San Diego   (619) 299-7812

Saturday before St. Patrick's Day. 200,000. 12 years. Free. Balboa Park. Hwy. 163, exit Sixth Ave., west to Balboa Park.

"There are just two kinds of people in this world: those who are Irish and those who wish they were," says Chuck Fox, chairman of the board for the San Diego St. Patrick's Day celebration. It's not an empty claim. This parade is believed to be the largest St. Patrick's Day march west of the Mississippi. At least 200,000 people turn out for the event, which begins at 9 a.m. with performances by Irish dancers, followed by a flag-raising ceremony an hour later.

By 11 a.m. the sidewalks around Balboa Park are lined with spectators. The parade lasts close to two hours and is never boring. There are floats, bands, clowns, equestrian groups, llamas, and surprise celebrities. After the parade, a sea of green-clad spectators and marchers continues celebrating in the park. Those who forget to wear the color that pays tribute to Emerald Isle can buy some greenery at booths around the park. Commemorative parade T-shirts are sold to raise funds for the next year's event. Booths also offer shamrock pins, ribbons, top hats (cardboard), flags, and buttons with messages such as "PBI" ("Proud to be Irish"). The prices are modest and the event so enjoyable even non-Irish visitors are sure they have some Irish blood in them somewhere.

Irish imports on sale include glassware, walking sticks, and sweaters. Booths also sell cookbooks, music books, and recordings of Irish music. A sampling of Irish food includes Irish soda bread, which is deliciously sweet, and traditional corned beef sandwiches. Hamburgers and hot dogs are also sold. Some spectators bring picnic baskets and buy a glass of dark Guinness beer for a taste of Ireland.

California Festivals — March

Entertainment is offered on two stages, where dance troupes of all ages demonstrate Irish steps. However, the highlight of the event is nonstop music until just before sunset. San Diego's top Irish performers play folk songs and lively jigs and reels that bring the crowds to their feet. Expect to hear "Danny Boy" a few times, plus a few American rock and roll songs. Rousing tunes such as "Finnegan's Wake" provide playful interplay between performers and the audience. Spectators clap during the singing, but when the music stops, those still clapping are teased amicably, and several more verses are sung to practice the timing.

When the day ends many hearty celebrants adjourn to one of San Diego's Irish pubs to carry on the singing and dancing. Long live the Irish! —L.S.

San Francisco International Film Festival
San Francisco   (415) 931-FILM

April-May . 50,000. 35 years. $7 per event; discounts for festival members, seniors, and students. Daily screenings at "AMC Kabuki 8Theatres" in San Francisco (Post and Geary Streets) the Pacific Film Archive in Berkeley (University Art Museum, Durant and College Avenues) and the Agugrius Twin Cinemas in Palo Alto, with a special day at the Castro Theatre, San Francisco's historic movie palace. Call ahead for schedule and directions to each theater.

This festival is a filmgoer's delight, a movie lover's dream: 14 days of films, seminars, and the chance to speak directly with many of the film makers whose films are shown. Held at three major locations in San Francisco and Berkeley—the Kabuki theatres, the Castro Theatre, and the Pacific Film Archive—this oldest of the U.S. film festivals has many of the directors introduce their films. After each showing, the director takes questions from the audience concerning everything from how much the film cost to how a particular scene was plotted and shot.

Unless you like popcorn, don't come to any of the showings hungry; and if you're looking for entertainment other than what's on the screen, you might be disappointed. But for all you aspiring film makers, being at the movies and talking to the folks who make them is a dream come true.

California Festivals   March

Santa Barbara International Film Festival
Santa Barbara   (805) 963-0023

Begins mid-March. 21,000. 7 years. Full festival pass $150, individual screening $6.50. Downtown Santa Barbara. From Hwy. 101, exit State St. toward the mountains.

Well, the San Francisco Film Festival may be the oldest and one of the most prestigious, but the Santa Barbara folks deserve an A+ for effort at this event. This film festival features premieres of U.S. and international films; documentary and archival films; workshops led by industry professionals; tributes to film luminaries; and special focuses on cinema of a particular country. There are also gala parties and receptions, where you can mingle with fellow movie buffs and rub elbows with a star or two while you sip champagne and listen to background jazz and rock.

The workshops are really something, with the screenwriters, directors, and producers of some of the best-known current films conducting sessions on their specialities. Also not to be missed are the special evenings with celebrities. In 1989, actress Lynn Redgrave and animator Chuck Jones delighted sold-out audiences.

You'll also find a little movie history at this festival, with special programs on the Flying A Studios that were in operation in Santa Barbara from 1912 to 1920. And then there's Santa Barbara itself, with its beautiful beaches and enviable climate. How much more could you ask for?

Shasta Dixieland Jazz Festival
Redding   (916) 244-5870

First weekend in April (Friday-Sunday). 15,000. 7 years. $40 for all-event badge; $35 for advance tickets. Six different sites along the motel strip; Elks Club and city convention center. From I-5, exit at Cypress Ave. or Hwy. 44 in Redding.

Dixieland jazz may have its roots in the South, but it's found its way to Northern California. For three days and nights, 12 bands from around the world rock the town of Redding and help perpetuate this purely American art form. The bands perform continuously at six different locations, and some performances are free to the public. There are also impromptu jam sessions after each evening's final performance, a special Sunday morning jazz hymn sing, and performances at the Saturday morning pancake breakfast. The final day features a grand finale performance with all the bands.

California Festivals   March

Redding is located just 10 miles from Lake Shasta, a popular boating, fishing, and camping lake. Nearly 20 hotels and 10 resorts offer accommodations, some right on the lake. Local restaurants run the gamut in types of food and prices, and some food is provided at each performance. If you like jazz, pine trees, and good times, don't miss the Shasta Dixieland Jazz Festival.

Snowfest Winter Carnival
Tahoe City   (916) 583-7625

Begins Friday before the first Sunday in March. 100,000. 11 years. Most events are free. Events are located throughout the region. Hwy. 89 from I-80 to North Lake Tahoe.

Whether you like to spend your winter days flying down ski slopes or curled up in front of a fire, the Snowfest has something for everyone. It's the largest winter carnival in the West, with over 140 events—just what anyone suffering from cabin fever needs.

If you're a ski buff or just enjoy playing in the snow, this festival offers a multitude of winter contests: skiing, snowboarding, snowmobiling, softball on skis, golf, and volleyball. If you're more a social butterfly than a snow bunny, you can take in the Snowfest Queen coronation and dance (just to be fair, there's a Mr. Lake Tahoe contest, too), great food, live music and street dance. And if you're looking for something in between, you can enter these competitions: Trivial Pursuit, pool, backgammon, dancing, ice sculpturing, and the annual Dress Up Your Dog contest. And be sure not to miss the firework displays (quite dazzling over the snow!), the torchlight ski parade, the snow palace, the arts and crafts fair, or the children's theater and penny carnival.

You say the mountain air makes you hungry? Well, there's no shortage of food at this festival, whether you enter the pizza or ice cream eating contests or the wild game and fish cook-off or pig out at the spaghetti, crab, pasta, or taco feeds. And of course the Tahoe/Truckee area offer dozens of restaurants and lodgings, from motels to lodges, condos to bed and breakfasts.

Nearly 20 ski areas participate in this 10-day winter extravaganza, with the opening ceremonies at Squaw Valley and the closing ceremonies at Boreal Ridge. Many lift passes are interchangeable from one ski area to another.

California Festivals   March

Sonora Celtic Celebration
Sonora (209) 553-3473 or (209) 532-7045

Second weekend of March. 6,000. 6 years. Sat. $10. Sun. $7.50, both days $15. Sonora Fairgrounds. From Hwy 99 go East on Hwy 120 to Sonora (take downtown exit to Sonora Fairgrounds).

It's a gathering of the clans —where you can discover the Celtic cultures, including Irish, Scottish, Cornish and Welsh peoples. This weekend festival recreates a Celtic village in the foothills of the Sierra with authentic Celtic music, dance, fine arts and crafts, tournaments, genealogy and ethnic food and drink.

Try some British bangers or Bubble and Squeak (cabbage and potatoes). There's also fish and chips, pasties (meat pies), hearty stews, baked potatoes, East Indian cuisine, Scottish shortbread, soda bread, cookies and scones. You can sip tea with your scones at the English Tea House or wander over to the Ireland Eye Pub where you'll find Guinness Stout, Harp Lager and other spirits.

Music is a big part of this weekend, with over 20 performances of Celtic bands, harpists, singers and pipe bands. Groups include the 24-member San Francisco Scottish Fiddlers, the Welsh a capella singers, the Gwen Dandridge's Swords of Gridlock's exhibition of English sword dancing, bawdy Border Morris and Clog Morris dancers—all rarely performed on the West Coast.

Stroll through the village-center Marketplace and you'll find Welsh, Irish and Scottish sweaters, shawls, hats, handwoven woolens and mohairs; oil paintings and photographs of Celtic landscapes and town scenes; perfumes; armor displays; musical instruments; Celtic designs in pottery; silver, bronze, gold and pewter bracelets, earrings, rings and goblets; and figurines featuring ancient mythological motifs.

Combatants recreate medieval battle scenes in authentic armor. (Photo by Ron Pickup.)

California Festivals
March

The kids will enjoy the Penny Royal Puppet Theatre for a Punch-and-Judy style show. For the grownups drama, poetry and prose classics are performed all day long.

Everyone will want to watch the armored clashes staged four times a day near the "encampment on the green." Here the White Rose Society will engage in armored swordfighting with, the War of the Roses, the Appian Regiment or the Crusade for the Innocents Knights. These battles are conducted with all the pomp and heraldry of a full armored encounter from the time of the knights of King Arthur's court. Authentic costumes and handmade armor make you feel as if you lived during this period. Watch craftsman fashion helmets and armor parts on the spot, or watch a Scottish Army black powder demonstration. See the White Rose Society fire 18th- century-style Scottish Army weapons while the pipes blare, frightening the enemy into submission.

If you suspect you have Celtic roots, and many of us do, you can visit the Glen of Clans where the regalia and clan tartans are on display. Over 26 clans attended last year. So come on down yee bonee Burnett, Blair, Campbell, MacArthur, Bonnachaidh, Hannah, MacKay, MacAlister, (Mother Lode Scots), MacLaughlin, Donald, Ross, Sinclair, Gregor, Keith, Ian, Henderson, Lamont, Shaw—ye know who ye are. - S.R.

California Festivals   April

Adobe Tour
Monterey   (408) 372-2608

Last Saturday in April. 2,500. 44 years. $10 adults, $7 students, children under 12 with parents free. The tour begins at the bay on the "path of history" in downtown Monterey. Monterey is located on Hwy. 1, 2 hours south of San Francisco.

During the Adobe Tour approximately 25 historic buildings are opened to the public, many of them for this day only. The buildings are beautifully restored and furnished with early artifacts and heirlooms, and hostesses in period costumes are available to talk about each structure's history. One of the buildings is the Custom House, considered the most important historical building in California. Another is the Robert Louis Stevenson House, where this famous author did much of his writing.

In addition to the self-guided walking tour, there is a baker's breakfast, a garden luncheon, an afternoon tea, and a wine and cheese reception. Each of these events is open to the public for a small fee. Also available throughout the day is musical entertainment, including classical guitar, banjo, and piano; a complimentary trolley service that takes you along the same route as the walking tour; and posters and gifts commemorating the day and Monterey's history.

Apple Blossom Festival
Sebastopol   (707) 823-3032

Weekend closest to April 10, depending on Easter (Saturday and Sunday). 20,000. 45 years. Free. Ives Park and area around the Veterans Building. Take Hwy 12 or Hwy 116 West to Sebastopol.

California Festivals — April

Apples are to Sebastopol what wine is to Sonoma County, and for over 40 years the folks in Sebastopol have been celebrating the beauty of where they live, when the apple trees are in full bloom. Organizers of the festival describe it as "a refreshing country experience"-- but Sebastopol is just an hour's drive north of San Francisco. If you've ever been there, you'll agree that it is in many ways a charming country town, and this festival highlights this side of Sebastopol.

There's a parade down Main Street, featuring floats, bands, and every local group; a craft fair; apple blossom tour; live music at the park, ranging from the U.S. navy band to country/western and jazz; 10K and 2-mile Apple Juice runs; two art shows; children's games, and a model railroad show. And what country fair would be complete without lots of good homecooked food, including barbecued chicken and many apple treats (the apple crisp can't be beat!).

Though the crowds get bigger every year, somehow this festival manages to keep its small-town flavor.

Sebastopol's Apple Blossom Festival keeps growing, but the parade manages to keep its small-town flavor. (Photo courtesy of the Sebastopol Area Chamber of Commerce)

Arvin Wildflower Festival
Arvin   (805) 854-2265

Last weekend in April (Saturday and Sunday). 13,000. 13 years. Free. Di Giorgio Park. Hwy. 99 to Bear Mountain Blvd. east to South Hill. Park is at South Hill and Franklin.

A musical kaleidoscope featuring rock, mariachis, Top-40, salsa, jazz, and reggae await the visitor at the Arvin Wildflower Festival. What began as an effort to raise money to reseed hillsides that were devasted during a catastrophic wind storm in 1977 has turned into the community's top social activity, combining music with abundant varieties of ethnic food, games, merchants, and the ever-popular greased pig contest for youths.

For the athletic, the weekend begins with 5K and 10K runs early Saturday morning. For those who prefer to sleep in, the parade starts at 10 a.m. Afterwards, the crowd moves to Di Giorgio Park and the festivities continue, with bands (a different one performs every hour on the grandstand), booths, a petting zoo for children, and lots of great Thai, Mexican, and other ethnic foods, as well as hot dogs, hamburgers, and barbecue.

California Festivals — April

As the sun begins to set and the weather turns cooler, the young and young-at-heart usually take advantage of the music with a few turns around the dance floor in front of the grandstand.
—L.M.

Two youngsters attempt to latch onto slippery porkers during the greased pig contest at the Arvin Wildflower Festival. (Photo by Leonel Martinez)

Bodega Bay Fisherman's Festival
Bodega Bay   (707) 875-2111

Third or fourth weekend in April—determined by the tides (Saturday and Sunday). 10,000. 17 years. Free. Westside Park. Hwy. 1 north from Bodega Bay, left on Eastside Rd. to Westside Park.

Many superstitions and traditions surround the sport and business of fishing, and this festival has its roots in the blessing of the fishing boats at the beginning of each salmon season. While they still bless the boats in Bodega, the festival has grown into a two-day event highlighted by a Sunday morning boat parade, featuring 100+ gaily decorated boats.

Besides the parade, there's a 6K run, a bathtub race, a kite-flying contest, pony rides, dog cart rides, face painting, and over 100 crafts booths, with many unique, locally made creations. Other booths feature such goodies as fish and chips, barbecued oysters (you gotta try 'em!), barbecued lamb (the secret's in the marinade), lamb sausages, hot dogs, snow cones, popcorn, soft drinks, beer, wine, doughnuts, and coffee (you might need it when the wind comes up!). The music's as diverse as the food, with a Navy band, Scottish bagpipes, an oompahpah band, and a local country/western group.

This festival is a lot of fun, and Bodega Bay is one of many lovely towns along this stretch of the California coast.

California Festivals — April

Butter and Egg Day Parade
Petaluma   (707) 762-9348

Weekend after last Wednesday in April (Saturday). 20,000+. 10 years. Free. Petaluma Blvd. North in Historic Downtown. North of San Francisco on Highway 101. 39 miles north of Golden Gate Bridge. Exit E. Washington, and travel west to Petaluma Blvd.

This festival is a salute to Petaluma's history, when from 1918 through the 1940s it was known as the "World's Egg Basket." A lot of family fun is packed into the one-day affair, starting with a pancake breakfast. You can also enter or just attend several egg- and dairy-related contests (including the Cutest Little Chick in Town, an Egg Toss, and Butter Churning) and tour historical homes, buildings, and a butter- and cheese-making facility. For the kids there are games and a moon bounce. Of course, the event of the day is the parade, two hours of 100+ entries: kids groups, local school bands and organizations, and floats of all kinds. Food booths are open all day, offering cuisine from Greek, Thai, Italian, to downhome barbecue . With the new marina and golf course completed and the coast and wine country close by, there's every reason to visit this charming city and its lighthearted festival.

Cherry Blossom Festival
San Francisco   (415) 563-2313

Two weekends in April (Friday-Sunday). 150,000. 25 years. Most events free. Japan Center and surrounding blocks of Japantown. Hwy. 101 to Van Ness Ave. Take Van Ness to Geary. Go west on Geary four blocks to the Japan Center.

Asian cultures are such a part of San Francisco's identity you'd think it would be difficult to find an event that could capture even more of the spirit and atmosphere than just walking through Chinatown or the Japan Center, but this festival gives visitors a chance to see many of the more treasured Japanese traditions. Japanese dances (with fans and kimonos, in groups and solo) are performed by Northern California dance groups, with the dancers' ages ranging from 4 to 60. There are also martial arts demonstrations, flower arranging and bonsai display and deminstrations, traditional tea ceremonies, art and photo exhibits, taiko drum and koto performances, contemporary music and entertainment, Akita dogs, Japanese carp exhibits, cooking demonstrations,sword and handmade doll exhibits.

Japanese foods, such as sushi, cooked chicken and rice, and tempura, are sold at the food bazaar, and Japanese music, both folk and classical, plays over loudspeakers. In addition, Japanese merchandise of all kinds is available at stores around the festival site.

Other events include a film festival featuring outstanding Japanese and Japanese-American movies, and a children's village with arts, crafts, storytelling, games, and magic shows. Four city blocks are closed off for this two-weekend celebration of Spring, which concludes on the last Sunday with a spectacular two-and-a-half hour parade.

The two-weekend Cherry Blossom Festival in Sanfrancisco's Japan town is one of the largest celebrations of Japanese culture and customs this side of the Pacific. (Photo courtesy of the San francisco Convention & Visitors Bureau)

Dolbeer Steam Donkey Days
Eureka   (707) 445-6567

Late April (Saturday and Sunday). 5,000. 10 years. Free. Fort Humboldt State Historic Park. Turn off Hwy. 101 on Highland Ave— go 1/2 block and turn on Fort Ave. (this is the only way you can go at these turns).

Eureka's not only gold country, it's also redwood country, and this festival salutes the logging industry that is still so prominent in this area. A "steam donkey" is a steam-driven machine that pulls logs (they long ago stopped using real donkeys), and you'll be able to see these impressive engines in operation, plus ride behind a steam locomotive. There's also a logging competition, an antique car show, and displays of all kinds of logging equipment and operations from the 1850s to the 1940s.

All this activity is bound to make you hungry (and thirsty!), so it's a good thing there's lots of chili, hot dogs, home-baked goods, and soft drinks available. (This festival is held in conjunction with Eureka's Rhododendron Festival.)

Festival of the Springs
Desert Hot Springs   (619) 329-6403

Second weekend in April (Friday-Sunday). 3,000. 34 years. Free. Downtown Desert Hot Springs, I-10 to Palm Dr. exit. North on Palm Dr., 3 miles to the intersection of Palm and Pierson.

Enjoy the rejuvenating mineral waters of the hot springs for which this city is named. This weekend festival celebrates the fantastic weather this time of year and focuses attention on visitors who come from around the world to enjoy hot mineral water and desert fun.

The center of this event is downtown Desert Hot Springs, where you'll find exhibitor booths (including arts and crafts), food booths (featuring international cuisine), and lots of activities. Just sit back and enjoy the weather, the mineral baths, the food, the people, and even some toe-tapping bluegrass, jazz, country/western and big band music. It's fun in the desert sun!

Gold Nugget Days
Paradise   (916) 872-8722

Last weekend in April (Thursday-Sunday). 20,000. 32 years. Ranges from $3.50 to $5 depending on the event. Downtown Paradise, Hwy. 70 through Oroville and then Clark or Pentz Road to Paradise. Or Hwy. 99 to the Skyway and then to Paradise.

This festival is a chance for the small community of Paradise to relive its beginnings as a gold-mining town. Seems that back in '59 (that's 1859, mind you), a 54-lb. nugget, known as the Willard Gold Nugget, was found in these parts, and this discovery put Paradise on the map for quite a few folks. This festival was first held in 1959 to commemorate the 100th anniversary of the discovery of this nugget.

By the look of this festival, the folks up on "the Ridge" sure do like to have a good time. The annual "Dogtown Nugget," a souvenir program that looks like a small-town newspaper, really sets the tone for the four-day affair: "If'n you aint bought your 'Paleface' or 'Petticoat' badge by now, the gold Shirted Deputies will be lookin' fer ya. It is tradition up here on the Ridge during Gold Nugget Days that gentlement that are clean shaven and ladies not adorned in petticoats must wear a badge. The Deputies will be checking every miner, farmer, school teacher, merchant, cooper, baker, fancy lady, gambler, and any stranger in town to make sure they are proudly wearing their badges. Just to be on the safe side, get one for your horse or mule, too." These badges are the main source of income for Gold Nugget Days Inc., which established and supports the the Gold Nugget Museum.

Some of the many activities during the four-day event include a home arts exhibit; craft fair; a Miss Gold Nugget contest; costume contests; country-style and pancake breakfasts; a bean feed; deep-pit barbecue; the Dogtown Revue and Gold Nugget Ball; a parade and awards ceremony; a donkey derby; and contests such as beard-growing.

And whatever you do, don't forget to pick up a copy of the "Dogtown Nugget." It gives some glimpses of miner life in the 1800s that you won't soon forget.

Great Sutter Creek Duck Race
Sutter Creek (209) 267-0252

Last full weekend in April (Saturday and Sunday). 5,000. 5 years. $5 per duck entry, onlooking is free. Minnie Provis Park. From I-80, Sacramento to Hwy. 16 to Hwy. 49. Sutter Creek is 8 miles from Hwy. 16 and 42 miles from Sacramento.

This truly silly event can't help but bring a chuckle or two from everybody present, except maybe the plastic ducks that are the stars of the show. Almost 6,000 gaily colored ducks bob and splash their way merrily down the stream in quest of $7,500 in prizes (proceeds are donated to charities). Each duck has its own parents (you can adopt a duck for a mere $5), who cheer their kids on to watery victory. Heats are held both days, with the big race on Sunday.

The "rules" of the game are about as serious as the event itself; for instance, parents cannot give their adoptive ducks mouth-to-mouth resuscitation if the ducks flounder or sink. In addition, ducks may not fraternize, commingle, associate, or touch any adoptive parents, any member of the human race, or any extension thereof. Ducks who do so are disqualified, and the parents lose a chance to win some of the prizes.

Following the races, winners and losers repair to local watering holes to recap the weekend. They leave the ducks behind.

California Festivals   April

Jackass Mail Run
Porterville and Springville   (209) 784-7502

Saturday preceding the Springville Sierra Rodeo. 2,000. 28 years. Free. Main St. and Cleveland, Porterville to Springville, Hwy. 99 to Hwy. 190. Take the Porterville exit.

This one-day event is the reenactment of the mail run to the mining camps in the foothills of Porterville during the late 1800s. They use real horse-drawn wagons to go from Porterville to Springville, 22 miles in all, with a barbecue lunch stop by Success Lake. Anyone who wants to can go along, and 200-400 people usually ride in the wagons led by people chosen especially to drive the wagons and deliver the mail each year. Actual U.S. mail is carried and delivered, and each piece is adorned with a special Jackass stamp in addition to a U.S. postage stamp. To add to the fun and excitement, a fake hold-up and robbery are staged along the way.

Once the wagon train arrives in Springville, the party begins, with live music (country/western), a Miss Jackass contest, food and game booths, and horseshoe contests. After a day on one of those wagons, you'll need a beer or two to get the dust out—just in time to kick up your heels and do a little two-steppin'.

Jazzaffair
Three Rivers   (209) 561-4321

First weekend of April (Friday-Sunday). 1,500. 18 years. Badges $35. Veterans Hall and White Horse Inn. Hwy. 99 to Visalia (north of Bakersfield, south of Fresno); east on Hwy. 198; 35 miles to Three Rivers.

In an effort to preserve this uniquely American style of music, this beautiful community, known as the gateway to Sequoia National Park, has been hosting the Jazzaffair for the past 18 years. Eight bands, mostly from California, join the host band (appropriately named "High Sierra") at three concert sites for three days of Dixieland jazz. There's also a cabaret and a deep-pit barbecue dinner. For other food, look to the many restaurants around Three Rivers.

April is the time to visit Three Rivers, when the wildflowers are in brilliant bloom in the foothills. If you like to camp or have an RV, lots of sites surround this area, but you can also find "regular" accommodations in town.

While Three Rivers may be small, the jazz is still plentiful and good, and the location makes this festival worth a trip.

California Festivals   April

KQED Wine and Food Festival
San Francisco   (415) 553-2200

Late April (Saturday). 4,000. 13 years. $45. Concourse Exhibition Center, 8th St. and Brannan St. From Hwy. 101, take 9th St. exit. Continue past light one black to 8th. Go right. Building is one block down at 8th and Brannan.

Over 120 restaurants and wineries join forces--and flavors--to create a block-long banquet. It's the largest tasting of paired wine and food in the country, and proceeds go to the local Public Broadcasting Station KQED. The ticket price may seem a little steep, but it's an all-you-can-eat affair, featuring appetizers, entrees, and desserts, plus at least 10 varietal wines, including champagne and dessert wines. No attempt to list all the restaurants, wineries, and types of food served will be made here--suffice it to say if you've ever wanted to taste it, it's probably here. Some of the more exotic dishes include squash and pear pate on garlic rounds, crab and avocado mini tostadas, duck tamales, satin potato soup with Vermont cheddar and pesto, prawns and scallops wrapped in pancetta with Chardonnay saffron sauce, and dungeness crab tarts with scallions and shitake mushrooms (see what we mean about gourmet?). And if you haven't made your way to the Napa or Sonoma valleys, you probably won't have to after visiting this festival; just about every major (and some minor) winery seems to be represented here. A live band lends a little background music to the atmosphere.

Forget the diet; this is an afternoon-long gourmet extravangaza!

You can't be shy at KQED's Wine and Food festival. (Photo courtesy of KQED)

California Festivals   April

Lilac Festival
Palmdale   (805) 273-3232

Early April. 5,000. 42 years. Free. Palmdale Cultural Center. Take I-5 to Hwy. 14 east to Palmdale Blvd. Go east to Sierra Hwy.

This spectacular flower show takes place during early April (Mother Nature helps determine the exact date) and is a must for anyone who loves floral beauty. As well as being an aromatic exhibit for lilac enthusiasts, the festival is also a competition. Flower growers from all over the Antelope Valley present their lilac specimens and lilac bouquets, some of which are truly grandiose arrangements, for a winning ribbon.

If lilacs alone aren't your cup of tea, wander over to the African Violet exhibit. There are also prize-winning tulips, lilies, and irises.

Enhancing the festival is an art show that showcases the diverse talents of local artists. The Antelope Valley is proud of its thriving art community and proudly displays craftwork ranging from pottery and sculpture to paintings, drawings, and etchings.

Plan to spend a few hours touring the Lilac Festival, which is sponsored by the people of Palmdale. The folks working the event are helpful volunteers and are happy to share information with visitors. They even have a decent concession stand! If it all seems too beautiful to leave behind, don't fret. Huge lilac bouquets can be had for a mere $10, and the artwork is on sale as well. Do arrive early in the day to see the flowers at their best.
--E.C.

Mother Lode Dixieland Jazz Benefit
Jackson   (209) 267-5632

Early April. 2,000. 14 years. $9.50 in advance, $11.50 at the door. Seven bistros and restaurants in the downtown Jackson Main Street area. Sacramento to Hwy. 50 to Hwy. 16 to Hwy. 49 to Jackson.

Well, April seems to be the month for jazz festivals, and if you're a jazz lover, you've probably travelled all over the state by now. Maybe it's a form of Spring fever, or maybe jazz is just one of those things that gets into your blood and you can't get enough of.

At this jazz festival, 10 Northern California jazz bands perform at Jackson bistros and restaurants from 11 a.m. to 6 p.m. each day, with all proceeds going to local charities. It's sort of like a progressive jazz feast, with the audience wandering from pub to pub and hotel to hotel to sample

California Festivals   April

each new "dish." It's a great chance to check out some Gold Country scenery and hear some of Northern California's best Dixieland jazz.

Pacific Coast Collegiate Jazz Festival
Berkeley   (510) 642-5062

Second weekend in April (Friday-Saturday). 5,000. 15 years. $5 one day; $8 both days plus Saturday evening. Take the Ashby exit from I-880; travel east on Ashby; turn left onto Telegraph; north on Telegraph; turn left onto Bancroft; travel one block to ASUC parking garage.

This festival is another big one—the largest student-run collegiate jazz competition in the U.S.—and is located in a part of the Bay Area where you can hear all the music you want just walking down the street. UC Berkeley is known for many things, and while jazz may not be the first thing you think of when you hear this school mentioned, it may be after you attend this festival.

During the two-day event, you can attend clinics, concerts, and a major musical competition in the categories of big band, combo and vocal ensemble. Student participants are critiqued and recognized for outstanding musical achievement by a panel of judges who are professional musicians, clinicians, jazz educators, and jazz writers.

With its focus on competition, the quality of the jazz you'll hear is quite high. And in between performances, you can stretch your legs with a stroll down Telegraph Avenue, where many street vendors display their wares and you'll be able to do some of the best people watching around. (The pizza-by-the-slice isn't bad either!)

Picnic Day
Davis   (916) 752-6320

Mid April. 70,000. 79 years. Free. UC Davis campus. I-80 from San Francisco going east toward Sacramento, take UC Davis exit.

Put on your walking shoes for what some consider the largest student-run event in the nation. Picnic Day is a huge family event on the UC Davis campus with so much diverse activity going on in one day that there's sure to be something interesting for everyone at every hour or half hour interval.

Start the day off by watching the old-fashioned parade, where the participants are always cheery and humorous. See antique tractors rumble down the street, several university bands trying to "out-weird" each other, floats, low-rider bicycles, etc. Bring a big picnic lunch to enjoy on the grass under one of the campus' many shady trees, then pull out your schedule to pick an event that suits your fancy. Favorites include the Dachschund races, the Battle of the Bands at pleasant Putah Creek, a rodeo, performances by jazz artists, barbershop quartets, the UC Davis Symphony, dance troupes (such as the Black Repertoire and Danzantes Del Alma), many dog events, farm animal exhibits, university department exhibits, lectures, and campus tours. There are also many sporting events, including polo, lacrosse, rugby, body building, water polo, water ballet, and horse shows. Come celebrate as UC Davis proudly opens its doors to the public. --P.R.

Rhododendron Festival
Eureka   (707) 442-3738

Last Saturday in April through the next week. 11,000. 25 years. Most events free. Humboldt County (parade in Eureka). Take Hwy. 101 to Eureka.

With the cry "the rhodies are coming, the rhodies are coming!" Eureka begins its annual celebration of the north coast's favorite flower. A huge parade, with all entries decorated in hundreds of rhododendrons, highlights the week-long event, but there's a lot more too: golf tournaments, square dancing, historical logging exhibitions, train rides, and, of course, a flower show and demonstrations of how to care for rhododendrons. The folks up here should know—thanks to the climate, the area surrounding Eureka is the best place on the West Coast to see blooming domestic and wild rhododendrons.
A twist on the usual beauty pageant has male and female youth ambassadors chosen to represent the county at various functions throughout the year.
Smelling all these flowers will probably make you hungry, so be sure not to miss the spaghetti and polenta feeds and the big breakfast on the last day.

San Dimas Festival of Western Art
San Dimas   (714) 599-5374

Last weekend in April (Saturday-Sunday). 6,000. 15 years. Free. San Dimas Civic Center Plaza. I-210 to Arrow Highway to Bonita Ave. Go east to the corner of Bonita and Walnut.

Sponsored by the San Dimas Festival of Western Arts, this three-day salute to Western and Indian art and culture is billed as "a way to preserve our western heritage through art." Approximately 40 national artists exhibit and sell their artwork and judge pieces by student artists.

A gallery and trading post are open to the public all weekend, and an auction is held on Sunday. Old-West-style foods are available, from pancake breakfasts to a chuck wagon featuring chili, hot dogs, and Indian fried bread. Special events include a Western dance featuring a live Western band, Indian dancing, an awards banquet, and various seminars and demonstrations about Indian and Western culture and history.

Santa Barbara Arts Festival
Santa Barbara   (805) 966-7022

Early April through early May. 18,000. 11 years. Varies. Throughout Santa Barbara. From Hwy. 101, exit at Santa Barbara St., travel north past Mission Ave. to Los Olivos; left on Los Olivos, past Old Mission, look for signs.

If you want to take in everything the Santa Barbara Arts Festival has to offer, plan a three-week holiday in this fair city! Initiated to bring tourists to Santa Barbara during the off-season, the annual Arts Festival is impressive in its scope of events. Previously housed in the Museum of Natural History, local artists now converge upon various downtown locations to present virtually every aspect of the arts: visual, theatrical, musical, literary, and dance. Highlights of the three-week fest include a food fair/competition, a community paint-by-number mural, a photography exhibit chronicling 48 hours of life in Santa Barbara, a dance art exhibition, folk art, and original Indian art. All these, and more, are conveniently located in and around Santa Barbara's central downtown area.

The Arts Festival is sponsored by the Downtown Organization in affiliation with the Santa Barbara Arts Council. The opening weekend festivities feature several simultaneous events taking place in the lovely De La Guerra Plaza. The food fair/competition is made up of entrants from some of Santa Barbara's finer restaurants and the food is judged not only for taste but for presentation. Foods from South America, Greece, Asia, and America are among the unique fare. As you sample the food, the Festival Stage in the plaza provides entertainment by several talented local bands.

After you savor the treats and listen to the tunes, pick up a paintbrush and add your efforts to the colorful community paint-by-number mural, outlined by a local artisan who devised an excellent paint-by-number scheme. The finished mural is prominently displayed for the duration of the festival. The festival also boasts a fine book fair featuring local publishers. Authors autograph books and give readings.

California Festivals — April

If you're concerned about bringing the kids to an art fest, don't be! The artists and organizers of this event are to be commended for including children into their themes. Children's art-in-action, sketch sessions with local architects and designers, a performance by the Santa Barbara Youth Symphony, and original art exhibits by children's book illustrators are some of the youth-oriented activities.

As of press time, the organizers of this festival were contemplating moving the festival from early Spring to the Fall. Either season is beautiful in Santa Barbara, but be sure to call ahead to verify the date! --E.C.

Scandinavian Festival
Thousand Oaks   (805) 493-3151

Second Saturday in April. 3,000. 19 years. $3 Adults, $1 Children. California Lutheran University. Take the Ventura Freeway (101) west from L.A. and go onto 23 North (Fillmore freeway). Exit Olsen road and turn left. Campus is located at Mt. Clef and Olsen.

Join Hands and learn some traditional folk dances. (Photos by Brian Stethem)

Local Scandinavian women unpack their heirloom cooking irons and waffle-iron-like presses every year to bake traditional pastries for the Scandinavian Festival. It's a way to show their pride in their heritage while they raise money for scholarships to California Lutheran University, on whose grounds the festival is held.

Highlights of the one-day festival include a piano concert featuring the music of Norway's native son Edvard Grieg, a play (usually by Henrik Ibsen), a Vasa Hambo dance contest that draws contestants from around the state and a traditional Scandinavian smorgasbord.

For smorgasbord fans, you'd better make your reservations in advance. Even with two seatings, it invariably sells out quickly. Here you can sample such traditional delicacies as spicy pickled herring, Scandinavian cucumbers, pickled beets, Swedish limpa loaf, Danish pumpernickel, baby red potatoes with cabbage, pork loin with crab apples and Swedish meatballs with gravy. Tickets are $12.50 for adults and $5 for children 10 and under.

Using old family dessert recipes, volunteers bake Danish coffee cakes,

California Festivals   April

breads, kringla, brune dager (Danish Christmas cookies) and lefse, a Norwegian potato tortilla-like pastry to sell. They also use special irons to make krumkake, a paper-thin cracker shaped into a cone.

The Festival attracts people of Scandanvian ancestry from all over the states.

Stockton Asparagus Festival
Stockton   (209) 477-6674

Last weekend in April (Saturday and Sunday). 80,000. 6 years. $5. Oak Grove Regional Park. I-5 to the Eight Mile Road exit.

    A county fair atmosphere prevails at this festival, which salutes the tasty asparagus plant. California produces 70% of the U.S. asparagus crop, and the area around Stockton produces most of California's crop.
    A walk down "Asparagus Alley" will give you a chance to visit the many booths located there, featuring such tasty treats as deep-fried asparagus, asparagus soup, asparagus salad, asparagus pasta, asparagus sandwiches, and gourmet asparagus entrees. These booths also sell non-asparagus foods and drinks (the wine-tasting booth seemed to be particularly busy), as well as arts and crafts. Exhibitors selected by the Stockton Arts Commission display and sell a variety of original arts; some 80 artists from California and Oregon are on hand.
    In addition to all this asparagus mania, there is an extensive antique and collectors car display (over 100 cars) on the grass near a small lake, and many of the owners are present to tell you all about their prized possessions, from a 1909 Sears Runabout to a 1973 Masserati. Also, musical entertainment (country/western, rock, blues, and pop) can be heard at any of several pavilions all day long.
    On a sunny Spring afternoon in the Central Valley, it is also pleasant to just wander about the park or sit by the lake and watch the passing scene.
—D.J. and M.J.

California Festivals   May

Berryessa Art and Wine Festival
San Jose   (408) 258-0952

Saturday before Mother's Day. 10,000. 17 years. Free. Noble Park. I-680 to Berryessa Rd. east exit. Turn right on Piedmont Rd. and follow signs.

While Sonoma and Napa may be the best known of the California wine producing areas, the Santa Clara Valley has a few wineries of its own. Several of them participate in this wine and arts festival, giving you a chance to sample some lesser-known (but quite good) wines, plus check out the wide variety of arts and crafts from 160 local artists.

In addition, this community- and area-wide celebration of Spring features continuous free entertainment, including country/western music, a concert band, jazz, and wandering musicians. And of course there's food—who wouldn't want to picnic on a sunny Spring day in the Bay Area?—from Mexican and Portuguese to Japanese and Filipino, plus some American favorites.

The Berryessa area of northeast San Jose is part of the original Palo Rancho Spanish land grant, and the 10+ acres of oak trees and grassy meadows that make up the park in which this festival is held are reminders of why the Spanish were so taken with the Bay Area when they first landed here.

Bidwell Bar Day
Oroville   (916) 538-2219

First Saturday in May. 2,000. 12 years. Free. Bidwell Canyon. From Hwy. 70 take Hwy. 162 east out of Oroville for 7 miles, turn left onto Kelly Ridge Rd., go 1 1/2 mi., then turn right onto Arroyo Dr. and follow it for 1/2 mi. to Bidwell Canyon.

This annual event celebrates the 1856 opening of the Bidwell Bar Bridge, the first suspension bridge west of the Mississippi River, and the 1848 discovery of gold at the same site. Get a taste of the Gold Rush Days first hand as you pan for gold, participate in a Victorian wedding (complete with a license, ceremony, and pictures), make pioneer crafts, churn butter, or dance to bluegrass, folk, and 1850s band music.

You'll see characters in historic dress as you browse through the museum and gift shop, and you can enjoy foods from then and now, including pioneer sausages, Bidwell beans, sweet potato pies, and Indian tacos. Enjoy the northern Sacramento Valley in the Spring, and learn history the fun way.

Cajun Crawfish Festival
Fairfield   (916) 361-1309, (707) 424-3076

First weekend in May. 8,000. 3 year. $3 adults, $2 seniors, children under 12 free. Travis Air Force Base, New Expo site. I-80 to Fairfield (west of Sacramento), Air Base exit to site.

First held in 1989, this festival celebrates Cajun culture, especially its food and music. The site is an open field dotted with colorful awnings, under which food is prepared and sold. A flatbed truck serves as bandstand, fronted by a plywood dance floor and folding chairs.

The food is strictly Cajun, with all the ingredients brought in from Louisiana, including two renowned Louisiana chefs, who prepare such dishes as spicy boiled crawfish and crawfish stew, jambalaya, gumbo, softshell crabs, seafood fettuccini, Gulf scallops, and catfish. Most popular was the alligator (!), served fried or barbecued. It sold out the first day.

Irresistible music was provided by Al Rapone and the Zydeco Express, the California Cajun Orchestra, and Bon Ton Mark St. Mary and his Red Hot California Band (zydeco is Creole Cajun music: a mixture of delta blues, rhythm and blues, rock and roll, country, bluegrass, and jazz). In addition to zydeco, which all the bands played, festival goers were treated to a broad spectrum of traditional Cajun French dance tunes from waltzes and two-steps to Louisiana blues.

Other activities include periodic dance workshops so you can learn some of the traditional dance steps, and crawfish races. Each day's activities conclude with a spirited Fais Do Do (Cajun for "street dance"). --D.J. and M.J.

California Festivals   May

Calico Spring Festival
Barstow   (619) 254-2122

Mother's Day weekend (Friday-Sunday). 10,000. 20 years. Adults $5, juniors $2, children under 5 free, camping $9. Calico Ghost Town. I-15, 10 miles north of Barstow. Take Ghost Town Rd. exit.

This old-time bluegrass hootenanny is one of the oldest such celebrations in the state. The three-day event includes a two-day fiddle, banjo, guitar, and band contest; clogging (with the chance to learn this classic country dance); bluegrass and country music; and singing for apple pies. Also featured are lots of games for kids (and, in some cases, adults), such as egg tosses, greased pole climbs, and searching for nickels in a haystack.

Situated in an actual ghost town and based on an 1893 schoolhouse festival, you'll find lots of old-fashioned fun, entertainment, and food, with a restaurant and confectionary right in town. Camping is also available.

This is the place to load up on snake oil if you're running low. (Photo courtesy of Calico Spring Festival)

California Festival of Beers
San Luis Obispo   (805) 544-2266

The Saturday of Memorial Day weekend. 2,000. 6 years. $15 advance, $20 at the door. $5 designated driver. The Graduate. Take Hwy 227 south of town near the airport to 990 Industrial Way.

This fun festival, sponsored by the wonderful people at the local hospice organization, has turned into the largest regional beer-tasting event in the country. You can sample beers from more than 60 state breweries, representing almost 25% of the country's breweries. Plus, you can enjoy gourmet food and a wide range of music in a festive outdoor setting. All proceeds go to Hospice of San Luis Obispo, an organization that provides in-home volunteer care to terminally ill people and their families.

California Strawberry Festival
Oxnard   (805) 984-4715

Third weekend in May. 100,000. 9 years. Adults $5, seniors and children $2. Strawberry Meadows at College park. 101 to Victoria Ave. Follow signs to festival site.

Located in the "Strawberry Capital of the World," this festival is a strawberry lover's delight. This event offers gourmet food and wine, fine arts and crafts, and musical entertainment (jazz, country, big band, and rock and roll) on three different stages, plus strolling musicians.

You and the kids can visit Strawberryland (featuring clowns, a petting zoo, crafts, and coloring projects), enter the 10K Strawberry Festival run, and watch contests of all kinds: tart tossing, a waiter's race (where waiters carry glasses of strawberry wine through an obstacle course and try not to spill a drop), a "strawberry blond" contest (resulting in the crowning of Miss Strawberry Blond), and a strawberry shortcake eating contest.

Besides strawberry-based creations of all kinds, you'll also find cajun treats, pizza, tamales, and other edibles at booths and restaurants around the festival site.

California Wine Exposition
Redondo Beach   (213) 376-6913

First Sunday in May. 1,000. 9 years. $25 in advance, $30 at door. Seaside Lagoon, 260 Portofino Way. From Los Angeles International Airport, 7 miles south to Catalina Ave. Turn right, go 1/2 mile to Beryl. Turn right to Seaside Lagoon.

Southern California is home to a variety of festivals, and the Southern California Wine Expo is among the finest! Imagine tasting wine from over 50 different wineries and enjoying delectable goodies from fine restaurants at a charming waterfront location. What began several years ago as a $100-a-plate moonlight feast for charity is now billed as the largest outdoor wine tasting event in southern California, with a far more modest admission price.

California Festivals   May

Winemakers offer at least three varietal wines to taste from and winery representatives are available to give detailed information about their product; not to mention generous samples! Local restrauteurs and caterers present tasty samples ranging from crepes suzette to Mexican brownies (just a touch of jalapeno!). Other tasty morsels include sausage muffins with goat cheese and rosemary spread. Beer drinkers don't despair; many well-known beer distributors are present (with samples!), including a local microbrewery with some excellent ale. There is also an abundance of nonalcoholic beverages.

This festival is more like a giant party thrown by 1,000 of your closest friends. The grounds are not typical of most; in fact, the Wine Expo is held at Seaside Lagoon, a compact and protected recreation area at Redondo Beach's King Harbor. Most of the crowd mills about under the huge umbrellas sipping wine, savoring the foods, and socializing. Picnic tables are set up, and a mariachi band provides the background music. Festival organizers are contemplating a full weekend event for future Wine Expos and plan to offer a charity auction as part of the agenda. All proceeds for this event are donated to seven local charities. --E.C.

Carlsbad Village Faire
Carlsbad   (619) 729-9072

First Sunday in May. 80,000. 13 years. Free. Village of Carlsbad. Take I-5 to Elm off ramp, head straight for the ocean (5 blocks).

California's largest one-day street faire features over 800 arts and craft exhibitors. Begun as an effort to revitalize the original village of Carlsbad, this festival has grown into an event that meanders throughout the city's streets and attracts some 80,000 people. The festival starts off with a pancake breakfast and Certified Farmers Market. In addition to the arts and crafts, you'll find booths featuring Greek, Thai, Italian, Polish, Chinese, and Japanese foods, plus continuous music (country, rock, and jazz). For the kids, there's a petting zoo and pony, llama, and elephant rides. It's a fun-filled day in this beautiful beach city just north of San Diego.

Chocolate Lovers Fantasy Faire
South Lake Tahoe   (916) 544-2118

Sunday of Memorial Day weekend. 1,000. 6 years. $5 Heavenly Valley Lodge take Hwy. 50 turn right on Ski Run Blvd. follow signs to Heavenly Valley Lodge.

"Fantasy" is the right word to describe this one-day sugarfest whose proceeds benefit the Lake Tahoe Women's Center, which takes care of abused women and the homeless. Over 300 chocolate treats are featured, including brownies, cookies, petit fours, ice cream, truffles, and fudge. Local gourmets and chefs compete for the "chocolate kiss" award for the most decadent treat, the best fudge, and the best all-around dessert. Champagne, milk, and coffee are also served.

Kids and adults alike can burn off all the sugar and calories by participating in a variety of games. For the kids, there's face painting, balloons, clowns, and a magic show. And for the adults, there's raffles, a slient auction, and a bake-off. Live entertainment from a string quartet adds to the flovor of this faire. And who wouldn't enjoy a Spring day in the mountains?

Cinco de Mayo
Borrego Springs   (619) 767-5035

Saturday closest to May 5. 1,500. 7 years. Free. Christmas Circle Park. I-8 or I-15 to Hwy. 163 at Ramona to Hwy. 79 to S-2 to S-22 to Borrego.

Festivals like this one, which recognizes an important date in Mexican history—the end of the French occupation and rule over Mexico—and honors the Mexican-American population, are held on this day throughout the United States and Mexico. In Borrego Springs, located in the mountains just northeast of San Diego, they celebrate Cinco de Mayo with Mexican food (a wide variety of dishes, including chili rellenos, chimichangas, beans, and fresh tortillas); dancing to the sounds of mariachis, vocalists, and a contemporary dance band; and lots of native arts and crafts displays. The Mexican Ballet Folklorico also performs.

Cinco de Mayo Fiesta and Art Fair
El Monte   (818) 580-2200

Sunday closest to May 5. 5,000. 7 years. Free. Arceo Park, 3130 Tyler Ave. Off I-10, take Santa Anita Ave. Go south to Mildred, turn left on Mildred to Tyler. Turn right on Tyler.

This city celebrates Mexico's liberation from France with an outdoor fiesta and art fair. Activities include a carnival, food booths, moon bounce, Folklorico dancers, and Mexican music. There are also pony rides for the kids, a chile salsa cook-off, a poster display, and the crowning of the Cinco de Mayo king and queen. The flavor of the festival is definitely Mexican-

American, as is the food: hamburgers, tacos, taquitos, chili, tamales, menudo, and assorted beverages.

Cinco de Mayo Kermesse
Lamont   (805) 845-3580

First Sunday in May. 1,500. 10 years. Free. St. Augustine Church Patio. Hwy. 99 to Hwy. 58 east. Turn off on Hwy 184. Go south 7 miles to Lamont.

The sights and sounds of Old Mexico come alive at the Cinco de Mayo Kermesse, held annually in the bustling rural town of Lamont. For one afternoon, the Kermesse (which means "a country fair held in the lowlands") duplicates almost exactly the countless details essential to a fair held in the Mexico of old. Banderitas, brightly colored sheets of paper cut with intricate designs, stream from booths and are strung high across the St. Augustine Church patio grounds where the fiesta is held. The rich smells of Mexican food waft through the air, mixing with the sounds of music, dancing, and laughter.

Not to be missed is the program presented by the Grupo Bailarin de San Augustin. Dressed in colorful costumes, this group of young dancers performs traditional dances from various states of Mexico. Singers serenade the crowd with mariachi songs and corridos (story ballads). Mixed in with the singing and dancing are "marriages" and "divorces" conducted by the "judge" on unfortunates who have been cast into the carcel (jail) by the Alguaciles (police) for various offenses such as frowning, flirting, etc.

Visitors should come early to take advantage of the rich, tasty Mexican food. The familiar enchilada, tamales, and flautas are offered, as well as tacos de birria (made with goat meat), escamochas (fruit cups), and aguas frescas, a punch made with various fresh fruits. Arts and crafts are available as well as activities that both young and old can enjoy, such as loteria (bingo) and a goldfish pond. Vendors are dressed in authentic Mexican costumes to add to the color of the event.

As day turns to evening, the music continues with a public dance starting at 7:30. Local bands play Top-40, Latin jazz, and salsa. —O.A.

California Festivals   May

Cinco de Mayo—San Diego
San Diego   (619) 237-6770

First weekend closest to May 5 (Saturday and Sunday). 100,000. 8 years. Free. Old Town San Diego State Historic Park. I-5 south into San Diego, take the Old Town Ave. exit.

With its close proximity to Mexico, San Diego has many Mexican-American citizens, and this two-day cultural celebration of one of Mexico's most important holidays is also one heck of a party. The 100,000+ attendees are treated to a variety of Mexican singers, musicians, and dancers (the music is a mixture of Mexican, Spanish, and South American), with performances by over 30 acts, including the Battle of Puebla reenactment commemorating the Cinco de Mayo celebration and several mariachi bands. In addition, there's a special Mexican rodeo with splendid equestrian groups.

The food, of course, is great, with such Mexican treats as tacos, fajitas, burritos, and freshly made tortillas, and the atmosphere is pretty traditional. Relive a little bit of Mexican history in one of the prettiest beach cities this side of the Pecos.

Coalinga Horned Toad Festival
Coalinga   (209) 935-2948

Memorial Day weekend (Friday-Monday). 7,000. 55 years. Free. Olson Park. I-5 to Hwy. 198 West. Hwy. 198 brings you directly into downtown Coalinga.

Don't get horned toads confused with jumping frogs—horned toads are lizards, and these suckers are quick! This event has been pitting horned toad against horned toad for over 50 years in Coalinga, where the town motto is "A nice place to live." And despite this seasonal influx of lizards, Coalinga really is one of the nicer towns in the Central Valley.

But it's not just all lizards and snakes at what the locals call "Derby Days." You'll find such other events as a parade, a dance, a carnival, a 10K run, a whisker-growing contest, water fights, tricycle races, and a barbecue featuring tri-tip beef. You can enter any of the contests, ride rides and play games at the carnival, and munch on a wide variety of food from the concession stands. You can pick up a few lizard souvenirs too, but if someone offers you a lizard skin wallet, beware—it may have been somebody's pet.

Coulterville Coyote Howling
Coulterville   (209) 878-3074

First weekend in May (Saturday and Sunday). 1,500. 6 years. Free. Coulterville Public Park. Hwy. 99 to Modesto, then east on Hwy. 132. Located at the junction of Hwy. 132 and Hwy. 49.

The highlight of the Olde Tyme Miner's Country Faire is the Coyote Howling competition, where contestants in several categories perform their best imitations of a coyote howl and try to win prize money. Throughout the weekend you'll find all kinds of activities, all in keeping with the country fair atmosphere. There are lots of games for the kids, plus raffles and contests for the adults: gold panning, shingle-splitting, and spinning and weaving. Plenty of homemade food too, including hamburgers, hot dogs, chicken, Polish sausages, ice cream, cakes, and pies. And what music would you expect to hear in this historic gold mining town? Why, bluegrass and country, of course.

Festival of Greece
Oakland   (510) 531-3400

Third weekend in May. 20,000. 19 years. Adults $3, children under 12 free. Greek Orthodox Church of Ascension, 4700 Lincoln Ave. Take I-580 to Fruitvale exit if traveling east, go one block to Champion. Turn left, go to Lincoln, head up hill until you see the church on the right.

Nestled in the Oakland hills with a commanding view of the San Francisco Bay, the grounds and community center of the Greek Orthodox Church of the Ascension make a perfect setting for the annual Festival of Greece. Held in late May when the weather is usually warm, the festival has a decidedly Mediterranean ambience. If you'd like to take a trip to Greece without leaving the states, this is the way to go. You can sample the sights, sounds, and tastes of Greece and experience the warmth of her people.

There is something for all ages at this festival. It kicks off with a businessperson's lunch on Friday. At the lunch you can begin to sample one of the real treats of this festival: the food! From the marinated shish kebabs to the rich mousaka, a beef and eggplant dish, the food is all authentic, lovingly prepared, and delicious. For dessert there are Greek pastries including melt-in-your-mouth baklava and loukoumades, Greek donut holes topped with honey. Greek wines are also available to wash down your meal. All the foods can be purchased to go, and there are areas outside the community center where you can sit and sip a glass of wine and enjoy calamari and other foods "al fresco."

Entertainment over the three-day festival includes cooking demonstrations, colorfully costumed Greek dancers and live music for dancing. Boutiques sell imported Greek items, including jewelry, records, tapes, and books. Greek cookbooks are also sold. If you're ready to really experience Greece, buy a raffle ticket. Top prize is usually a trip to Greece, cash or a car.

Fiesta de las Artes
Hermosa Beach   (213) 376-0951

Memorial Day weekend. 100,000. 24 years. Free. Pier and Hermosa Ave. I-405 7 miles south of Los Angeles International Airport. Take Artesia Blvd. exit. Go to the intersection of Pier and Hermosa.

This three-day outdoor festival, which takes place both Memorial Day weekend and Labor Day weekend (see September), has a lot of the best of most festivals. Over 450 booths feature unique handmade arts and crafts and fine art. Over 40 booths, assembled in the Food Pavilion, offer a diversity of international foods. And at the May version of the festival, jazz bands from five western states compete at many levels, with the winner opening for the Hollywood Jazz Festival. In addition, this festival hosts the collegiate playoffs for the prestigious Playboy Jazz Festival.

Located just one block from the beach, this event offers many outdoor activities, such as volleyball games. In addition to the jazz competition, other entertainment includes jazz, raggae and salsa bands, saw playing, jugglers, and mimes. And if the 100,000+ crowd gets to be too much, you can slip off to the beach to catch some sun, cool off with a dip in the ocean, or join in that ultimate spectator sport, people watching.

Fiesta del Sol
Solana Beach   (619) 755-4775

Third weekend in May (Saturday and Sunday). 7,000. 13 years. Free. Solana Beach. I-5 to Lomas Sante Fe Dr., head west to the beach.

California Festivals   May

Imagine a beach party that starts at 7 a.m. with a pancake breakfast for early birds. Naturally, there will be a surfing contest and a rough water swim. There will also be some games on the shore, like tug-of-war and a gunny sack race across the sand. The food will come from local restaurants, and several local musicians will play.

Solana Beach has been putting on this two-day event since 1979, concentrating on the theme "Fun in the Sun." It began as "Howdy Neighbor," a community event in October. When Solana Beach became a city in 1986, there was talk of holding a March birthday celebration, but the weather is so much better in May that they decided to hold it then.

The fiesta begins early Saturday morning, and by 10 a.m. more than 100 booths are open. There is art on display, crafts and jewelry for sale, information on nonprofit organizations, and a merchants fair, plus food booths selling hot dogs, hamburgers, tostadas, tamales, and "A Taste of Solana Beach," samples of cuisine from local restaurants. An hour-long parade starts at 11 a.m. and features floats, marching bands, equestrian groups, etc. A music extravaganza starts in the beach parking lot at 1 p.m. Bands play country music, rock, jazz, reggae, and nostalgic tunes.

With the nightfall, visitors can walk down to the beach for the community bonfire. Fiesta organizers devise unique ways to ignite the large blaze—even lasers!

The party starts again Sunday, with more music, booths, and fun in the sun. Solana Beach started out saying "howdy" to about 3,000 people; the free event now draws around 20,000 people each day. —L.S.

Fiesta La Ballona
Culver City   (213) 202-5689

Third Saturday in May. 10,000. 15 years. Free. Veterans Park. I-405 to Culver/Washington exit. Take Culver Blvd. east to Overland.

This one-day community event is considered a "festival of the people" and is primarily an opportunity for families from the area to gather in a local park and spend the day eating, listening to music, and enjoying a Spring day in Southern California.

The day begins with 5K and 10K runs and a pancake breakfast. By mid-morning, booths around the park are selling arts and crafts and a variety of ethnic foods, including tacos, burritos, teriyaki meat, and Indian dishes. Throughout the day many bands perform, from country and swing to jazz, big band, and rock-n-roll. There are also many games, rides and a petting zoo for the kids, plus an antique car display featuring antique army trucks, army tanks, and fire engines. Special demonstrations are put on by the local police department and their K9 team.

California Festivals   May

Fiestas Patrias Celebrations
San Jose   (408) 258-0663

Closest Sunday to May 5. 150,000. 9 years. Free. Downtown San Jose. From Hwy. 101 take the Alum Rock exit west. From I-280 take Guadalupe south.

This festival takes place on two different days, one in May and one in September, and honors Cinco De Mayo and Mexican Independence Day. It features a large parade (150 units) in the morning, food and craft booths, a Mexican art and cultural exhibit, and lots of live music, including mariachis and Folkloric dancers.

If you're a Mexican-food lover, you may want to spend the day tasting the variety of traditional Mexican and contemporary Chicano foods, including fajitas, tamales, fried chicken, corn on the cob, hot dogs, chili burgers, and ice cream. If you're more interested in education than eating, be sure to check out the art and culture exhibits; they offer a look into Mexican life both long ago and today. Whatever your pleasure, don't miss the parade or the music, both colorful and full of life, with a touch of history.

Frontier Days
Lake Elsinore Valley   (714) 674-2577

Memorial Day weekend (Thursday-Sunday). 20,000. 18 years. Rodeo $6, dances $5, barbecues $6. Lake Elsinore Rodeo Grounds. I-15 between San Diego and Corona passes Lake Elsinore—follow the signs.

If you've been hankering for a taste of frontier life or just always wanted to see a real live cowboy or watch a rodeo, then don't miss Lake Elsinore Valley's Frontier Days, featuring three days of Professional Rodeo Cowboy Association rodeos and lots of cowboy fun.

Located in the mountains just north of San Diego, this three-day affair attracts some 45,000 people, cowboys and otherwise. Each morning begins with a big breakfast, and before each rodeo there's a barbecue featuring Western-style hamburgers and hot dogs. The more adventurous can get a taste of Saturday night in a cowboy town at the two dances following Saturday and Sunday's rodeo. And don't miss the Saturday parade, featuring an Old Frontier theme and horse-drawn vehicles.

For anyone in your family who isn't a cowboy buff, there's also a carnival, with many rides and games. In addition, Lake Elsinore and the surrounding area offers many other activities, including picnicking, camping, fishing, and waterskiing.

California Festivals   May

Great Monterey Squid Festival
Monterey   (408) 649-6547

Memorial Day weekend (Saturday and Sunday). 30,000. 8 years. $4 adults, $2 children ages 6-12, free for children 5 and under. Monterey Fairgrounds. Exit Hwy. 1 at Camino Aquajito and then follow special signs to the festival.

The Great Monterey Squid Festival really holds true to its name. Besides being great fun and great entertainment, it's also a true celebration of the Monterey squid industry. If you've ever wondered how squid are caught, cleaned, or prepared, or anything about the life of a squid, this is the place to go. Through several films, videos, demonstrations and educational displays you can learn anything you ever wanted to know about this interesting cephalopod.

But of course the main attraction of this festival is the food. If you're squeamish about eating squid, the Great Monterey Squid Festival will make a convert out of you. In addition to fried, broiled, sauteed, marinated, and barbecued squid, you can sample delicious squid pizza, ceviche, fajitas, chowder, and empanadas, plus squid parmesan (excellent!), squid Siciliano, Cajun- or Greek-style squid, and much more.

While you're enjoying squid delicacies you can sit at one of several bandsites and enjoy great music (jazz, rock, country/western, and bluegrass) and entertainment. Or you can wander around and shop for squid theme gifts and other arts and crafts. There are several activities and even entertainment for the kids, as well as strolling clowns and mimes, and you can purchase wonderful octopus balloons. You can even have your picture taken with Mr. Squid!

All in all, this is a wonderful event for all ages. Besides benefiting community nonprofit organizations, the Great Monterey Squid Festival spotlights the fishing industry and the incredible edible squid. —K.L.

These squid balloons are about the only thing you can't eat at the Great Monterey Squid Festival. (Staff photo)

California Festivals   May

Grubstake Days
Yucca Valley   (619) 365-6323

Memorial Day weekend (Friday-Monday). 20,000. 41 years. Free except for PRCA rodeo. On Hwy. 62 behind the American Savings and Loan Bank. I-10 to Hwy. 62 east. 30 miles north of Palm Springs.

Memorial Day weekend is prime time for a good ol' Western celebration, and that's just what Yucca Valley's Grubstake Days is. It began over 40 years ago as a celebration for the gold miners in the area, and continues today as a fun festival for people from all over this area and beyond.

There's a carnival with games and rides for the kids, a parade with all kinds of decorated floats and marching bands, horseshoe contests, a tug-of-war competition, and, of course, the PRCA rodeo. There's lots of food too, from Mexican to Chinese and Thai (plus the usual carnival fare). And what Western weekend would be complete without dances Friday and Saturday nights? After a day in the fresh desert air, you'll have plenty of energy to take in some rock and roll and Western tunes.

Hometown Festival
Greater Ukiah   (707) 462-4705

Memorial Day weekend and throughout the following week. 10,000. 9 years. Free (fee for some events). State St. and School St. Off Hwy. 101 to Ukiah, take Perkins St. exit or North State St. exit

This community-oriented festival lasts 10 days and features 33 groups from three communities in 33 major events, highlighting just about every activity this area has to offer. Each year there's a different theme, and the number of activities and participants just keeps growing.

The festivities begin Memorial Day weekend with two parades, a rodeo (featuring bronco riding, calf roping, chute dogging, wild cow milking, cow riding, and a pig scramble), a golf tournament, barbecues, breakfasts, woodcutting, a turkey shoot, and a dance. There's also a street fair, with food booths (Chinese food, hot dogs, hamburgers, drinks, etc.), exhibits, and entertainment.

Other events throughout the festival include a chili cook-off, jazz and pop concerts, a street fair, a street dance, the Russian River Run (with distances of 8K and 10K), softball games, and museum exhibits.

California Festivals   May

Hughson Fruit and Nut Festival
Hughson (209) 883-4740

Third weekend in May (Saturday-Sunday). 30,000. 3 years. Free. Downtown. From Hwy 99 take Whitmore exit east approximately 6 miles.

Hughson is one of the towns you'd miss if you blink while driving by. But one weekend in May a year you can't miss it. Over 30,000 people jam tiny downtown Hughson for this big, family-type party. The center point of the festival is the farmer's market where you can buy all locally grown fruits and vegetables, and even herbs to olive oil. Of course, you won't want to miss the wide variety of tasty nuts—even orange and BBQ-flavored—although the most popular flavor is still natural! A stop by Food Alley will net you some linguisa, Chinese food or great homemade Mexican foods. Entertainment includes a petting zoo, tractor pull, car show, fun run and orchard harvesting equipment show with live demonstrations.

I Madonnari Italian Street Painting Festival
Santa Barbara (805) 569-3873

Memorial Day weekend (Saturday-Monday). 25,000. 5 years. Free. Old Mission Santa Barbara. From Hwy 101 take the Mission St. off-ramp and travel east to Laguna St., turn left and continue to Los Olivos St. and the Old Mission entrance.

An Italian tradition since the 16th century, street painting—using chalk as the medium—is enjoying a renaissance in cities throughout Western Europe and the U.S. The granddaddy of this event takes place every year in the village of Grazie di Curtattone, Italy, and its sister festival in the U.S. is held at the Old Mission piazza in Santa Barbara. Some 200 pavement squares are sponsored by local businesses, organizations and individuals and local artists are invited to become "madonnari,"

For one day Santa Barbara's Old Mission Piazza looks like it's italian sister city Gragie di Curtatone. (Photo by Macduff Everton)

or street painters. To round out the experience, the organizers have created an authentic Italian market nearby where you can get a bite to eat and shop for imported Italian specialities.

Imperial Sweet Onion Festival
Imperial City (619) 353-1900

First Saturday in May. 15,000. 6 years. Free. California Mid-Winter Fairgrounds. Go 4 miles west of El Centro on Highway 86.

We'll go anywhere for free onion rings! Yes, it's onionmania every year in Imperial City, where you can sample 15 different onion ring recipes. But the onion fun doesn't stop there. Among the day's activities are an onion ice cream contest, onion cooking contest, onion eating contest, onion clipping contest, onion crafts, onion golf and a floral competition with — you guessed it —ONIONS. Other highlights include an oompahpah band, square dancing and many local bands.

Jumping Frog Jubilee
Angels Camp   (209) 736-2561

Third weekend in May (Thursday-Sunday). 52,000. 64 years. Adults $9.00-$6.00; children and seniors $7.00-$4.00. Angels Camp. On Hwy. 49 south of Hwy. 4. Follow signs to the fairgrounds.

You KNOW this festival is going to be different when you drive into Angels Camp and see laundry lines sporting flannel shirts, Levis, long underwear, and calico dresses strung across Highway 49.

The first frog jump in Angels Camp (settled in 1849) was held in the bar of the Angels Hotel and made

Laundry lines festooned with Levis, long underwear, and flannel shirts and strung across downtown Angels Camps tell you you've arrived at the Jumping Frog Jubilee. (Photo by Mary Lou Johnson)

California Festivals   May

famous by Mark Twain's story "The Celebrated Jumping Frog of Calaveras County." Those Gold Rush days are the theme of this famous jumping frog contest, held at the county fairgrounds.

Hundreds of the little green fellows are jumped daily in special contests ranging from Kid's Day, Senior Citizen, and Scouts jumps to the Media, International, Junior, and Senior division jumps and the Grand Finals on Sunday.

You get a clear view of the jumps from bleachers in front of the stage. Lots of excitement is generated as the "jockeys" drop their frogs onto the launching pad of green felt then clap their hands, stomp their feet, or blow on their green friends to get them to leap. Jumps are measured from starting point to landing point of the third hop. The world record of 21 feet, 5 and 3/4 inches, set in 1986, is held by Rosie The Ribiter.

Part of the fun is hearing the names of the entries. How about Buzzard Bait, Dog's Breath, Lord of the Flies, or Road Pizza?! If you want, you can rent a frog right there, come up with a catchy name, and enter history as a frog jockey!

The Jubilee is held in conjunction with the county fair, so there are lots of exhibits to look at, and the carnival rides are included in the price of admission. New in 1991 was a Marathon Water Ski Race at Lake Mendocino. The rodeo and some of the other events are held in the arena, just a few hops past the frog jump stage. Viewing is from a pleasant, partly shaded hillside. Many people bring blankets and picnic lunches—it's a down-home crowd, and jeans and shorts are the standard uniform. Food is also available at the fair, and you'll hear lots of country music. —D.J. and M.J.

Kingsburg Swedish Festival
Kingsburg   (209) 897-2925

Third weekend in May (Thursday-Sunday). 25,000. 27 years. Free. Memorial Park. Kingsburg is 20 miles north of Visalia and 20 miles south of Fresno on Hwy. 99.

This is no "yuppie" festival—it's one of those community-oriented events that captures the spirit of small-town America, where the spectators and participants know one another by name and the lady selling quilts or the seniors selling cupcakes could be your next-door neighbors.

The four-day event, which commemorates this community's Swedish heritage, began as the Midsummer Festival, named after the annual celebration of the harvest in Sweden. The first one, held in Kingsburg in 1924, was a luncheon for the residents of the Fernholm Concordia Home. But today this festival features booths of all kinds, manned by local students and seniors, with everything from games and crafts to homemade ice cream.

There are many events as well, such as the Swedish Pea Soup and Pancake supper, a Swedish smorgasbord, "Finlandia" travelogue, Parade of the Trolls, youth dance, Dala Horse Trot run, decorating and raising the May pole, a Swedish pancake breakfast, Swedish children's stories, live entertainment all day Saturday and Sunday, arts, crafts and food booths and a parade. Thursday night at the Swedish Pea Soup is the annual crowning of the Queen.

This festival doesn't overwhelm the town of Kingsburg, which must be an awfully nice place to live; high school classes from decades ago can be seen riding on the floats in the parade, and many past festival queens still reside in the community. —K.J.

La Fiesta de San Luis Obispo
San Luis Obispo   (805) 543-1710

Begins Tuesday after the second weekend in May. 40,000. 51 years. Free for most events (charge for breakfast and family concert). Mission Plaza. San Luis Obispo is located on Hwy. 101.

Four days of music, dancing, parades, arts and crafts, food, and live entertainment celebrate this city's Spanish heritage and its founding by Father Junipero Serra in 1772. Strolling mariachi bands and the smell of Mexican food sets the mood at Mission Plaza each day, as do the many costumed participants.

Besides the arts and crafts fair and a family concert, one of the highlights of this festival is the bonfire burning of Zozobra, the "Old Man of Gloom." This Indian tradition has people throw sticks on the fire to burn away all ill feelings and gloom in preparation for the fiesta. There's also a costume breakfast: restaurants from downtown San Luis Obispo donate the food, and if you wear a costume, you get in for half price.

Booths set up around the plaza feature a variety of foods, including Mexican, Spanish, Filipino, Indian, Chinese, and barbecue. You'll hear a wide variety of music as well, including big bands, jazz, rock and roll, blues, and traditional Mexican.

Lamb Derby Festival
Willows   (916) 934-8150

First week in May (Monday-Sunday). 7,500. 59 years. Variety show $5-$8. Jensen Park. Willows is located on I-5, 85 miles north of Sacramento.

California Festivals   May

The sheep industry is big business in this part of the Sacramento Valley, and this festival provides an opportunity for those not familiar with the industry to learn more about it as well as savor some of its tasty products.

Among the more educational activities you'll be treated to are demonstrations of working dogs herding sheep (impressive no matter how many times you see it), sheep shearing, and sheep dog trials. The other side of the coin are the many sheep dishes you can taste, with two favorites being Basque-cooked lamb and barbecued lamb.

The rest of this festival is a fun, community-oriented event, featuring a high-quality variety show, parade, carnival, 5K and 10K runs, crafts fair, food concessions, contests (including a diaper derby, muscle man competition, and bathing beauties), a softball tournament, dances, clowns, face painting, and live entertainment.

Lemon Grove Old Time Days
Lemon Grove   (619) 469-9621

Early May (Friday and Saturday). 15,000. 29 years. Free. School Lane—from Lincoln to the Recreation Center. In downtown Lemon Grove, Hwy. 94 east from downtown San Diego, Lemon Grove exit. Parking on side streets.

You may think this two-day community festival has something to do with lemons, but you're wrong. It's just a good, old-fashioned community fair, with lots of activities for the whole family in a town that claims (with tongue somewhat in cheek) to have the best climate on Earth.

The festivities begin Friday night, with a barbecue dinner, country/western music show, and fireworks. Saturday begins early with a pancake breakfast, followed by a parade, a crafts show, and the old-time fair. Booths display and sell locally made arts and crafts plus all kinds of food: hot dogs, pizza, Mexican dishes, beer, soda, and margaritas. Other activities on Saturday include a cake-decorating contest and art demonstrations. There's also lots of live entertainment both days.

Living History Days
Petaluma   (707) 938-1519

Third Saturday of May. 1,000. 21 years. Adults $2, 18 and under $1, children under 6 free. Petaluma Adobe State Historic Park. Exit from Hwy. 101 39 miles north of San Francisco at 116 East. 1 mile east on 116/Lakeville, turn left on Casa Grande Rd.

Step back into the 1840s in this historic setting—the largest adobe in California, on General Vallejo's Mexican land grant. You'll see demonstrations of blacksmithing, weaving, candlemaking, basketmaking, and breadmaking in adobe ovens, plus a showing of period horse back riding.

Artisans in costumes from the time demonstrate period arts and crafts, and the house is filled with period furnishings. You can participate, too, making a visit to Living History Days both educational and fun.

Long Beach Lesbian and Gay Pride Celebration
Long Beach (213) 435-5530

Third weekend of May (Saturday and Sunday). 35,000. 8 years. $10. Shoreline Aquatic Park. Take the South Long Beach Freeway (710) to Shoreline Drive. The park is at Pine and Shoreline Drive.

Now the fourth largest gay pride event in the United States, this festival/parade commemorates the birth of the gay rights movement. The festival features live entertainment, dancing, information and artisan booths, games and food. Over 140 exhibitors participated last year. Entertainers such as Jimmy James, Dena Kaye, Lynn Lavner, Jane Edwards, E.G. Daily and Mona Caywood have appeared recently.

May Festival
Fillmore   (805) 524-0351

Third weekend in May (Thursday-Sunday). 15,000. 45 years. 50 cents. Downtown Fillmore. Hwy. 101 to Ventura, east on Hwy. 126 to Fillmore.

The Fillmore May Festival originally was held to celebrate the annual harvest and have an old-fashioned fun get-together with your neighbors. Now it has become a money maker as well for the clubs and organizations sponsoring the many food and game booths at the carnival.

Each year the theme is different, but the emphasis is always on community history. You'll see old-timers' costumes (1890s) and western attire, as well as beautiful old buildings around town. The focus of the festival is the midway and the carnival booths, which are sponsored by local folks, so all revenues from the community go back to the community. The food booths feature country to Mexican foods, hot dogs, cotton candy, and barbecue. The music, of course, is country/western. Special events at the festival include honoring the citizen of the year as grand marshal of the parade and the crowning of Miss Fillmore at the beauty pageant. And make sure you pick up a copy of the *Pole Creek Bugle*, the special satirical edition of the local newspaper.

Activities and times are listed in the paper, so schedule your visit around the parade, barbecue, and carnival, and make sure you make time to discover Fillmore's past. Walk down Central Street to Main and see the ornate scrolls on old buildings and the railroad boxcar, and visit the Historical Society. You'll feel the struggles of life in this railroad and farming community and understand why the May festival means so much to the folks in Fillmore. —S.F.

Monrovia Days
Monrovia   (818) 358-7627

Third Saturday in May (Wednesday-Saturday). 20,000. 77 years. Free. Center of town. East of Pasadena on I-210. Exit on Myrtle Ave. North to Library Park.

You may not see anyone wearing silly hats or playing pin-the-tail-on-the-donkey, but each May the city of Monrovia takes four days to celebrate its birthday (105 years old in 1991). Nearly 20,000 people turn out for the event, which has a different theme each year.

The festivities begin Wednesday with a kick-off parade and a carnival that runs through Saturday. The high point of the festival is Saturday's parade, featuring over 115 entries including, floats, bands, antique cars, equestrian units, and novelty displays.

Other activities include a community luncheon, and a pancake breakfast. There is also a variety of ethnic foods, hamburgers, barbecued chicken, and pizza for sale.

Morgan Hill Mushroom Mardi Gras
Morgan Hill   (408) 779-9444

Memorial Day weekend (Saturday-Sunday). 35,000. 13 years. Adults $5, children $2. Community Park, Monterey and Tennant. Hwy. 101 to Tennant Ave. Go west one mile.

If you like your steak smothered in sauteed mushrooms, spinach and mushroom quiche, stuffed mushrooms, and mushroom and cheese omelets, this festival is your meal ticket. Over 40 food and drink booths feature a variety of mushroom (and other) dishes. Good thing Morgan Hill is the largest mushroom-growing area in California!

But there's more to do than just eat at this festival. There are over 200 arts and crafts booths, continuous entertainment (featuring jazz and country/western music), and a large play area for the kids including clowns, and a petting zoo.

Mule Days Celebration
Bishop   (619) 873-8405

Memorial Day weekend (Thursday-Monday). 50,000. 22 years. Free. Fee for some events. Tri-County Fairgrounds. Hwy. 395 to Bishop. Turn off on Sierra St. from Hwy. 395. Entrance to fairgrounds off Sierra St.

If you're looking for something a little different this Memorial Day weekend, get your camping gear together, grab the family mule, and head for Bishop and the kick-off of the summer mule-packing season in the High Sierra. For four days, the spotlight is on mules, those equestrian marvels that mule lovers are determined to prove can do anything a good horse can do—only better. From trail riding to show classes, mules do it with a grace unique to this animal.

Among the many exciting events at this festival are chariot races, where several wheelbarrow-size chariots are pulled around a racetrack by teams of two mules, leading to an exciting and sometimes disastrous finish; steer roping and penning, where cowboys can prove their roping and riding skills astride some of the best working mules in the U.S.; and English classes, hunter classes, and jumping, where the mules are tested in their ability as riding animals and taken through a course of jumps to demonstrate their versatility. Other events include barrel racing, Western racing, packing, trail riding, obstacle courses, chuck wagon races, and hauling demonstrations.

But the wildest event of the weekend is the packers scramble, where some 50 packers, 40 horses, two dozen cattle, and 80 mules mix it up in the main arena.

In addition to these competitions, there is also a parade featuring more than 250 nonmotorized entries, country and western dances, barbecues, pancake breakfasts, an arts and crafts show, and the Professional Invitational Western Art Show.

California Festivals   May

Newport Beach Salute to the Arts
Newport Beach   (714) 644-3150

Middle of May. 10,000. 8 years. Free. (Fee for some events.) Different locations within city of Newport Beach. Hwy 1 to Newport Blvd. to village.

This festival is a cornucopia of visual, performing and culinary arts. Music, dance, and dramatic events take place throughout the festival days, including a juried art competition. Special menus are offered by area restaurants for food sampling. Musical offerings include opera, jazz, steel band, big bands and symphonic orchestras.

Chamber music is just one of the many musical events at Newport's Salute to the Arts. (Photo courtesy of Newport Salute to the Arts)

Pacific Beach Block Party
San Diego   (619) 483-6666

Second Saturday in May. 50,000. 14 years. Free. Garnet St., from Cass St. to Mission Blvd. I-5 in San Diego, take Garnet St. exit and head west.

Don't let the name fool you. The free Pacific Beach Block Party actually spans several avenues. There's dancing in the streets to performers such as the Ravells, a 60s band. There are blocks of food offerings and a half-mile of exhibitor booths. The rest of the festivities get under way at 9 a.m. The party is usually the day before Mother's Day, so it's a great excuse to have fun while shopping for a present for Mom.

The more than 400 booths are staffed by businesses and local groups. Their wares include jewelry, pottery, paintings, photographs, stained-glass pieces, clothing, and tarot card readings. Since the party is only blocks from the beach, it's not surprising to find plenty of booths with swimwear, sunglasses, and T-shirts. Some exhibitors offer samples, such as a free 15-minute massage and a spinal check.

All the walking you'll do is bound to build up an appetite, so turn down "food street" and try to decide between a Hungarian sausage sandwich, teriyaki chicken, or Siam beef on a stick. There are also hot dogs, gyros, pita sandwiches, pizza, fish tacos, churros (a cinnamony Mexican dessert), barbecued meats, and more.

Pan American Festival
Lakewood   (213) 866-9771, ext. 417

Second week in May (Thursday-Sunday). 30,000. 45 years. Free. Mayfair Park, 5720 Clark Ave. 91 Freeway to Lakewood Blvd. south; east on South St. to Clark Ave. The park is at the corner of South and Clark.

Begun 45 years ago as a show of friendship between the U.S. and Central and South America, this four-day event now features live entertainment, 100 craft booths, 20 food booths, amusement rides for all ages, lots of live entertainment, and displays of police and fire equipment. Other events include softball and volleyball tournaments, a flag exchange, and a Spanish "speak-off."

The food booths offer a wide variety of refreshments, including baked potatoes, hot dogs, hamburgers, chili, nachos and other Mexican food, pizza, pretzels, baked goods, shaved ice, ice cream, and cotton candy. Craft booths feature country crafts, silk flower arrangements, children's furniture, toys, stuffed animals, face painting, and balloons. There is also a "Make It/Take It" booth, where participants can create their own buttons and hats.

Among the live entertainment is 50s and 60s rock and roll; country/western; big band; Hawaiian music; Spanish guitar and flute; Mexican music and dances; and a barbershop chorus.

Patterson Apricot Fiesta
Patterson   (209) 892-2701

Last weekend in May (Saturday and Sunday). 20,000. 20 years. Free. Downtown Patterson on the circle. I-5 to Patterson exit, Sperry Ave. 3 miles to Patterson. Do not take Patterson Pass Rd. if coming from the north.

The entire town of "The Apricot Capital of the World" gets involved in this two-day event that promotes both apricots and the community of Patterson. Streets are blocked off, booths set up around the park and central plaza, and bales of hay set out for seating.

California Festivals   May

Saturday begins with hot-air balloon rides and the "Run for the Apricots." Later in the day there's a horseshoe tournament, arm wrestling, art displays, craft fair, parade, barbecue, petting zoo, and lots of food and free entertainment. The evening is capped with a fireworks display and community dance. Sunday features the popular public breakfast, more hot-air balloons and crafts, a fireman's muster, and a skydiving exhibition, plus more food and entertainment. Other activities include an apricot recipe contest, the Little Mr. and Miss Apricot pageant, a car show, a bike race with almost 300 riders, and Spanish, rock, and country/western music.

At the food booths downtown, you'll find lots of apricot goodies, such as pies, tarts, ice cream, and fresh apricots. Other food available includes Mexican and Chinese dishes, linguicia sandwiches, steak on a stick, and barbecued chicken.

Prunefestival Wine and Arts
Campbell   (408) 378-6252

Third weekend in May (Saturday and Sunday). 40,000. 13 years. Free. Campbell Community Center, 1 W. Campbell Ave. Hwy 880 to San Jose, Exit Hamilton Ave. to Winchester Blvd. corner of Winchester and Campbell Ave.

You might not think a town would want to herald its past glory as the Prune Processing Capital of the World, but Campbell takes pride in its heritage, and this festival helps to preserve that pride. As you can probably guess, you'll find many creative prune products here, such as prune wine, prune bread, and prune mustard.

Some 200 craft vendors offer a wide variety of hand-crafted items. And don't worry—there's lots of non-prune food, including hot dogs, hamburgers, Italian and Polish sausage, fajitas, nachos, shish kebabs, and stuffed pizza (calzone).

As for entertainment, there's a variety of music and a Kiddie Korner with puppets, face painting, a clown, and a "bounce about."

Raisin Festival
Selma   (209) 896-3315

First weekend in May (Thursday-Saturday). 8,000. 12 years. Free. Pioneer Village and downtown. 15 miles south of Fresno on Hwy. 99.

California Festivals — May

The Raisin Festival is a celebration of Fresno County's number one agribusiness, the raisin industry. Highlights include: Gourmet Row featuring raisin cuisine from outstanding valley restaurants (Thursday night), national raisin tray rolling competition, forklift truck rodeo, horseshoe tournament, stitchery, horticulture, baking and art compititions. Entertainment includes live bands, a melodrama and special acts throughout the day. There is also a pancake breakfast, a family fun run/walk and a parade and over 75 food and craft booths.

Rancho California Balloon and Wine Festival
Temecula   (714) 676-5090

Third weekend in May (Saturday-Sunday). 100,000. 9 years. Adults $5, Children $2.50, children under 6 free. Lake Skinner. From I-15, take the Rancho California Rd. exit. Go east 10 miles to the Lake Skinner turn-off.

When most people think of California's wine country, they don't think of Southern California, but a visit to this festival may just open your eyes to what's going on in the south (besides beaches and traffic, of course). Rustic, rolling hills provide the backdrop for the two-day event, filled with the majestic beauty of brightly colored hot-air balloons, lots of good local wine (from 11 of the Temecula Valley's wineries), plenty of food, a variety of family activities, and the sounds of cool jazz.

Believe it or not, the festival gates open at 3 a.m. each day (that's right- 3 o'clock in the morning), with dawn champagne balloon flights lifting off at 7 a.m. and lasting until 10:30 a.m. More than 60 balloonists from all over the U.S. participate in this event. If you've never seen a balloon festival of this sort, the ascensions alone are worth almost any price of admission--they're exciting, colorful, fun, educational, and inspiring. The whole crowd gets involved, with everyone cheering each time a balloon takes

Balloons fill the sky and wine your glass at the Rancho California Balloon & Wine Festival. (Photo courtesy of Rancho California Balloon & Wine Festival)

off and the balloonists and their passengers waving and taking pictures.
There's plenty to do besides taste wine if you decide to remain on the ground. Activities for the whole family include an antique car exhibit, games, arts and crafts, swimming, fishing, boating, a puppet show, clowns, and magic shows for the kids, live entertainment and walks through the historic town of Temecula, a town preserved by law in the architectural style of the 1890s. Other events include pancake breakfasts, a gourmet cooking contest, a grape-stomping contest, amateur wine-making competitions, magic shows, a dance exhibition, a lip-synch contest, and a variety of musical entertainment.

Red Suspenders Days
Gridley   (916) 846-3142

Third Saturday in May. 10,000. 30 years. Free. Daddow Park and Fairground and downtown Gridley. 50 miles north of Sacramento on Hwy. 99.

They've been honoring the fire fighters in this community for 30 years at Red Suspenders Days, with a parade, a dinner and dance, an arts and crafts show, pancake breakfast, and, of course, bed races. This event also features a "mule kicker" dance with a country band, barbecue, chili cook-off, walkathon, 5K and 10K run, draft horse (Clydesdale) show and competition, games for the kids, and face painting.
There's lots of live music, including jazz and country/western, and good food too, including Spanish dishes, barbecued beef sandwiches, and homemade desserts.

Russian River Wine Festival
Healdsburg   (707) 433-6935
1-800-648-9922 (CA only)

Sunday after Mother's Day. 4,500. 20 years. $10-$15 (includes glass and 5 wine tastes). Healdsburg Plaza Park. From Hwy. 101 (north of San Francisco), take central Healdsburg exit to Healdsburg Ave., two blocks to the plaza.

The purpose of this festival is to promote wines of the Russian River Wine Road, a cooperative organization of 59 Sonoma County wineries located near the Russian River. More than 30 member wineries set up tasting tables around the perimeter of Plaza Park. $10 buys you a souvenir wine glass and tickets to taste five wines (tickets for additional tastings are 50 cents each). Also around the park are several food booths and many arts and crafts booths.

This is a five-hour festival, from noon to 5 p.m. Within the pretty tree-shaded park, a band plays jazz. And it is possible to lounge around and listen without spending a cent. If you are a wine enthusiast, though, you will want to part with $10 or more, as you can taste some wines here that are difficult to find elsewhere. A few are sold only at the wineries.

A free festival guide includes a map of the plaza showing the location of each winery's table, as well as a description of each wine being poured. Also included is a story about each winery participating and information on its winemaking style.

Can you think of a nicer way to spend a Spring day? --D.J. and M.J

Sacramento Dixieland Jubilee
Sacramento   (916) 372-5277

Memorial Day weekend (Friday-Monday). 100,000. 17 years. $65 for a 4-day all-event pass. Over 40 sites throughout Sacramento. I-80 or I-5 to Sacramento.

This four-day musical extravaganza is known as "America's International Jazz festival." Jazz, jazz, and more jazz is what you'll be treated to, with more than 100 bands playing over 1,000 sessions at over 40 venues, from 10 a.m. to midnight each day, plus impromptu jam sessions well into the wee hours. Sets average about an hour.

Bands from as nearby as, well, Sacramento and as far away as Australia and Russia all travel to Sacramento to celebrate the music of America. You just can't be grumpy listening to this music. And it takes quite a bit of will power to just sit and listen. Pretty soon the ol' fingers start snapping, the toes start tapping, and you may just find yourself compelled to boogie up and down the aisles, or even onto the dance floor.

In addition to all this great music, many special events are scheduled, including piano/tuba/washboard-a-ramas, a hymn sing-along, banjo bash, red hot mamas, all-night jam sessions, big band show, ragtime piano, and best of all, the crazy crowd. Beer, mixed drinks, sodas, pizza, and a variety of specialty foods and snacks are available at all performance sites, and Old Sacramento is worth exploring for its restaurants, bars, shops, and such freebies as steam locomotive rides. There's also an honest-to-goodness paddlewheel riverboat!

The number of bands and the quality of the music at this festival really are incredible. It's four days of jollies, with the crowd becoming more entertaining itself as the hours roll on and the refreshments roll down. The bands seem to thrive on lack of sleep, and their enthusiasm is contagious. But you've got to love Dixieland, and lots of it. —K.J. and B.B.

San Fernando Fiesta
San Fernando   (818) 361-1184

First weekend in May (Saturday and Sunday). 50,000. 64 years. Free. Recreation Park. San Fernando is easily accessible from I-210, Hwy. 118, I-5, and I-405.

This festival celebrates both Cinco de Mayo and San Fernando's cultural heritage. San Fernando was the first settlement in the Los Angeles area, and you can probably guess by its name that that first settlement was Spanish. Same goes for this festival.

The entire event has a Spanish and Mexican flavor, in both the food and entertainment. The live music features nationally renowned Latin, country, and pop acts, and the food, though primarily Mexican, also includes American and Thai dishes, falafels, and pizza.

Some 50,000 people attend the two-day event, enjoying the great Southern California weather, the carnival rides and game booths, the ethnic foods, and themselves.

San Francisco Examiner Bay to Breakers—"Footstock"
San Francisco   (415) 777-7770

Third Sunday in May. 100,000. 80 years. $12-$15 for race. Spear St. and Howard St.; Golden Gate Park. Take Hwy. 101 or I-80 to downtown San Francisco. For Golden Gate Park, take Hwy. 101 north, get off at Fell St. exit, follow Fell to the park.

Whether you're a runner or not matters very little at this event, known in the *Guinness Book of World Records* as the world's largest footrace. It certainly seems like the largest when you're in the middle of that pack of 100,000 on a foggy Sunday at 8 a.m. The race travels 7.5 miles from the bay side of the city to the breakers at Ocean Beach, and unless you're one of the seeded runners (and they get world-class runners, including Olympic gold medal marathon winner Rosa Mota, so good luck), the first mile can only be navigated at a shuffle at best.

But believe it or not, running isn't really the focus of this event for most of the crowd. The fun is in watching all the crazy participants, dressed in everything from bathrobe and slippers to a plastic bubble butt that bounces and bobbles its way in and out of the crowd—you may even see the Golden Gate Bridge or the Transamerica pyramid navigating their way through Golden Gate Park! Lots of skiers, skaters, wheelchairs, and bike riders also make the trip.

Some of the best costumes are worn by the "Centipede" entries, where groups of 5, 10, 15, or more (often sponsored by local corporations) remain attached throughout the race via ropes or ribbons or the costumes themselves. Past races have seen a giant pig and a huge red lobster, which the runners carried from underneath, and some couch potatoes who finally got out of the house but just had to bring the couch along.

Once you get to the end, the crowd continues on to the Polo Field in Golden Gate Park, where "Footstock" awaits. Here you can meet up with non-running friends for a picnic, pick up your official T-shirt, sip some free beer (which tastes amazingly good at 10 a.m.), and do some more people watching. There are also awards presentations, entertainment, and food.

The two days before the race are also full of events, from a block party at Embarcadero Center (where the race begins), featuring live music and dancing, to an expo of running wear, equipment, food, and entertainment. The night before the race, you can attend a free outdoor comedy show and concert. And be sure to stop by the pasta feed, where you can load up on some delicious carbos and get your body, as well as your mind, ready for the big race.

Santa Cruz Spring Fair
Santa Cruz   (408) 425-5645

Third weekend in May (Saturday and Sunday). 35,000. 22 years. Free. San Lorenzo Park. Hwy. 17 to Ocean St. Go down three lights, turn right at the County Building.

Though any time of year is the right time to visit Santa Cruz, Spring is one of the best (as long as the fog cooperates!). This two-day fair celebrates the coming of Spring to the California coast, with over 100 arts and crafts booths and 50 food booths.

Nearly 30,000 people cruise the park where this event is held, munching on all kinds of food (with 50 different booths, there's just about everything you can imagine), checking out the arts and crafts, and listening to five bands each day play country music, mellow rock, jazz, etc. It's a fun way to spend a weekend, and Santa Cruz is one of the nicer places to be this time of year.

California Festivals   May

Shafter Potato 'n Cotton Festival
Shafter   (805) 746-3982,
          (805) 746-1517

Third weekend in May (Friday-Saturday). 6,000. 21 years. Free. Downtown area. From Hwy. 99 (10 miles north of Bakersfield) take the Shafter exit and go west past the airport approximately 5 miles.

You might not think potatoes and cotton have much in common, but agriculture is the number one industry in this part of the San Joaquin Valley, and for 20 years the town of Shafter has been celebrating its "agricultural paradise" with a two-day festival in the middle of Spring.

The celebration begins Friday with a Junior Miss beauty pageant. Saturday features a big parade and an arts and crafts fair. Among the booths you'll find crafts and many games for the kids as well as Chinese, Mexican, Thai, and "Oakie" food, locally made goodies, and an assortment of fast foods. The booths are all decorated and judged, with the winners getting trophies.

Some of the other events over the two days include a fun run for the sports-minded, contests of skill, a fireman's muster, and a Saturday night dance. There's also live entertainment throughout the festival.

Sierra Madre Art Fair
Sierra Madre   (818) 355-7186

Third weekend of May (Saturday-Sunday). 20,000. 30 years. Free. Memorial Park. I-210 east of Pasadena. Balwin off-ramp to Sierra Madre Blvd. Left to Memorial Park.

130 artists turn Memorial Park into an outdoor gallery during this two-day event that's been going on for almost 30 years and has come to be known as one of the best fine art fairs in Southern California. Juried oils, watercolors, photographs, and sculpture from around the U.S. are featured, and many up-and-coming artists show their work here. Many artists also demonstrate their techniques. Another tradition of this festival are the T-shirts, with each year's shirt featuring the best artwork from the previous year. 1989's T-shirt sported a colorful bird-of-paradise flower.

The park setting offers a recreational play area for the kids, and a variety of foods (ethnic dishes plus hamburgers and hot dogs) are available. Strolling musicians add a relaxing touch to this friendly festival. Artists say this is one of the most pleasant shows to participate in.

Sierra Showcase of Wine
Plymouth   (209) 274-4766

First Saturday in May. 1,200. 10 years. $12.50 advance, $15 at the door. Amador County Fairgrounds. Take State Hwy 49 to Plymouth, follow signs to Amador County Fairgrounds.

The clear mountain air of the Sierra Foothills sharpens the senses and draws discriminating wine buffs from all over to this wine-tasting extravaganza, where you can sample opulent Chardonnays, traditional Zinfandels and rich Cabernet Sauvignons from Nevada, El Dorado, Amador, Calaveras and Tuolumne counties. Altogether, 35 foothill wineries participate, each proud of their regional specialities, which this year include bold Zinfandels from Amador county, Cabernets and a late-harvest White Riesling from Nevada County, Sauvignon Blancs and a mountain-grown syrah from El Dorado, and from Calaveras County berry-flavored Zinfandels, oak-aged Chardonnays and Merlots and elegant Cabernet Sauvignons. Plenty of fresh fruits, crackers and cheeses are provided to help complement the flavors of the wines.

As in years past, designated drivers will be entitled to complimentary coffee, soft drinks, snacks and a gift mug.

Spring Wine Festival
Gilroy   (408) 778-1555

First Saturday in May. 700. 17 years. $27.50. Hecker Pass. Take U.S. 101 North or South to Hwy 152 (Hecker Pass Highway) west to 3050 Hecker Pass in Gilroy.

One of the unique aspects of the Spring Wine Festival is that you can talk to the proprietors of the 20 local wineries that participate. Bring your wine questions along with your appetite and taste for wine.

For one price, you receive a souvenir glass to sample the great Santa Clara Valley wines, eat a complete BBQ dinner and enjoy the barrel races and bocciball tournaments. Plus, the setting is spectacular with lush gardens and a cute train that wends its way through the park.

Strawberry Festival
Arroyo Grande   (805) 473-2250

Memorial Day weekend (Saturday-Sunday). 250,000. 9 years. Free. Village of Arroyo Grande. Take any Arroyo Grande exit off Hwy. 101 and ask directions to the village or to the High school, where shuttle buses run every 10 minutes to the festival site.

Strawberries may be the excuse for this festival, but family fun and entertainment are what it's really all about. Sure, strawberries have been a major part of the Arroyo Grande Valley farming industry since 1890, and sure, this festival features a strawberry prince and princess contest, the 10K strawberry stampede, a strawberry pancake breakfast, strawberry shortcake, and dipped strawberries, but there's plenty of other activities, entertainment, and food to satisfy the whole family. A "battle of the bands" showcases 25 bands at eight locations. Other entertainment includes dancers, baton twirlers, gymnastic exhibitions, and wandering minstrels, mimes, and jugglers. There are lots of activities for the kids, too--puppets, clowns, and games, including tug-of-war, an egg toss, and a three-legged race.

And strawberries aren't the only food you'll find--you can choose from 60 food vendors, featuring Greek, Chinese, Mexican, Filipino, Cajun, and German dishes, plus an oak-pit barbecue.

Strawberry Festival
Garden Grove   (714) 638-0981

Memorial Day weekend (Friday-Monday). 200,000. 34 years. Free. Village Green. Garden Grove Freeway (Hwy. 22) to Euclid. North on Euclid to Village Green. The grounds are on the left, approximately 1 mile.

Sure, strawberries are a popular item when they're in season, but would you believe 200,000 people turn out for this four-day salute to strawberries? Garden Grove was once the largest producer of strawberries on the West Coast and, though times have changed, this is still the second-largest city festival in California.

And strawberries are what you'll find here. You can enter the strawberry pie-eating contest, watch the strawberry cake-cutting ceremony, or help try to build the largest strawberry shortcake (do the winners get to eat it too?). Red is also the dominant color of the day, with a "Redhead Roundup" and a contest to see who has the most freckles.

Other events include a parade, a carnival, a large talent show, live country and modern music, and an arts and crafts fair. There's lots of food, of course, both strawberry and otherwise, and you can guess what the specialty is: strawberry shortcake.

Vacaville Fiesta Days
Vacaville   (707) 448-4613

Third weekend in May (five days). 20,000. 33 years. Some events have fees. Andrew's Park on East Monte Vista Ave. I-80, exit at downtown Vacaville.

This week-long tribute to the city's Spanish and Western heritage is seven days of Western family fun in the sun. There are so many events it's hard to list them all here, and it seems like everyone in the city gets involved.

Here's just some of the things you'll find at Fiesta Days: a queen pageant, a golf tournament, a talent contest (featuring everything from tumbling routines to rock and roll bands), a whiskerino contest (participants are kept in the local "jail"), eating contests, a parade, a carnival, a store-decorating contest, employee costume contest, photo contest, western dances and barbecues, wristwrestling competition, olympic skills and body-building contests, and a turkey shoot. One of the funniest events is the tug of war, which often turns into a real war!

With so much to do it's a good thing there's plenty to eat, including Mexican, Vietnamese, Chinese, and American food and lots of beer. In addition to the many contests and events already listed, there's also different entertainment every day, including western and polka bands, a big band, impersonators, and jugglers.

Maybe the folks in Vacaville should think about changing this festival to "Fiesta Month"...

Whole Earth Festival
Davis   (916) 752-2568

First or second weekend in May (Friday-Saturday). 20,000. 23 years. Free. UC Davis campus. I-80 from San Francisco going east toward Sacramento, take the UC Davis exit.

The Whole Earth Festival, a popular crafts fair, celebrates our interdependence with Mother Earth. Reminiscent of the 60s, the festival includes tie-dye clothing of all types and emphasizes healthful living, awareness of our environment, harmony, peace, tolerance, acceptance, and good times. As you meander through the crowd you'll see booths where quality handmade items such as ceramics, jewelry, textiles, clothing, sandles, and candles are sold. Curried Indian dishes, vegetarian pizza, and freshly squeezed fruit juices are some of the culinary delights offered at the festival. You can also enjoy live rock and roll dance music and several lectures on campus that follow the theme of the day. --P.R.

Windsor Laff-Off
Windsor (707) 838-7285
(707) 838-9766

Third Saturday in May. 300. 12 years. Adults $5, children free. Landmark Vineyards. From Hwy. 101 take the Windsor exit. Turn left on Old Redwood Hwy., left on Windsor River Rd., through old downtown Windsor and left again at Keiser Park.

They say that laughter is the best medicine, but it's even better when it's combined with lots of fresh air and sunshine at this afternoon and evening event.

The day begins with a morning parade that ends at the park, where booths of food, crafts, live entertainment, and games are set up. But the focus of the day is the comedy show, which is a state-wide competition for amateur comedians. People come from all over Northern California to try their hand at stand-up. The finals go all evening, making for some great entertainment while you picnic under the stars (bring your own picnic basket!) on the Green at Landmark Vineyards.

California Festivals   June

Annual Italian Benevolent Society Picnic and Parade
Sutter Creek   (209) 223-0350

First week in June (Friday-Sunday). 5,000. 110 years. Fee for some events. Italian Picnic Grounds, Sutter Hill and Main St. Hwy. 16 east from Sacramento to Hwy. 49. Sutter Creek is 8 miles from Hwy. 16, 42 miles from Sacramento.

When you think of the Gold Country you think of history, but you probably don't think of four Italians in 1881 founding an organization for widows and families of deceased members that has endured into the late 20th century. This three-day community festival, located on the Italian Picnic Grounds, continues the tradition with a children's carnival, bingo games, beer and wine booths, entertainment, and a Sunday morning parade with some amusing participants, including a "Win A Dago" truck sponsored by a local sanitation company and an out-of-step troop of marchers that defies any attempts at synchronization.

As for food, you can enjoy a traditional Italian feast of ravioli, chicken, and all the trimmings on Saturday evening (be sure to get your tickets early--only 400 people can attend) and a barbecue after Sunday's parade. In addition, the park's many acres of oak-shaded grass dotted with picnic tables is the perfect setting for a family-style picnic.

Art & Wine Festival
Walnut Creek   (415) 934-2007

First weekend in June (Saturday-Sunday). 30,000. 10 years. Free. Heather Farms Park. From Hwy 680 take the Ygnacio Valley Rd exit in Walnut Creek. Go several miles, then turn left on San Carlos to Heather Farms Park.

Sure, it's free to get in. But the whole idea behind the Art and Wine Festival is to stroll around looking at fine art while sipping wine and beer from some of California's finest wineries and breweries. And in order to do any tasting, you'll have to buy a commemorative glass for $4 and tasting tickets are $1.25. In years past such notables as Kendall Jackson, Barefoot Cellars, David Bruce, Concannon, Louis Martini, Felton Empire, Windsor, Sutter Homes, Wente, Weibel and Napa Ridge wineries participated along with the microbreweries of Anchor Steam, Pete's Wicked Ale and Lind Brewery. We recommend getting your tasting glass ahead of time; they're a dollar cheaper that way, and in past years have sold out quickly.

Over 130 artists and craftsmen present their works while continuous live music plays—everything from rock 'n roll, country and jazz quartets to a 17-piece big band. Top local restaurants sponsor over 20 food booths, including ethnic foods and more traditional festival fare such as pizza, pasta, hamburgers, chicken sandwiches, etc. Other popular attractions include a kit car display, karate and gymnastics exhibitions, face painting and a petting zoo for the kids.

Carnaval San Francisco
San Francisco   (415) 826-1401

Memorial Day weekend (Friday-Sunday). 300,000. 12 years. Free. Parade: Mission St.; festival: Harrison between 16th and 21st. Hwy. 101 to Army St. west, right on Harrison to 21st.

Carnaval San Francisco is a multiethnic Mardi Gras parade and festival featuring carnival contingents representing New Orleans, South America, and the Caribbean. In addition to the parade running through the Mission District of San Francisco, you'll find a festival featuring five entertainment stages filled with the sounds of Latin, rock, Dixieland, Samba, African, Caribbean, and Zydeco music, plus ethnic foods of all kinds: Puerto Rican, Cuban, African, Brazilian, Greek, Chinese, Japanese, and Panamanian.

This celebration is attended by more than 300,000 people annually.

Over 300,000 Mardi Gras revelers shed their inhibitions at San Francisco's multicultural Carnaval. (Photo by Debra Netsky)

California Festivals   June

Cherries Jubilee
Placerville   (916) 626-6521

Father's Day Weekend (Saturday-Sunday). 3,000. 4 years. Free. Goldbud Farm. From Hwy 50 take Carson Road exit and go east to Goldbud Farm, 2501 Carson Road.

Have you ever wondered how far someone can spit a cherry? At Placerville's Cherries Jubilee the record is 67 feet (only 5 feet short of the world record). And when people aren't spitting cherries, they're tying the stems together in their mouths. Believe it or not, someone has done that in about 5 seconds. But the real highlight of the festival are the wonderful cherry desserts. Treat yourself to a cherry pie, chocolate-covered cherries, or the ever-popular cherries jubilee. Goldbud Farm is a great place to kick back while listening to good bluegrass music, enjoying a picnic and eating some fresh cherries.

Cherry Festival
Linden   (209) 887-3767

First weekend in June (Saturday and Sunday). 10,000. 33 years. Free. Downtown Linden. Linden is east of Stockton, 10 miles from Hwy. 99.

Located in the fertile San Joaquin Valley, the area surrounding Linden is one of the largest cherry producing areas in the country. The festival features games, carnival rides, a parade, and a variety of entertainment and music, including country/western, pop, Dixieland, jazz, and big band. And of course you'll find all kinds of cherry treats: fresh cherries, cherry cakes and pies, and cherry ice cream. A farmers market is also featured.

If you find after a while that you just can't eat another cherry, other foods you can sample are barbecued ribs and chicken, hot dogs, and pizza. Wine tasting is also available.

Cherry Festival
Beaumont   (714) 845-9541

Third week in June (Wednesday-Sunday). 10,000. 73 years. Free. Stewart Park and Beaumont Ave. I-10 from Los Angeles past San Bernardino. Take the first Beaumont exit. Take Beaumont Ave. north two blocks.

California Festivals   June

This annual celebration of the area's cherry industry is several days of family fun. For the kids there's a carnival and parade (Saturday), sky divers, games, and arts and crafts of all kinds. For the adults there are stage shows featuring local bands, plus a beer garden where you can beat the heat. The whole family will enjoy 72 arts and craft booths, pancake breakfast, horse show, and talent contest. Or try your hand at cherry picking! You'll find the usual carnival food—hot dogs, hamburgers, etc.—plus lots of cherry favorites and some interesting creations.

Columbia Diggin's
Columbia   (209) 532-4301

First weekend in June (Thursday-Sunday). 8,000. 10 years. Free. Columbia State Historic Park. 2 miles off Hwy. 49. 4 miles north of Sonora.

This popular four-day event isn't just a festival—it's a "hands-on" experience of life in a gold-mining town in the mid 1800s. You can take part in the reenactment of events that actually occurred in this area—the heart of California's Gold Country—visit an old-time saloon, and see live entertainment. The food is from the 1800s too: home-baked bread, lemonade, sasparilla, and more. It's a living history of life in the Old West.

Davis Street Faire
Davis   (916) 756-5160

First Sunday in June. 20,000. 5 years. Free. Downtown Davis. From Hwy 80 take the Davis exit, go three blocks to the downtown area.

There's a wholesome charm to this small town dominated by academics (home to the University of California at Davis). So when they put on a street faire—it draws a crowd. After all, at least 20,000 students and faculty live within walking distance.

Music is a big part of the day with rock 'n roll, jazz, bluegrass, and 50s and 60s tunes rounding out the mix. The Aggie Maverick Band wakes things up with a quick march through downtown, and for the rest of the day a new group plays every half hour.

The centerpiece of the faire is the classic car show sponsored by the Western Vehicle Association. Over 300 entrants vie for Best of Show. Visitors are just as likely to see a mini-truck parked next to a horseless carriage or an exotic foreign sports car parked next to a chopped-top custom car. You'll also find restored classic race cars, trucks, motorcycles, boats, sportscars, hand-built creations, and vans.

A stroll through downtown will take you past over 120 booths with fine arts and crafts. A visit to the Beer Garden or the wine tasting area is a good way to cool off while deciding whether to enjoy snacks or a complete meal from ethnic food to the American summer staples — hot dogs and hamburgers. For the kids they've added a five-ride kiddie carnival to the petting zoo and special games.

East Palo Alto Juneteenth Festival
East Palo Alto   (415) 853-3100

Saturday and Sunday closest to June 19. 10,000. 19 years. Free. East Palo Alto Recreation Center. Hwy. 101 to University Ave. exit. Go east on University to Bell Ave.

East Palo Alto's Juneteenth festival is one of the largest annual gatherings in that city. The two-day celebration commemorates the date when African Americans in the western states finally recieved word of the Emancipation Proclamation Act. The festival features local and international entertainers, arts and craft booths, and a lot of delicious ethnic food for your eating enjoyment. The festival attracts vendors and visitors from all over the state.

Eastfield Ming Quong Strawberry Festival
Los Gatos   (408) 379-3790,

First weekend in June (Saturday and Sunday). 50,000. 32 years. Free. Grounds of the Los Gatos Civic Center. 110 East Main St. Hwy. 17 to Los Gatos.

You can indulge in strawberries to your heart's content and know you're benefitting a good cause at this two-day festival whose proceeds go to Eastfield Ming Quong, a nonprofit mental health agency for emotionally troubled children and families. Some 50,000 people gather at the Los Gatos Civic Center to enjoy strawberry shortcake, strawberries dipped in chocolate, strawberry daiquiries, and strawberry milkshakes, along with some non-strawberry burgers, steaks, and other goodies. If you're a breakfast lover, be sure to show up early each day for the festival's famous strawberry pancakes, a delicious twist on an old stand-by. You can also purchase crates of strawberries to take home.

Food's not all you'll find here, though. The two entertainment stages feature classical, jazz, blues, country, folk, and rock and roll; a carnival with rides and games; over 70 artists selling their work, including jewelry, baskets, pottery, paintings, and photography; clowns, magicians, and belly dancers; the coronation of the Strawberry Festival Youth Ambassadors and her court; and a baby picture contest.

Encinitas Flower Festival
Encinitas   (619) 591-3769

Weekend after Mother's Day (Saturday-Sunday). 40,000. 15 years. Concert $2; festival $1. Downtown Encinitas. I-5 east to Encinitas Blvd.

This coastal city—known as the "Flower Capital of the World"—blossoms during its flower festival. The organizers of this event strive for a funky, hometown atmosphere, and the parade certainly embodies this feeling; spectators are welcome to join in, and it's not unusual to see a unit of spontaneous bicycle or roller skating teams. Saturday you can bike or walk a 20-mile stretch of the Southern California coastline, then settle down and enjoy the parade or check out the surfing competition.

But the focus is on flowers, and there are many "living art" displays—local landmarks depicted in floral and photographic arrangements, the floats in the parade, and the fellowship garden at the Self-Realization Retreat. In addition, you'll find over 200 booths, offering everything from handcrafted jewelry to a dunking stall, even a complete physical check-up! Food booths offer hot dogs, hamburgers, teriyaki chicken, falafel sandwiches, barbecued ribs, shaved ice, and snow cones. No liquor is allowed. —L.S.

Festival Red Bluff
Red Bluff   (916) 527-6220

First Sunday in June. 4,000. 13 years. $1. Sun Country Fairgrounds. I-5 to Hwy. 99 east. Follow Hwy. 99 east to signs for Red Bluff.

Located in the northern part of California's Sacramento Valley on the Sacramento River, Red Bluff is known as the gateway to Mt. Lassen National Park. This western-flavor town shows its hospitality and community spirit each year during this festival. In addition to the arts and crafts show, there is a fashion show, a variety of food booths, business displays, a petting zoo, costumed character parade at noon and demonstrations. Local musicians, vocalists, dancers, and clowns show off their talents with live entertainment and something special for everyone.

Festival at the Lake
Oakland   (510) 464-1061

First weekend in June (Friday-Sunday). 122,000. 9 years. $5. Lakeside Park—north side of Lake Merritt in downtown Oakland. I-580 to Harrison or Grand Ave. exits. Go west to Lakeside Park.

Diverse music on four stages, international cuisine from dozens of Bay Area caterers and restaurants, and an array of art exhibits, crafts and special programs for children, seniors and folklife programs --that's Oakland's Festival at the Lake. Northern California's largest and most popular cultural event, the festival draws 122,000 people to the shores of Lake Merritt each year and features music ranging in styles from blues and jazz to reggae and gospel.

The arts are a major focus of this festival and include a citywide maskmaking project, a nationally recognized craft market, sculptural installations, children's billboard art and a juried photo exhibition. An award-winning mini-festival for children— "Kids Kaleidoscope"— offers such hands-on activities as a petting zoo, puppet making, mask making, fire trucks, talking police cars, face painting, a portable Rain Forest, as well as a Story Telling tent and a Young Artist Stage. The Folklife program features performances and demonstrations by traditional artists, showcasing their indigenous foods, dance, music, and arts. Garden demonstrations, International Food Fair, and special activities for seniors add to the Festival's diversity.

Fort Ross V.F.D. Summer Music Festival
Fort Ross   (707) 632-5911

Fourth Saturday in June. 1,500. 17 years. $15. From Santa Rosa take Hwy 101 to River Road (Russian River Area). West on River Road through Guerneville and Monte Rio to Cazadero Highway. Right on Cazadero Highway to Cazadero. The festival takes place 2.8 miles north of Cazadero on Fort Ross Road.

Since 1974 the local "back to the land" community has supported its all-volunteer fire brigade with this yearly bash. And over the years this festival has become well known for scrumptious food and a wide variety of music.

For that reason, you may want to arrive early because the food sells out fast. Their famous oyster bar and popular salad bar are devoured quickly. But there's also a Mexican canteena, BBQ for carnivores and vegetarians, an espresso bar, and a fabulous dessert table loaded with chocolate tortes, cheese cakes, fruit smoothies and pastries. Wines from all over Sonoma County are also available for tasting.

The music is continuous and diversified and includes folk, rock 'n roll and ethnic music. Plus, kids are entertained by storytellers and Scorby the Clown. All in all, the community puts on a great show in a wonderful setting surrounded by redwood trees.

Health & Harmony Music and Arts Festival
Santa Rosa   (707) 575-9355,

Second weekend in June (Saturday-Sunday). 15,000. 13 years. Adults $6, seniors $4, children 6-12 $2. Sonoma County Fairgrounds. One mile east of Hwy. 101 on Hwy. 12 in Santa Rosa.

The Health & Harmony Festival is Northern California's largest crafts fair and health and environmental expo, with an outdoor music celebration. It's outdoors, it's Spring, and health-consciousness fills the air, along with the sounds of country, folk, rock and roll, reggae, jazz, and new age music (past artists have included Crystal Wind, Jolt, Brazilian Beat, O.J. Ekemode and The Nigerian All-Stars, Pride & Joy, Pete Escovedo and Taj Mahal). Other entertainment includes dancers, magicians, clowns, and jugglers. 250 exhibits display arts and crafts, fine imports, health and environmental products and services, and information about alternative energy sources, computers, videos, new technology, organic plants and gardening, and children's products. You can also attend ongoing lectures and demonstrations by professionals on such topics as holistic health care, body therapies, the preservation of our environment, and alternative lifestyles.

For the kids there's the Rainbow Center, an area where they can play games, share activities, and enjoy entertainment. Each day also features a kid's parade, led by Bubbles the Clown and Clo the Clover Cow and made up of any children who want to participate (they can wear costumes and play instruments).

You will find a delicious assortment of natural foods, including Mexican, Italian, and Chinese dishes, plus sweet treats and fresh fruit smoothies.

California Festivals — June

Hilmar Dairy Festival
Hilmar   (209) 668-2855, (209) 668-BULL

Third Saturday in June. 5,000. 10 years. Free. Hilmar High School. 6 miles south of Turlock on Hwy. 165.

This small, pleasant festival—celebrating the lifestyle and products of this dairy farm community—attracts mostly families from the surrounding area. The theme of the day is dairy products: you can purchase decorated milk cans, mailboxes with a wooden cow head and legs, cow T-shirts, and cow magnets from the many arts and crafts booths, or treat yourself to free cartons of milk on ice and, of course, ice cream. Other foods are also available, such as tacos, pizza, hot dogs, hamburgers, and cinnamon rolls.

Not to be missed are the interviews of the candidates for Little Milkmaid and Little Milkman. These cleverly costumed 4-to-6-year-olds answer questions about their favorite foods and how they help Mom and Dad. One Little Milkmaid explained her duties as riding in parades and waving. "Everyone thinks I'm so cute!" she added. You also shouldn't miss the Pet Parade. Past parades have featured a chicken wearing a bonnet, a dog with a Mohawk hairdo, a bride and groom dog couple (she wearing a veil and train and he a tophat), plus various calves and goats. First prize went to the "Chow cow," a hapless Chow dog fitted with a plastic udder. Ya gotta see it to believe it!

Entertainment includes Portuguese folk dancers, old-time fiddling, Sweet Adeline singers, and "Debbie's Dancers" (mostly kids). If you like to try new things, enter the cow mooing contest. There are four categories: calf, heifer, cow, and bull (honest!). But you'd better know what you're doing if you enter the cow milking contest!
—M.J. and D.J.

One of the highlights of the Hilmar Dairy Festival is the Little Milkmaid and Little Milkman contests. (Photo by Marylou Johnson)

California Festivals / June

Huck Finn Jubilee
Victorville   (714) 780-8810

Father's Day weekend (Friday-Sunday). 12,000. 16 years. Adults $6, juniors $3, under 5 free; camping $9/night. Mojave Narrows Regional Park, Victorville. South of Victorville, I-15 to Bear Valley cut-off, East to Ridgecrest Ave., then north to park entrance.

Mark Twain would be proud of the organizers of this event, which has been featured on *Good Morning America*, thanks to its authenticity. The life and times of Tom Sawyer and Huck Finn are recreated at a 500-acre park, with river-raft building, fence painting, greased pole climbing, a catfish derby (the winner gets $1,000), Injun Joe's treasure hunt, Miracle Tonic medicine shows, and a series of skits all day long that retell the adventures of Huck Finn. It's a kid's day in heaven—they can join in the treasure hunt (which takes them all over the woods) and keep whatever treasure they find, build a raft and ride it, fish off the riverbank, climb a greased pole—actually relive a day in the life of one of the original American folk heroes.

There's entertainment for the grown-ups, too, with one of the largest bluegrass country shows in the West, Dixieland jazz, clogging demonstrations, a crafts fair, mountain man village, a circus, and an RV show and expo. And when everyone gets hungry, the many outdoor food booths offer hot dogs, chili, barbecue, corn on the cob, hamburgers, popcorn, ice cream and drinks.

Bring your own pole for some Huck Finn fun.
(Photo courtesy of Huck Finn Jubilee)

Humboldt Folklife Festival
Arcata   (707) 822-7150

Second Saturday in June. 800. 13 years. Adults $8, HFS members $6, children under 12 and adults over 60 free. Lazy L Ranch, Fickle Hill Rd. From Hwy. 101, take the Sunnybrae exit at Arcata. Go east to first left (1 block), turn left at Union St. Head up the hill to the stop sign, take Fickle Hill Rd. 3 miles to ranch.

California Festivals — June

Folk music, dance, and song are the focus of this one-day event, sponsored by the Humboldt Folklife Society. The day begins at 10 a.m. and ends at 1 a.m. and is filled with various workshops and performances by mostly local musicians. Workshop topics include instruction in international folk dance, pennywhistle, bluegrass, mandolin, Scottish country dance, musical saw, Appalachian dulcimer, and finger-picking guitar. The performances are just as diverse, with bluegrass, jazz, blues, gospel, fiddles, slide guitar, dulcimers, Irish music, banjos, Cajun performers, a musical saw, big band sounds, country swing, contra music and dancing, international folk dancing, and square dancing. Other related events include storytelling, kids songs and games, and an open mike night.

You'll no doubt work up an appetite, and lots of good food is provided throughout the day, including burritos, bagels and cream cheese, enchiladas, salad, fresh fruit, guacamole and chips, cheesecake, cookies, popsicles, and a variety of beverages, both alcoholic and nonalcoholic. Childcare is provided from 10 am to 5 pm.

Be sure to bring your instruments and your dancing shoes!

Be sure to bring your instruments and your dancing shoes to the Humboldt's Folklife Festival. (Photo courtesy of Humbolt Folklife Society)

Isleton Crawdad Festival
Isleton   (916) 777-5880

Second weekend in June (Friday-Sunday). 75,000. 3 years. Free. Isleton. Take Hwy. 160, Isleton is located 5 miles north of Hwy. 12 on Hwy 160.

Three quarters of a million TONS of crawdads are taken from the waters of this area—the Sacramento/San Joaquin Delta—each year. This festival celebrates and promotes the growing popularity of the wily crustacean with a crawdad cookoff, crawdad eating contest, crawdad races, the Crawdad Queen competition, a parade, fun run, carnival, bingo, pancake breakfast, crafts booths, and lots of food.

This is primarily a two-day river party, with lots of food (but those crawdads go fast!), beer, music, people, and fun. In addition to crawdads, you can taste Cajun food and different fast foods, and beer isn't the only thing you'll find to drink. The music is country/western, rock and roll, 50s and 60s, bluegrass, and Cajun, and you can dance to all these at the street dances. And you can purchase lots of crawdad-related souvenirs, such as buttons that read "Permit To Pinch Tails."

If you groove on large, boisterous crowds, this festival's for you! —M.J. and D.J.

Jazz on the Lake
Garberville   (707) 923-3368

Fourth Saturday in June. 7 years. $16.00 advance Mateel Members, $18.00 advance, $22.00 at the gate. Benbow Lake State Recreation Area, 1 mile south of Garberville on Hwy 101 in Humboldt County.

A weekend in the woods of Southern Humboldt and a day of fine jazz are combined to turn this event into a fun summer getaway. Benbow Lake State Recreation Area in scenic Southern Humboldt County makes a beautiful backdrop for jazz. Featured performers in past years have included Hugh Masekela, Jimmy Smith, The Blind Boys of Alabama with Clarence Fountain and Band, The Persuasions, John Handy, and Bobby Hutcherson.

Juneteenth
Berkeley   (510) 655-8008

Third or Fourth Sunday in June. 20,000. 55years. Free. Adeline St. I-80 to Ashby Ave. exit. Ashby to Martin Luther King Jr. Way, turn right to the intersection of Alcatraz and Adeline.

Juneteenth celebrations are new to California, but the holiday has been celebrated for over a hundred years in Texas. Although Abraham Lincoln signed the Emancipation Proclamation on January 1, 1863, news of its signing did not reach the slaves in Texas until June. The slaves coined the word "Juneteenth" for the day they were freed.

South Berkeley merchants, who viewed this African-American celebration of freedom as a viable opportunity to encourage growth and development in their community, staged their first Juneteenth celebration in 1987. Today, the festival draws several thousands of people. Three stages (including the Black Repertory Theater) featuring nationally known local talent, is one of the highlights of the festival. The festival is geared toward emphasizing the positive contributions of Black Americans and attracts festivalgoers from all sectors of Berkeley and the surrounding communities.

While listening to soul music, rock, jazz, and reggae, you can sample various ethnic foods, such as sweet potato pie, barbecue, and red beans and rice. Also of particular interest at this festival are the booths featuring African textiles, clothing, and jewelry.

Klamath Salmon Festival
Klamath   (707) 482-7165

Weekend after Father's day in June(Saturday-Sunday). 4,000. 21 years. $2. Klamath townsite. Directly off Hwy. 101, 20 miles south of Crescent City in Klamath.

This festival is a celebration of the salmon fishing industry along the Klamath River. The thought of eating fresh, barbecued salmon prepared from a special recipe by the Yorok Indians is sure to lure anyone to this very scenic area of California. A long hike through the park will be enough to whet your appetite for the salmon or specially prepared barbecued beef.

On Sunday you can take a picnic lunch to the river to enjoy the hydroplane races, arm wrestling and a tug-o-war. A barbecue takes place both days. If you enjoy learning about the salmon industry or if you just want to mix with the folks in Klamath, you will surely have a good time at this festival. The people are very hospitable and do their best to make sure you enjoy your dinners and participate in the singing and dancing that takes place. You can learn to square dance or learn some authentic Indian dances. Or you can simply sit back and enjoy the country/western or rock and roll music. There are also local entertainers who will do some fine fiddling, drumming, and singing.

You might want to spend the weekend enjoying the spectacular beauty of the Redwood Forest and the Klamath River Valley before or after attending the festival. If you plan to stay overnight anywhere in the area, be sure to make reservations. Camping and weekend visits are very popular in the summer! —L.F.

La Jolla Festival of the Arts and Food Faire
La Jolla   (619) 232-7655

First weekend in June. 20,000. 5 years. $3. La Jolla County Day School. 1-805, La Jolla Village Dr. west to Genesee Ave., turn right. Located on the corner of Regents Rd. and Genesse.

This festival, rated the number one art show in San Diego County, features more than 110 artists displaying works valued at a total of $2 million.

The art portion of the festival ranges from watercolors, jewelry, and oils to serigraphs, sculpture, and photography. Past displays have included such award winning art as Don Carter's waterfront and rural watercolors, Frank Giku's Oriental and nature watercolors, and Christian "Dutch" Mostert's marine settings in various media.

Turning from palette to palate, as the name says this is not just an art show and sale. Visitors can sample international fare from more than a dozen of San Diego's best ethnic restaurants. The food includes Moroccan, Indian, Chinese, Vietnamese, Greek, Jewish, and Mexican dishes. Desserts include chocolate fondue. There is also European coffee and espresso for those who fill up on the great food.

But this feast for body and soul is also a fundraiser, with proceeds going to numerous programs for the disabled. Even each year's festival poster, featuring designs by local artists, is used to raise money for this good cause. --L.S.

Lakeport Revival on Clear Lake
Lakeport   (408) 438-1957 or (707) 263-5092

Second weekend in June (Thursday-Sunday). 5,000. 4 years. Lake County Fairgrounds. From Hwy 29 to Lakeport Blvd. east to Main St., North to Martin St., West to 401 Martin St.

This four-day nostalgia event is patterned after the Beach Street Revival held in Santa Cruz for the past 14 years. It features a car show, dance parties, bikini contests (male and female), a rolling museum parade and a two-day festival with many food booths. Music at this year's event will be provided by Daddy-O, Sha-Boom and the Charms.

Living History Days
San Jose   (408) 287-2290

Weekend after Father's Day (Saturday-Sunday). 20,000. 10 years. Adults $6, seniors $4, children $3. San Jose Historical Museum. From Hwy. 101, take the Story West exit to 10th St. and Alma St. From Hwy. 280, take 10th St. south to Alma St.

Living history museums have become very popular, and with good reason--what better way is there to learn about the past than by literally walking through it? San Jose's Living History Days recapture the late 1800s with a village of 22 historical buildings, demonstrations of period skills and crafts, old-time parades, "townspeople" dressed in turn-of-the-century costumes, and many fun and entertaining activities for every member of the family. Women are invited to join the Women's Christian Temperance Union as they picket the beer and wine booths, or join the suffragettes as they protest their inability to vote. Those "feeling poorly" will want to buy a bottle of miracle medicine at Dr. Sage's Shangri-la Family Medicine Show. The kids will be delighted by the high-wheel bicyclers and a puppet show, plus a chance to participate in a Maypole dance.

The museum features several exhibits in the original and restored buildings that include a Victorian home, doctor's/dentist's offices, and the Bank of Italy (which later became the Bank of America). Nearly 80 different historical crafts and skills are demonstrated, including blacksmithing, wood carving, china painting, eggery, spinning, quilting, weaving, broommaking, calligraphy, printing, gold mining, lace making, and stained glass work. Three stages feature a wide variety of entertainment, including gun fights, piano music, can-can dancers, several ethnic dance groups (Scottish, English, Chinese, Greek, and Mexican), puppet shows, and a banjo band. Food booths feature old and new foods, and the Victorian garden party gives everyone a chance to relax under umbrellas with a cool lemonade and a tasty pastry.

But don't be surprised if your peaceful afternoon is disrupted by a band of desperadoes robbing the bank.

Lompoc Valley Flower Festival
Lompoc   (805) 735-8511

Third weekend in June (Wednesday-Sunday). 90,000. 39 years. Free (fee for some events). Ryon Park, West Ocean St. and O St. From Hwy. 101 (north of Santa Barbara), take the Hwy 1. exit. It's 20 miles into Lompoc. At the stop sign turn left into Lompoc.

Each June the Lompoc Valley in Central California turns into a myriad of color with the blooming of thousands of acres of flowers, from alyssums to zinnias (A to Z, get it?). Known as the Flower Seed Capital of the World, the town of Lompoc takes this opportunity to celebrate the fertile valley and the beautiful flowers (varieties of sweet peas and marigolds dominate the landscape) with a five-day festival. Activities include a spectacular floral parade on Saturday morning, featuring floats completely covered with natural material and blossoms, many of which are grown solely for this event. There's also a carnival with many rides and games, giant bingo competitions, arts and crafts (over 100 booths with the artists present), lots of entertainment including rock, pop, and country music, plus comedy, mimes, clowns, and dance groups, and nearly 40 food booths (take your pick: barbecued steak and chicken, hot dogs, quesadillas, lo mein, lumpias, tacos, chocolate mousse, homemade strawberry pies, milkshakes, funnel cakes, cotton candy, and more).

Despite all this fun, for many people the highlight of the festival is still the flowers. Lompoc is a large agricultural community nestled in a valley that's covered with flowers this time of year. You can take guided bus tours of the flower fields, and there's also a judged flower show with many arrangements by amateurs and children. Even just driving into the valley for this event should leave you with a lasting impression of its beauty this time of year.

North Beach Fair
San Francisco   (415) 346-4446

Third weekend in June (Saturday and Sunday). 75,000. 38 years. Free. Grant Ave. from Columbus to Filbert. Hwy. 80 to San Francisco, take the Broadway exit.

Whether or not you're Italian matters very little at this event, the longest-running street fair in San Francisco. The North Beach Fair presents the best of this city's historic Italian quarter, combining outstanding arts and crafts with exceptional rhythm and blues. Outdoor cafes serve California and Italian wines along with gourmet food, specializing in Italian delicacies. North Beach chefs compete for the "Best of North Beach" awards in nine food categories: pasta, pizza, calzone, gnocci, ice cream/gelato, cappucino, bread, Italian cake, and fortune cookies (fortune cookies?).

Besides being the home of some of the best Italian cooking around, North Beach is also well-known as a haven for aspiring writers, and the addition of the Literary Fair to this festival highlights this other North Beach speciality.

Just what we need—another great excuse to go to San Francisco for the weekend.

North Monterey County Strawberry Festival
Watsonville   (408) 663-4166

Second to the last weekend in June (Saturday-Sunday). 24,000. 11 years. Adults $5, seniors and children 6-12 $2, kids 5 and under free. Santa Cruz County fairgrounds. From Hwy. 101 or Hwy. 1, take Hwy. 152 to Watsonville. Follow signs to fairgrounds.

With the proliferation of strawberries in this area, it seems only natural that there'd be a festival to salute them. And these folks do it up right, with 75 arts and crafts booths of handcrafted items, 22 booths of gourmet food

California Festivals   June

and exotic drinks plus strawberries prepared in a variety of ways, and a stage featuring continuous music, from rock and roll to country. Other booths sell souvenirs such as wine glasses, T-shirts, hats, visors, posters, and jackets, and a second stage features entertainment just for the kids. There's also a wild animal display, clowns, jugglers, and puppet shows. Many years they also have a Wild West show.

Novato Art and Wine Festival
Novato   (415) 897-1164

Last weekend in June (Saturday and Sunday). 10,000. 9 years. Free. Grant Ave. in historic downtown Novato. Take Hwy. 101 to DeLong exit in Novato.

For two days every June, they close down the streets of Novato and turn them over to 200+ artists and craftspeople and some 10,000 art and wine lovers during this summer festival. Booths of unique arts and crafts line the streets, offering a variety of handmade wares. Local restaurants have booths as well, with such foods as Tex-Mex, Oriental, and ice cream, and continuous music from some of Marin County's top musicians can be heard. The local Marin French Cheese factory (worth a visit another day) offers free cheese samples to all who attend the festival. And, of course, many of the fine Napa and Sonoma County wineries are on hand to pour samples of their grape products.

Ojai Music Festival
Ojai   (805) 646-2094

Weekend after Memorial Day (Friday-Sunday). 5,000. 45 years. $12-$27. Ojai Festivals Bowl, Libbey Park. From Hwy. 101, take the Hwy. 33 exit and drive east 12 miles into Ojai; Libbey Park is located across from The Arcade, at the corner of Signal St. and Hwy. 33.

Founded in 1947, the Ojai Music Festival presents five concerts during the first weekend in June. Located in the Ojai Valley north of Los Angeles, the festival has earned an international reputation for excellence and innovation with a balance of well-known classical music and less frequently performed pieces.

The five concerts highlight mainly American music. A different musical director is featured each year, and since each has his or her own vision of the music and the shows, the content of the concerts differs quite a bit from year to year.

There is also an art and pottery show the same weekend as the music festival, and many art galleries with exhibitions of local artists' work are located in Ojai. While some food is available at the concerts (including soup, sandwiches, and Ojai orange juice and lemonade), the Ojai area also offers many unique restaurants and accommodations.

Railroad Days
Dunsmuir (916) 235-2177

Fourth week in June (Thursday-Sunday). 5,000. 47 years. Free. Downtown Dunsmuir on Pine St. 48 miles north of Redding on I-5. Take the Dunsmuir exit off I-5.

Railroad Days is Dunsmuir's annual celebration of the rich railroad traditions that put this community on the map. This historic railroad town was founded in 1886 in a box car by the side of the track that was a railroad stop for Southern Pacific. The town was originally known as Pusher, for the extra engines added at this stop to push northbound trains over the summit.

This event is four days of small-town fun and excitement in the shadow of beautiful Mt. Shasta. In addition to many historic railroading traditions, there's a parade, beauty pageant, softball tournament, fishing derby, carnival, street dance, 2K and 5K runs, game booths, sidewalk sales, and a river race. Live entertainment includes light rock, jazz, and Mexican guitar. Food booths sell American, Mexican, and Thai food; barbecued chicken; and beer and sodas.

Dunsmuir is located in the heart of some of the finest trout-fishing country in Northern California, and offers some beautiful camping and hiking areas as well.

Rocklin Jubilee
Rocklin (916) 632-4100

Saturday before Fourth of July. 12,000. 6 years. Free (fee for some events). Johnson-Springview Park, 5480 Fifth St. Take I-80 to Rocklin Rd. Drive west (away from Sierra College), cross Pacific/ Taylor to reach Fifth St. Take a left. Park is on the right.

The Rocklin Jubilee is a not-so-small Independence Day celebration in this hilly suburb of Sacramento. The event may not be small-town but the atmosphere sure is, which makes it that much more enjoyable. It all starts Friday night with a fireman's spaghetti dinner and dance. Saturday features a fun run, pancake breakfast, and parade, followed by a dog Frisbee contest, pet show, community barbecue, and lip-sync competition that people really go all out for. All-day stage entertainment features several local jazz and country bands. There are also games for the kids, including sack races and a balloon toss, and a poster contest with all entries designed by local school children. Food booths offer hot dogs, snow cones, baked goods, beer, and much more. There are also more than 50 craft booths. The festival ends Saturday evening with a big fireworks show.

San Anselmo Art and Wine Festival
San Anselmo   (415) 346-4446

Third weekend in June (Saturday and Sunday). 65,000. 9 years. Free. San Anselmo Ave. between Tamalpais and Mariposa. Hwy. 101 to Turnstead Ave.

Back in the 1880s, this little town was just a whistle stop junction on the North Pacific Coast Rail. Now one of the many communities that make up beautiful Marin County, San Anselmo is the home of the county's premier midsummer event, known as the "function on the junction."

This festival features outstanding arts and crafts, gourmet foods and California wines, and continuous musical entertainment, all in outdoor garden cafes in the Marin hills. The food includes fajitas, oysters, and hand-dipped ice cream, and the wines are from many of the area's fine wineries. The entertainment includes jazz, folk, and contemporary music, plus jugglers and magicians.

This two-day community festival is one more good reason to make a trip to Marin for a weekend.

San Marcos Chili Cook-Off
San Marcos   (619) 744-1270

Second Sunday in June. 8,000. 12 years. $3. Walnut Grove Park. Hwy. 78 to Twin Oaks Valley, then north to Olive. Turn right on Olive, then left on Sycamore.

If you like chili, mosey on down to San Marcos in San Diego County this June for the big chili cook-off, sanctioned by the International Chili Society. It's pretty entertaining watching each team's ritual; they spend all day cookin' up those secret recipes, and though the results are awfully tasty, you may not want to know what goes into every pot.

Along with the chili cook-off there's also a salsa contest (the two go hand-in-hand), country/western music and dancing, a battle of the bands, including seven bands. If you're not a chili lover, you can probably find a hot dog or two, shish kebabs, popcorn, cotton candy, and shaved ice. And if you are, you'll be happy to know they serve lots of beer to wash down all those spicy beans.

Saratoga Blossom Festival
Saratoga (408) 867-0753

Last Sunday in June. 10,000. 53 years. $1 donation. Big Basin Way in Saratoga Village. Hwy. 17 to Hwy. 9 to Saratoga.

This annual art and wine festival, set in and around Wildwood Park in the village of Saratoga at the base of the Santa Cruz Mountains, is a revival of the 1900-1941 Blossom Festival. In those days, people came by train and horse and buggy to this community to celebrate the coming of Spring in this lovely, quaint town. In 1977 the festival was reborn, making 1990 the 53rd anniversary of the event and the third year to honor the California Poppy.

Besides flowers, you'll find plenty of food booths, wine tasting (with commemorative wine glasses you can purchase), all-day entertainment, pony rides for the kids, and unusual arts and crafts.

Take a day off and head for Saratoga to catch Spring in full bloom.

Scandinavian Mid-Summer Festival
Ferndale (707) 786-9853

Third weekend in June (Saturday and Sunday). 1,000. 40 years. Free. Main St. in Ferndale. Hwy. 101 to Ferndale exit (Ferndale is the western-most city in the continental United States!).

This festival celebrates the longest time of the midnight sun in Scandinavia, encompassing traditions from Sweden, Denmark, Finland, and Norway. The dairy community of Ferndale, with its Victorian buildings and homes from the late 1800s, almost recreates a Scandinavian town, thanks also to the traditional food, music, and costumes.

The food ranges from Danish aebleskivers (something like a donut) to Norwegian lefse (close to a crepe), plus split pea soup, pastries, sandwiches, and such local specialties as shrimp cocktail. Scandinavian dances and folk music are performed by local kids and adults, and craft

California Festivals   June

booths feature many European folk crafts. A grand march through the streets of Ferndale features people in traditional costumes.

Ferndale is the home of the Scandinavian Midsummer Festival, a traditional celebration featuring native dances, costumes, food, and crafts. (Photo courtesy of the Ferndale Chamber of Commerce)

Secession Day
Rough & Ready   (916) 432-3725

Last Sunday in June. 2,000. 25 years. Free. Center of Rough & Ready. 3 miles off Hwy. 20 between Grass Valley and Marysville.

So you thought the South was the only place to secede from the Union in the 1800s? Thanks to the imposition of a tax on the miners, Rough & Ready's population of 3,000 in 1850 voted to form its own country, and this all-day celebration commemorates the Great Republic of Rough & Ready's three-month secession from the Union, which ended July 4, 1850.

Many buildings from the 1800s still stand, helping to set the atmosphere for the day. The festivities begin with a chuckwagon breakfast (featuring good ol' pancakes, ham, and eggs), followed by a return to the Old West as local thespians perform the ongoing saga of Rough & Ready in an open-air theater. Famous

Travel back in time when Rough & Ready celebrates its three-month secession from the Union in 1850. You'll see can-can girls, gunfights, and a reenactment of the town's early history. (Photo courtesy of Rough & Ready Chamber of Commerce)

gunfights are recreated, muzzle loaders fire away, and teepees dot the landscape.

The day also features music (country/western, of course), dancing girls, a cake walk, a children's parade, an antique car exhibit, a blacksmithing exhibition, and lots of good food, including hamburgers, hot dogs, sandwiches, homemade pies, cookies, and soft drinks and beer. It all adds up to an enjoyable day in the sun and a tribute to one of California's more bizarre pieces of history.

Summer Arts Festival
Garberville   (707) 923-3368

Fourth weekend in June (Saturday and Sunday). 13 years. $2 adults, $1 seniors and children, children under 5 and adults over 65 free. Benbow Lake State Recreation Area. 1 mile south of Garberville on Hwy. 101, in Humboldt County.

The Summer Arts Festival at Benbow Lake presents crafts, fine art, music, and dance in an exquisite lakeside setting. The festival has over 100 booths, with local artist's as well as crafters from all over California, Oregon, Washington and beyond represented. Each booth features a unique and individual talent from stained glass, leather and jewelry to burlwood bowls and boxes. Throughout both days two stages offer local musicians and dancers a chance to display their talents. Families can also enjoy such pastimes as swimming, boating, pony rides and face painting for the little ones.

In the evenings the festival presents "Jazz on the Lake", set amongst the redwoods where the bandstand is right next to the lake and the audience sits on the grassy shore.

Benbow Lake, outside of Garberville, is a beautiful setting for the Summer Arts Festival, which features many local artists and craftspeople. (Photo by Marc PoKempner)

Sunnyvale Art and Wine Festival
Sunnyvale   (408) 736-4971

First full weekend of June (Saturday and Sunday). 150,000. 18 years. Free. Downtown Sunnyvale. Hwy. 101 to the Mathilda exit. Go 3 miles south. Located at Mathilda and Washington Ave.

This two-day event is a cut above the usual art and wine festival, with 500 pre-selected artists and craftspersons, the chance to taste over 24 wines supplied by several different Bay Area wineries, and 30 food and beverage booths sponsored by local nonprofit organizations and serving a variety of ethnic foods. There are also special activities for the kids.

The quality of the food is as high as the arts and crafts, and as unique: you can sample buffalo wings, Chinese chicken salad, teriyaki steak kebabs, linguisa, pepper steak sandwiches, nachos, polish sausage, pizza, ice cream sundaes and more! Over 150,000 people attend over the two days, making this festival Sunnyvale's largest promotional event. Better plan on getting there early!

Union Street Spring Festival Arts and Crafts Fair
San Francisco   (415) 346-4446

First weekend in June (Saturday and Sunday). 100,000. 17 years. Free. Union St. business district. Union St. between Gough and Steiner.

The "Grand Dame" of San Francisco street fairs features outstanding arts and crafts, garden cafes with wine and fine foods, continuous entertainment, a tea dance, an uphill waiter's race, street performers, California wines and beer, and gourmet food.

Three stages of live entertainment feature music ranging from jazz to folk to big band. The arts and crafts are a gallery-scale exhibit of some of the best artists and craftspeople from California and the Western states. And San Francisco is known for its high-quality street performers, ranging from mimes and clowns to jugglers and musical "robots."

It feels more like an elegant Victorian garden party than a street fair.

Weed Carnevale
Weed   (916) 938-4624

Third weekend in June (Friday-Sunday). 3,000. 17 years. Free. Bel Air Park. Central Weed exit off I-5, left to College Ave., three blocks to Bel Air Park.

You'll greet old friends and meet new ones at this summer festival in Weed, at the foot of Mt. Shasta. What was once an Italian celebration is now one big community party with a more international flavor. There are softball, bocci ball, and horseshoe tournaments; a "Top of the State" run; watermelon eating contests; helicopter rides (you can just imagine the view!); a dance Friday night; a country/western concert; the crowning of the festival queen and king; and the big parade on Saturday.

Food, game, and crafts booths are set up around the park where the festival is held. Food booths feature quite a variety, including steak, hamburgers, hot dogs, Polish sausage, linguica, southern fried chicken, Mexican food, spaghetti, and cheesecake.

If you get tired of all this old-fashioned food and fun, you can always just sit back and enjoy the view.

Wine and Food Renaissance
Lakeport   (707) 263-6658

Last weekend in June (Saturday). Limited to 600. 8 years. $15 advance, $17.50 at door. Lake County Fairgrounds. From Hwy 101 go east on Hwy 20, then head south on Hwy 29 and take the Lakeport exit.

This is a fun garden party where they judge pairings of Lake County red and white wines and local beers with some unusual foods. How does Cajun Chicken fetuccini and steamed clams with Asiago cheese and a Konocti 1989 Fume Blanc sound? Besides all the great food and wine you can listen to a four-piece vocal group called "More than Meets the Ears", as well as a nice string quartet. If you want to attend make your reservation early—seating is limited to 600 people.

Arcata's Fourth of July Celebration
Arcata (707) 822-3619,
(800) 553-6569 (Calif. only)

July 4. 5,000. 14 years. Free. Arcata Plaza. Located where Hwy. 101 and State Route 299 cross. Take the Downtown Arcata exit.

What better way to spend the Fourth of July than at a local community gathering—especially when that community is Arcata, located on the northern coast of California. This festival in downtown Arcata features arts and crafts, bingo, antique fire engine rides, samba parade, food (veggie burgers, falafels, barbecued ribs, sushi, guacamole, etc.), and local bands playing all types of music (bluegrass, jazz, Irish folk music, reggae, rock). You can shop at the Farmer's Market, participate in the 10K run, and watch a doubleheader baseball game and root for the local favorite, the Humboldt Crabs. Other treats include train rides around Humboldt Bay and, of course, fireworks.

California Rodeo Salinas
Salinas (408) 757-2951

Third Thursday in July through following Sunday. 60,000. 82 years. $5-$12. Children and senior citizen discounts Thursday and Friday. California Rodeo Grounds, 1034 N. Main St. Hwy. 101 South to Laurel Dr. exit, turn left on Laurel, right on N. Main. Hwy. 101 North to N. Main exit, one block on right.

America's top cowboys compete for World Championship points on the wildest broncos and bulls in the country at this four-day rodeo that includes trick riders, horseshow competitions, and horse races. Other special events include a chili cook-off, round-up barbecue, rodeo queen contest, carnival, Western dance, and square dancing. Local charities run concessions offering burritos, hot dogs, hamburgers, and beer and sodas.

This competition has been upholding the tradition and heritage of the Old West for over 80 years by showcasing the skills used by cowboys and ranchers yesterday and today.

Carmel Bach Festival
Carmel   (408) 624-1521

Last three weeks in July. 19,000. 55 years. Free to $40. Sunset Cultural Center, 9th St. and San Carlos. Hwy. 1 to Ocean Ave. exit.

The focus of this festival is music, music, music. For three weeks each July, classical music lovers can travel to Carmel for some of the finest in baroque music. While much of the music is by Bach, the works of other major composers are featured as well. In addition to the Monday through Friday evening performances, each Saturday features an opera, and each Sunday there's a major Bach sacred work. There are also special concerts for young listeners, a classical camp for 8- to 18-year-olds, recitals, lectures, and symposiums on many aspects of classical music.

Carmel is a beautiful town on the coast just south of Monterey, perfect for a sophisticated event of this sort. It is also the home of many great restaurants, hotels, and bed and breakfast inns, though July is the height of the tourist season, so make your plans early!

Easter in July Lily Festival
Smith River   (707) 487-3443

Second weekend in July (Saturday and Sunday). 9,000. 30 years. Free. Ship Ashore Resort. Directly on Hwy. 101, 3 miles north of Smith River at the Ship Ashore Resort grounds.

Easter in July? Well, it's more the flower that's the focus of this festival in Smith River, known as the "Easter Lily Capital of the World." Ninety-five percent of the potted lily plants in the U.S. are grown from bulbs produced in this area's uniquely favorable climate.

The two-day event salutes the importance of the lily industry to this area, with floral displays, arts and crafts, live entertainment (including country/western and rock music), logging shows, a flea market, and plenty of food, including a pancake breakfast. Money earned from the festival goes to the

Rowdy Creek Fish Hatchery, and tours of the hatchery are continuous over this weekend.

Fourth of July
Bridgeport   (619) 932-7500

July 4. 5,000. 129 years. Free. Downtown Bridgeport. Hwy. 50 to Hwy. 395 to Bridgeport.

The tiny town of Bridgeport attracts nearly 10 times its size to this one-day, 125-year-old celebration of Independence Day. Located just northeast of Yosemite Forest on the eastern side of the Sierras, Bridgeport offers not only small-town hospitality and history but some great hunting and fishing and beautiful scenery as well.

The day begins with a bang (literally) as a 13-gun salute (for the original 13 states) goes off at 6 a.m. If that doesn't wake you up, the coffee and pancakes at the pancake breakfast will. The parade, with floats, bands, antique cars, and equestrian participants, begins at 10. The crowd then moves over to the historic Mono County Courthouse for a series of patriotic speeches and songs.

The afternoon is filled with such old-fashioned activities as a greased pole contest, diaper dash, arm wrestling, softball, and arts and crafts show. Kids can join in the haystack contest and pie-eating competition. The funniest events of the day are the tug-of-war across the river, where the losers really end up all wet, and the mud volleyball games.

The day ends with a barbecue, dance, and, of course, a fireworks display, just as they've done in Bridgeport for over 100 years.

Fourth of July—Exeter
Exeter   (209) 592-2919

July 4. 7,000. 100 years. Free. City Park. Hwy. 99 to Hwy. 198 east to Hwy. 65 (Kaweah exit). Two miles south to Exeter.

It's a full day of family fun in Exeter's beautiful city park, with something for everyone: games, arts and crafts, live entertainment in the park's gazebo, and all kinds of food, including deep-pit barbecue, hamburgers, hot dogs, bratwurst, tacos, ice cream, and more. Entertainment includes country/western music, gospel singers, dancers, soloists, fiddlers, and even rock and roll. Some of the events on this day of tradition include boccie ball and horseshoe tournaments, a 10K run, and, of course, a fireworks display after sunset.

California Festivals   July

Fourth of July Celebration
Crescent City   (707) 464-3174

July 4. 4,000. 27 years. Free. Beachfront Park. Turn west off Hwy. 101 onto Front St.

The North Coast really lights up during this Fourth of July celebration. The locals say it's the best in the area, with a huge parade, arts and crafts, flea market, live entertainment, and one of the largest and most spectacular fireworks displays in Del Norte County.
The music and entertainment really set the tone of the day, with a square dance demonstration, a melodrama performance by a local theatre group, a logging show, and many local bands performing a variety of music. They do it up right with the food too, with booths set up around Beachfront Park offering barbecued beef dinners, barbecued oysters, Indian tacos, corn dogs, and, of course, lots of cold beer.
What a way to celebrate our independence!

Fourth of July Festival
Martinez   (510) 228-2345

July 4. 20,000. 12 years. Free. Waterfront Park. I-680 to Marina Vista exit, follow to Ferry St., turn right into Waterfront Park.

Nearly 20,000 people gather at Waterfront Park for a day of arts and crafts, games, live music, dancers, and booths featuring ethnic and "down-home" food. The entertainment goes all day long, with local dance groups, country/western music, and jazz. There are also Bocci tournaments, a raffle, and games for the kids. The food—Filipino, Hawaiian, Oriental, and American—ranges from barbecue to fried rice. The day ends with a spectacular fireworks display over the waters of the Carquinez Straits.

Gasquet Raft Races
Crescent City   (707) 457-3267

Last Saturday in July. 700. 23 years. $4 registration fee to participate. Forks of the Smith River. Off Hwy. 199, between Crescent City and Cave Junction or in Gasquet at the forks of the Smith River.

Rain or shine, warm water or cold, they gather at the banks of the Smith River outside Crescent City for a race that some take seriously but most don't. Four categories of rafts work their way down the river: hand-paddled, sponsored, oar-driven, and most unusual. The last category is the most entertaining, of course, with past winners including "Ollie's Tank," whose commander stated in a pre-race press conference that win or lose, after the race the craft would be diverted to Nicaragua to help aid the Contra freedom fighters.

Non-contestants use inner tubes, air mattresses, and rubber rafts to traverse the river's rapids, while others race the rafters to the finish line via dry-docked vehicles. These land-lubbers are also in charge of the food, which includes hot dogs and chili boats (no pun intended), but it's every person for themselves when it comes to the beer.

The day begins with a pancake breakfast and ends with an awards ceremony and dance celebration.

Gilroy Garlic Festival
Gilroy   (408) 842-1625

Last full weekend in July (Friday-Sunday). 140,000. 13 years. Friday: adults $7, seniors and children $2; Saturday and Sunday: adults $8, seniors and children $2. Christmas Hill Park. Hwy. 101 south from San Francisco. Take the Gilroy exit. Follow the signs to the festival.

People from all over the world have heard about the Gilroy Garlic Festival. All this recognition and publicity might lead some people to think the Garlic Festival is all hype. Fortunately it is quite the opposite. This festival rightly deserves all the credit and recognition it receives. One visit will most definitely convince anyone—particularly if you are an aliophile (a lover of garlic)!

California produces 90% of all U.S. garlic, and most of it is either grown within a 90-mile radius of Gilroy or goes to Gilroy at some point for processing. The garlic industry in Gilroy surpasses the $54 million mark!

The 5,000 volunteers who put in over 250,000 hours have thoughtfully organized everything from the parking to the feasting on such delicacies as blackened shrimp, escargot kebabs, pork tamales, linguini pescadore, stuffed mushrooms, Thai cuisine, sushi, turkey legs, corn on the cob, fajitas, pizza, jambalaya, and seafood gumbo—all made from recipes featuring garlic, of course. You can even sample such desserts as garlic ice cream or garlic flavored peanut butter cups!

As we roamed the grounds of Christmas Hill Park, the comment we heard most often was, "I wish I hadn't eaten breakfast." Take it from me—don't eat anything before you go to Gilroy. In fact, you might want to get up early and run a few miles or play a few rigorous games of raquetball before you go so that you build up a good appetite. You will most certainly, without a doubt have plenty of opportunity to sample any type of food you desire.

By all means, make sure you spend time at Gourmet Alley. You will not only be entertained by the culinary wizards who toss spectacular skillets of flaming calamari, grill mountains of garlic bread, and stir-fry bushels of vegetables fresh from Central California fields, but you will also taste some delicious food. The talented chefs of Gourmet Alley perform to benefit their chosen charities, sauteing scampi in lobster butter sauce, stuffing giant mushrooms, and basting huge slabs of sirloin with rosemary mops dunked in garlic marinade. Make sure you try the the calamari and the artichokes, too!

Although the food is the most famous feature of this festival, there are also four stages of continuous entertainment, featuring country/western bands, rock groups, the big band sound, and puppeteers, mimes, belly dancers, and clowns. You can watch garlic braiding and garlic topping or observe celebrities cook their favorite garlic dishes. Those who enjoy arts and crafts will find 80 booths where artisans display or demonstrate many unique products. Other festival events include the 10K Garlic Gallop, the Annual Garlic Golf Tournament, the Garlic Squeeze Barn Dance, the Garlic Festival Tennis Tournament, and the Tour de Garlique Bicycle Tour.

You won't be disappointed if you go to Gilroy—just realize that there will be thousands of other people visiting, so plan to come early or stay late (or both). You will find dozens of souvenir items, from T-shirts to cookbooks, as a remembrance of your visit. The Gilroy Garlic Festival is truly an enjoyable experience—and a festival that deserves its fine reputation. — L.F.

International Beer and Food Festival

San Francisco   (415) 553-2200

First Saturday in July. 3,000. 9 years. $30 (adults only). Concourse Exhibition Center, 8th St. and Brannan St. Hwy. 101 in San Francisco to Civic Center exit. Proceed straight through light on Bryant. Turn right on block down onto 8th St. Next block is Brannan. Concourse is loated at southeast corner of 8th and Bryant.

You can sample over 200 beers (or maybe you can't!) from around the world at this three-hour festival, plus taste some of the best in "pub grub" from mostly local food vendors. Whether your tastes run toward Australian lager, English ale, German pilsner, or Swiss nonalcoholic beer, you'll find it here. Other countries represented include Belgium, Canada, China, Czechoslovakia, Denmark, El Salvador, France, Hong Kong, India, Ireland,

California Festivals — July

Jamaica, Japan, New Zealand, Norway, the Philippines, Scotland, Singapore, Sweden, Thailand, the U.S., and the West Indies. In addition, 20 Northern California microbreweries offer their finest for your tasting pleasure (ever heard of Buffalo Brew, Pete's Wicked Ale, Pelican Pale, or Bigfoot Barleywine Ale?).

The food offerings are about as varied as the beer. You can nosh on sausages, kosher pickles, Texas chili, gator tail (that's right--alligator), pizza, perogies, chips and salsa, cheese and crackers, and all kinds of other nibblies, including marinated garlic cloves (from Gilroy, where else?).

Some light background jazz adds to the sophisticated air of this event, which benefits the Public Broadcasting Station KQED.

Jazz And All That Art On Fillmore
San Francisco   (415) 346-4446

Weekend after Independence Day. 50,000. 7 years. Free. Fillmore St. between Washington and Post St. From Hwy. 101, take Geary Blvd. to Fillmore St.

San Francisco's Fillmore St. celebrates the city's jazz heritage with this free outdoor jazz, art, and wine festival featuring handmade crafts, fine art, garden cafes, gourmet food, wine, beer, street performers, and fabulous jazz music. It's a revival of Fillmore St.'s musical heyday, when it was known in the 40s, 50s, and 60s for its hot jazz and blues clubs.

You can stroll along Fillmore and check out booths of more than 150 local artists displaying their crafts and fine art, watch a fashion show or lounge in outdoor garden cafes and sip fine California wines that complement such treats as jambalaya, fajitas, and barbecue.

But the focus is on the music, with jazz performances all day each day of this weekend-long festival. It's a showcase for San Francisco's jazz roots and the city's continuing support of the creative spirit.

July 4th Celebration
Lemoore   (209) 924-6401

July 4. 10,000. 4 years. Free. City Park—Fox St. and Bush St. west of Hwy. 99 (about 25 min.) on Hwy. 198 to 18th Ave. exit north to Bush Street, east of I-5 (about 35 min.) on Hwy. 198 to 18th Ave.

The community of Lemoore and the local Naval Air Station join forces for a day-long celebration of Independence Day.

The festivities begin at 7 a.m. with a 10K run, and the day is filled with such events as a chili cook-off, bed races, face painting, children's games and races, clowns selling balloons, and live entertainment. Food booths set up around the festival site (the city park) feature all types of food, including Chinese, Mexican, and Filipino dishes, as well as barbecued tri-tip beef.

The evening is filled with fireworks and a music program at the high school stadium, a fitting ending to this community- and family-oriented day.

July 4th Independence Celebration
Modesto   (209) 524-1307

July 4. 30,000. 29 years. Free. Parade—downtown, festival—Graceada Park, fireworks—John Thurman Field. Hwy. 99 to Modesto.

A community parade through downtown Modesto kicks off the day-long festivities. The picnic in the park includes arts and crafts booths, food booths, and live entertainment. There's music for people of all age. Dixieland, barbershop, bluegrass, country/western, and rock bands play in the Mancini Bowl throughout the day, along with roving entertainers. In addition, the famous McHenry Mansion and Museum are open to the public throughout the day. The fireworks at dusk end this old-fashioned family celebration with a bang.

Mendocino Music Festival
Mendocino   (707) 937-2044

Two-week period in July. 600. 5 years. $11-$16 for concerts; Master classes and pre-concert lectures, Free; discount for series. The festival tent is located next to the Ford House on Main St. in downtown Mendocino. Take Hwy. 101 north from San Francisco, west on Hwy. 128, north on Hwy. 1 to Mendocino.

This educational and cultural event comprises 15 performances over 12 days, with emphasis on orchestral and chamber music, opera, jazz and ethnic music are also presented. The music touches on many of the classics, including Handel, Mozart, Dvorak, Strauss, Beethoven, Tchaikovsky, Shostakovich, Schumann, Schubert, Brahms, and Stravinsky, as well as more contemporary composers. Members of the San Francisco Symphony, Opera, and Ballet orchestras are featured, along with many of Mendocino County's most outstanding musicians. In addition, many internationally renowned soloists perform each year. Masters classes are also offered to aspiring vocalists, string players, percussionists and pianists.

The setting for this festival is as inspirational as the music and performers. Held under a huge white tent situated on the Mendocino headlands, the music of each performance blends with the cool sea air and the sound of the waves to create near-perfect listening conditions. Evening concerts begin at 8:00 p.m., afternoon concerts at 2. Coffee, wine, juice, mineral water, and cookies are sold at each performance, and two post-concert "galas" offer a chance to meet the artists, enjoy Viennese delicacies and coffees, and sip champagne while you waltz to the music of a live string quartet.

Be sure to make your plans early—besides its beauty, Mendocino is well-known for its many great restaurants, hotels, inns, and bed and breakfasts—sometimes too well-known! For music lovers, this festival is not to be missed.

Mozart Festival
San Luis Obispo   (805) 543-4580

Ten days in late July, early August. 7,000. 21 years. $3-$25. Locations throughout the county. San Luis Obispo is midway between San Francisco and Los Angeles on Hwy. 101.

Founded in 1971, this event is an annual summer music festival honoring Mozart and his music. Growing from three concerts in 1971 to 22 in 1991, the performances are held all over the county. Sites include California Polytechnic State University, the Mission San Luis Obispo de Tolosa, and the press room of one of America's finest champagne houses. Each year the festival presents international, national, and regional artists, from the well-known to the young and emerging.

In addition to the main performances, there is also the "Festival Fringe," a series of free, informal concerts held by festival musicians. And in 1986, the "Mozart Akademie," a series of lectures and demon-

The beauty of California's missions is combined with the classic music of Mozart at the Mozart Festival in San Luis Obispo. (Photo courtesy of the San Luis Obispo Mozart Festival Association)

strations that explore and illuminate the music of Mozart, was begun. There is also an arts festival that runs from the last week of July through the week of the music festival and features gallery showings, poetry readings, ethnic music and dance, studio tours, and exhibitions of different media, such as carving and fabric work.

If you're looking for artistic integrity, this festival provides it.

Music at Sand Harbor
North Tahoe   (916) 583-9048

July—five nights of events. 6,000. 10 years. $19 general admission. $17 NTFAC membership. I-80 to Truckee, then Hwy. 89 south or Hwy. 267 south to Hwy. 28. Follow Hwy. 28 east 5 miles past Incline Village, Nevada.

Enjoy five nights of music on the shores of Lake Tahoe at Sand Harbor State Park. You'll hear contemporary rock, jazz, and rhythm and blues. Past performers have included The Nylons, Nicolette Larson, Dave Mason, John Mayall, Tower of Power, and Maria Muldaur. Most people bring picnics to snack on during the performances. Opening acts have included The David Grisman Quintet, Commander Cody, The Lost Planet Airmen, Peter Rowman, The Free Mexican Airforce, Nicolette Larson, and The Bobs.

Fondly referred to by the locals as "Tunes in the Dunes," this event is sponsored by the North Tahoe Fine Arts Council, a bi-state community-supported nonprofit organization dedicated to fostering and nurturing the arts in this area. Profits go toward high-school scholarships, support of local artists, publication of a local arts newspaper, arts and crafts fairs, the upkeep of the Sand Harbor stage, and the Shakespeare at Sand Harbor Festival, which takes place in August.

Old Miner's Days
Big Bear Lake   (714) 866-4607

Begins end of July. 5,000. 40 years. $3. Various locations in Fawnskin, Big Bear City, and Big Bear Lake. I-10 to I-215 east. Exit on Highland Ave. near the mountain resorts. Go left to Hwy. 330. Go up the mountain to the dam. Take Hwy. 18 to Big Bear Lake.

The *Old Miner's Gazette*, the Old Miner's Days official program that looks more like an old-time newspaper, sets the tone for this 10-day event, with tongue firmly planted in cheek. The masthead blares: "Old Miner's Gazette—Published in the Hills Now and Then—Some News is Better than No News." The lead stories are full of such colorful writing as "The

Committe for Preservation of Natural Phenomena has undertook to see ifen the big crane whut part way sunk in the lake could be put back since mariners on big Bear Lake is havin a helluva time getting thar bearings without it." This area is rich in mining history, and this event pokes fun at and pays tribute to this history.

A dance kicks off the festivities, and over the next several days various events take place: a chili cook-off, a fashion show, the logger's jubilee ($2 per guest with an Old Miner's Days button), melodrama performances ($7 for adults and $5 for children), a country fair (two days of log sawing, log rolling, yodeling, and pole-climbing competitions), a doo-dah parade (featuring some wild outfits), a powder puff derby, donkey softball, team roping and penning, a three-day national burro derby (where wild burros are led along a winding, 42-mile course, despite the burros' bucking, kicking, rearing, twisting, and other uncooperativeness), the Miss Clementine contest, community breakfastsl, a whiskerino contest, clothing and crafts booths, wrangler presentations, children's events featuring a gunny sack race, water balloon toss, a wheelbarrow race and a carnival, the 24th annual square dance, the big parade, featuring a colorful procession of marching bands, antique cars, floats, drill teams, color guards and equestrian groups, and awards presentations.

Of course, food and live entertainment play a big part in all this too, and you'll find lots of Western specialities, including ribs, baked beans, corn on the cob, and hot dogs, plus lots of live country/western music. All in all, it makes for a fun, lively two weeks in the mountains, paying tribute to an area founded by miners in the 1800s.

Orange County Fiesta Days
Fountain Valley   (714) 962-4441

First week in July (Thursday-the Fourth of July). 55,000. 10 years. Adults $3, seniors and military $2, children $1. Mile Square Park, entrance on Brookhurst St. and Heil St. 405 Frwy. to Brookhurst north exit to park. Or Hwy. 22 to Brookhurst.

A big carnival is the highlight of this five-day event, with the emphasis on family fun. Besides all the rides and games at the carnival, there are a variety of children's activities, face painting, an arts and crafts exhibit, a baby contest and a pie-eating contest, and lots of live entertainment (mostly 50s and 60s music). One of the highlights is the chili cook-off, where 25-30 chili connoisseurs go head to head with some wild concoctions. There's also a rib cook-off, sure to satisfy even the most particular appetites. Topping off this festival is a free fireworks show, the largest such spectacle in Orange County. All the fireworks are purchased with donations made by the citizens of Fountain Valley, making the evening's finale that much more special.

California Festivals   July

Pear Fair
Courtland   (916) 775-1053

Last Sunday in July. 25,000. 19 years. Free. Bates School grounds. Hwy. 160 20 miles south of Sacramento, I-5 south from Sacramento to Hood Franklin exit, or I-5 north from Stockton to Twin Cities Rd. exit. Follow signs.

Set in the middle of the Sacramento Valley along the Sacramento River, Courtland is a small (only 600 people!) agricultural community surrounded by Bartlett pear orchards and open fields. Even though there's only one gas station, one grocery store, one pharmacy, one bar, one grammar school, one library, and one post office, somehow they accommodate the over 20,000 people who show up each July for this agricultural celebration.

The day begins with a 5 and 10-mile fun run and an all-you-can-eat pancake breakfast and continues with arts and crafts, entertainment (magicians, clowns, strolling minstels, puppets, storytellers, square dancing, a circus, and music), a parade, children's games, carnival rides, and more. The fair is known for its good eating, and besides the fresh pear pie, pear crepes, pear sundaes, pear ice cream, pear frappes, deep-fried pears, and pear bread, you'll find barbecued chicken, corn on the cob, tacos, burritos, hot dogs, shish-kebabs, Chinese food, and watermelon. And of course a quantity of fresh, ripe pears are on hand to take home. The true pear aficionado won't want to miss the pear pie-eating contest or the pear peeling contest. There is also an historical display about the pear industry.

Sandcastle Days
Imperial Beach   (619) 424-6663

Late July (ocasionally early August, depending on the longest tide). 180,000. 12 years. $1 charge for dance; other events free. Imperial Beach. I-5 to Imperial Beach exit Palm Ave. west or exit Coronado Ave. west to the beach. Free shuttle bus from parking

Only in Southern California, right? Where else would you find a full-fledged, three-day-long contest to see who can build the best sandcastle? They even have rules, like how big the building area can be, what kind of decorations you can use, what sorts of coloring are o.k., what tools are allowed, and how much water you can have on hand. And the prizes (for the Masters category)—$4,000 for first place, $2,000 for second, and $1,000 for third! Other categories have money prizes totalling $1,800. But if you saw some of these creations, you'd understand why they take it so seriously—this is hard work, not child's play!

California Festivals — July

The weekend begins with the Sandcastle Ball (featuring live music) at the Imperial Beach Fire Station on Friday. Although it is a "ball," casual dress is appropriate. On Saturday, the city's birthday party begins with a pancake breakfast for competitors and spectators alike. At 11 a.m. the Sandcastle Parade begins (complete with skydivers), followed in the afternoon by the children's sandcastle competition, an arts and crafts show, food booths (featuring hot dogs, pizza, Polish sausage, Chinese food, etc.), the cutting of the city birthday cake, and a fireworks display in the evening. On Sunday, the U.S. Open Sandcastle Competition begins, with entrants competing in the Masters, "Castle of Your Mind," "Best Replica," "Best Sculpture," "Creatures of the Sea," and "Executive Sandbox" categories.

Sawdust Festival
Laguna Beach   (714) 494-3030

July and August. 250,000. 25 years. $4 adults, $3 seniors, free for children under 12 with an adult. 935 Laguna Canyon Rd. From I-5 or I-405 take Hwy. 133 south into Laguna.

For 25 years this arts and crafts festival (sorry—it's NOT a tribute to sawdust!) has been home to some 200 exhibitors each summer. It is one of three major art festivals held in Laguna Beach each year, and attracts 250,000 visitors during its two-month run.

Many things make this festival different, and special. First, the artists and vendors design their own booths, blending their designs with the overall design of the festival grounds, a design that changes each year. In the past, artists have used such props as dragons, the Statue of Liberty, and Frankenstein on a surfboard to create their unconventional structures. Second, all artists are present and interaction is encouraged, especially at the kids booth, where they can learn many different crafts hands-on. Demonstrations of crafts also take place each day. Among the crafts exhibited at the Sawdust Festival are pottery, glass, handcrafted wood, drawing, sculpture, metalwork,

The Sawdust Festival in Laguna Beach gives visitors an opportunity to watch artists and craftspeople at work. (Photo courtesy of the Sawdust Festival)

weaving, porcelain, jewelry, silkscreens, toys, games, windchimes, quilts, masks, handstitched clothing, handmade dolls, enameling, baskets, ornaments, etchings, and paintings.

The festival got its sawdust label during its first year, when it was set up on a vacant lot and sawdust was used to keep down the dirt. While the organizers called the show the "Laguna Artists and Gallery Owners Exhibit," the press labeled it the Sawdust Festival, and the name stuck. It is now located in a beautiful eucalyptus orchard just minutes from the beach.

A smorgasbord of food awaits the hungry visitor, including Mexican dishes, yogurt smoothies, potato skins, salads, pasta, ice cream, fresh fruit...the list goes on and on. And there's a wide variety of music and entertainment as well, including jazz, folk, country, blues, pop, rock, reggae, Latino, bluegrass, and 50s and 60s rock, plus minstrels, troubadours, jugglers, mimes, clowns, puppeteers, and magicians.

Semana Nautica
Santa Barbara   (805) 969-2052

Saturday before July 4th through the following Sunday. 20,000. 57 years. Free. Most activities in East Beach. From Los Angeles, take Hwy. 101 to Cabrillo Blvd., one mile west to beach.

Looking for a festival where you can get physical? Santa Barbara has a week (and more) for you during Semana Nautica ("Marine Week" in Spanish), the Summer Sports Festival.

Imagine the thrill of fishing from an inner tube. It's called body boating, and it's one of the more than 30 competitions held on or near the ocean. Most are open to amateurs. There is no charge to enter the competitions, and out-of-towners are welcome to sign up and work out. The champions receive plaques and the benefits of exercise.

The festival opens with the Oceanfest competition, a contest drawing lifeguards from all over the state. Lifeguards surf ski, participate in dory races, and show their stuff on paddle boards. Other nautical contests throughout the nine days incluide the one, three, and six mile ocean swims, kayak, sailboat and jet ski races. Dryland contests comprise of tennis, squash/handball, racquetball, lawn bowling, horseshoes, soccer, softball and a 15K run. There's also the traditional beach biathlon made up of a 4-mile run and a mile ocean swim, and the annual cricket match.

The festival is scheduled around the 4th of July, and Santa Barbara celebrates in style with a 4th of July parade, Sports for Life Symposium, arts and crafts displays, sand sculpture and sandcastle competitions, entertainment, and the traditional visit by the U.S. Navy and coast Guard ships.

California Festivals   July

Sonoma's "Salute to the Arts"
Sonoma   (707) 938-1133

Third weekend in July. 20,000. 6 years. Free. Wine tasting tickets available for purchase: 8 wine tasting tickets and souvenir glass, $10. 11 food tasting tickets for $10. Sonoma Plaza. Hwy. 101 to Hwy. 37 east; go to Hwy. 121 north to Hwy. 12. North to the plaza.

    I should begin by stating a blatant bias: Sonoma is my favorite Northern California community, and my experience over the years indicates that anything the town undertakes is usually done right. And with the Salute to the Arts—Sonoma's celebration of the visual, culinary, and performing arts—the town has outdone itself.

    To begin with, there is probably no more pleasant setting for festivities of this sort than the Sonoma plaza. Events and displays are scattered around the plaza under the beautiful Sonoma spring sky. Events include a gathering of local authors and theatrical performances; some lovely paintings, photographs, and crafts by area artists; and a series of musical events, including jazz and classical artists in the plaza's amphitheater. There are also special activities for the kids, and the plaza has a fine playground and duck pond to help keep the little ones entertained.

    As for food and drink, this festival is a must for any self-respecting gourmet (or gourmand). A number of local wineries have booths featuring a great variety of local products (for $3 you purchase a glass, and $1 tickets will get you generous tastes of each wine). The food is a nosher's paradise. Not your usual collection of hot dogs and hamburgers but samplings of

Reenactment of Edouard Manet "Le dejeuner sur l'herbe, 1863"
(Photo by Ron Zak)

chicken caccitore and gnocci with basil sauce, prawns cooked in beer with black bean sauce, and twice-dipped strawberries (in both white and dark chocolate) are just some of the delicacies to be found.

As if all this weren't enough, the plaza is surrounded by some of the finest restaurants in the region and the park has ample room for tossing down a blanket and picnicking on items brought from home or purchased at one of the excellent nearby delis. —D.F.

Tapestry In Talent
San Jose   (408) 293-9727

Weekend closest to July 4 (Saturday-Sunday). 150,000. 16 years. Free. Downtown San Jose. Hwy. 101 to San Jose.

This multicultural arts festival incorporates visual, performing, and culinary arts with representation from the community's multiethnic population through the arts. It involves hands-on activities as well as an art gallery for the young, plus a wide variety of food and entertainment.

Seven stages feature live music, including jazz, rock, country/western, big band, classical, blues, top 40, folk, and ethnic, and performances include modern, ethnic, square, and folk dancing plus ballet and theater. The food booths feature dishes from Mexico, Vietnam, China, Portugal, the United States, and Italy. A screened arts and crafts from artists throughout the western states. In addition, an invitational fine arts gallery featuring Bay Area artists can be found.

This two-day event is one of the area's largest, bringing, as the organizers say, "arts to the community and the community to the arts."

Weaverville Fourth of July
Weaverville   (916) 623-6101

Weekend closest to Fourth of July (Wednesday-Sunday). 30,000. 11 years. Free. Tickets sold for melodrama. Main St. and Lowden Park. I-5 to Redding, Hwy. 299 west to Weaverville, approximately 48 miles (1 hour).

A Weaverville Fourth of July is a chance to travel back in time. Some of the magic comes from this old gold-mining town, which claims 119 historical sites. Many of the brick and wooden buildings were built during the California Gold Rush of the 1850s, and it is easy to celebrate several eras of Americana by walking through this small town tucked away in the redwood-covered mountains.

# California Festivals															July

Independence Day opens with the roar of an anvil firing at 6 a.m. The sound invites visitors to a pancake breakfast at Trinity Park. The breakfast is free with the purchase of a $3 collector's button that depicts a different historical site each year, and collector's wear their buttons as though they were medals. The anvil firing continues every 30 minutes at the park. The ice cream social begins at 10 a.m., and at 11, visitors gather around the bandstand (erected in 1901) to continue a tradition begun during the 1976 bicentennial: for one minute, freedom rings from bells in the old schoolhouse and pump engine.

The 11:15 parade features school bands and the best of local talent. After the parade is the perfect time to visit two museums that complete the view of what early pioneer life was like in Weaverville. The Joss House is the oldest, still-used Chinese temple in the state. Artifacts include items for worship and the weapons used in two Chinese wars. The Jackson museum has exhibits of toys, dishes, and the old jail cell. You can also check out the Art Center for the arts and crafts fair or take in a performance of a resurrected melodrama at the Trinity Theatre.

Over at the park, the old-fashioned Fourth of July oratory is soon replaced with band music. Booths sell food (hot dogs, hamburgers, pizza, Vietnamese and Italian dishes, Mexican treats, pita bread sandwiches, and ice cream) and beverages and the park kitchen serves up a meal at noon. Physical strength is tested in meets such as the Timber Ridge Run, a rodeo, a bucket brigade, motocross races, and softball games. As you might guess, as dusk settles the sky is filled with fireworks, a fitting end to an old-fashioned Fourth of July. —L.S.

California Festivals   August

Anderson Marsh Blackberry Festival
Lower Lake   (707) 994-0688,

Second Saturday in August. 5,000. 7 years. Free. Anderson Marsh State Historic Park. I-5 north from Sacramento to Hwy. 20 west to Hwy. 53 south. One mile south of the city of Clearlake.

Take a trip back to the turn of the century while you enjoy blackberries, blackberries, and more blackberries! The staff at Anderson Marsh State Historical Park have found a way to combine the celebration of the blackberry harvest with a living history demonstration of early 20th century life. Guided nature tours through Anderson Marsh State Historical Park are available to understand and appreciate the natural resources and archaeological resources that date back 10,000 years.

You can boo the villain and cheer on the good guys between bites of blackberry cobbler at the Anderson Marsh Blackberry Festival. (Photo by Len Fecko)

Anderson Marsh is a turn-of-the-century ranch house. Festival demonstrations include traditional home skills such as churning butter, laundering the family wash by hand, and spinning thread from wool on an antique spinning wheel. There are also demonstrations by blacksmiths, horseshoers, and other tradesmen.

One of the newest additions to the festival is a melodrama that runs

California Festivals — August

three times in the barn. You will laugh, cry, cheer, and boo (don't worry, the signs will tell you when) as you actively participate in the adventures of the cast.

The musical entertainment at the festival is country-oriented. You can listen to bluegrass, fiddlers, and classical folk songs while you enjoy homemade blackberry pie, cobbler, and pastries—all a la mode, if you wish. The arts and crafts displays also feature country items. The folks who have their crafts on display will gladly explain to you the steps taken to create such items as quilts, wood carvings, jams and jellies, and hand-woven scarves and sweaters.

This one-day festival is an enjoyable event for the entire family. You will find that your children will be entertained while they learn, with yo-yo demonstrations, cloggers, games, marble-shoots, and puppets. Other events are sponsored by the community of Lower Lake. —L.F.

Where else can you find girls cheerfully washing clothes together -- using washboards and tubs? (Photo by David Thom)

Annie & Mary Day Fair
Blue Lake   (707) 668-5066

First Sunday in August. 1,500. 21 years. Free. Perigot Park. Take Hwy. 101 north to Hwy. 299 (just north of Arcata). Follow Hwy. 299 east 5 miles to Blue Lake.

Inquisitive minds might be asking, "Who were Annie and Mary?" Well, if you want to know everything about these two remarkable ladies, visit the Annie & Mary Day Fair in Blue Lake. Sponsored by the Blue Lake Chamber of Commerce, this festival began as a remembrance for Annie and Mary, two well-loved secretaries who worked in the local railroad office early this century. Since that time, it has evolved from a fair and picnic into a full day of activities for the entire family, featuring the Annie and Mary Day Old-Time Fiddle Contest.

The day begins with a 10K run and 2-mile fun run. Following the races is a small-town parade, with horses and old cars. Breakfast is available all morning long.

The fiddle contest begins at lunch time and continues throughout the afternoon. Fiddlers of all ages compete for over $1,200 in prizes in various categories. At past festivals this free event has drawn over 1,500 spectators to Blue Lake, which more than doubled its population for the afternoon. Other features of the day include craft and food booths, pony rides, a children's area, a horse gymkhana, and junior all-star and old-timers baseball games. A specialty not to miss is the barbecued beef.

The Blue Lake Museum, located in the old railroad depot, is open all day for those who want to learn more about the railroad industry and this town's 100+ year history. Featured are many photos and artifacts of the old railroad and lumber industries. Walking tours of the town's many historical buildings are also available. And if you still find a little free time, you can visit the Mad River Fish Hatchery, just two minutes from town. So come to Annie and Mary Day for a free day of fun in the sun, something frequently not found in August in the surrounding foggy coastal areas. — L.F.

Banana Slug Derby
Orick   (707) 488-2171

Third Saturday in August. 350. 22 years. Free. Prairie Creek Redwoods State Park. Hwy. 101 50 miles north of Eureka, 40 miles south of Crescent City.

For over 20 years this spine-tingling event has drawn a crazy crowd of onlookers and competitors to race and cheer on their favorite slugs. Whether you bring your own slug or rent one at the park, the derby is open to anyone who wishes to participate in the "sticky" competition (sorry!). Competitors are grouped into three categories: adults, children, and government agencies, and the slugs go head to head (or is it tail to tail?) in a race for the coveted "Top Banana" award, which goes to the fastest banana slug of the bunch. Hand-crafted trophies are awarded to the winner in each category. The banana slug, known to scientists as *ariolimax columbianis*, is an important member of the redwood forest community. After the derby even the fastest slug is returned to its home in the forest so it can continue to munch on plants and return nutrients to the soil.

Each category has several heats. The races work like this: the slugs are placed in the center of a large circle about 3 feet in diameter. The first slug to cross the circumference of the outside circle wins the heat. A highly competitive race takes about 5 minutes for the victor to slime across the finish line in a blaze of glory. The winners of all heats in a category are then put in the center for the Big Slime Off.

The day begins with a pre-race parade through the park, followed by the crowning of the Banana Slug Queen and the singing of the banana slug anthem. Though a bake sale takes place in the picnic area, you should probably plan to bring a lunch, unless of course you've brought a weekend's worth of food and are camping.

Two banana slugs go head-to-head (or is that tail-to-tail?) as they slime their way to the finish line. (Photo courtesy of Banana Slug Derby)

California Dry Bean Festival
Tracy   (209) 835-2131

First weekend in August (Saturday and Sunday). 40,000. 3 years. Adults $5, seniors and children $3. Central Ave. and 10th St. Take I-205 to first Tracy exit to downtown Tracy.

You'll discover everything you ever wanted to know about dry beans—and more—at this two-day festival in the heart of California's agricultural area. Start with a trip down Bean Boulevard (recently renamed from 10th St.), where nonprofit organizations prepare the official bean dishes of the festival, including Mardi Gras pasta salad, Cajun black eyes, mixed California bean soup, Portuguese beans, chili, California creole beans, bean tostadas and tamales, and bean tacos. There's also a bean display and museum, with a remarkable exhibition of old and new harvesters and a complete history of the bean industry in Tracy.

This festival is only a few years old, but in its fourth year it attracted some 40,000 visitors. (Did you ever think there were so many bean lovers?) In addition to all those beans, other festival activities include an arts and crafts fair; a chili bean cook-off (anyone can enter); a 10K run, 2.5-mile fun run, and 1-mile children's run; an antique car show; and plenty of live entertainment, with three stages featuring continuous country, jazz, and Dixieland music, as well as strolling musicians and puppeteers.

The folks in Tracy take their beans seriously, and this festival was created not only to celebrate the bean industry but also to try and dispel all those nasty rumors about beans, "the magical fruit."

Dixon Lambtown Festival
Dixon   (916) 678-2650

First weekend in August (Saturday-Sunday). 8,000. 5 years. $4. First St. I-80 between San Francisco and Sacramento; south on Hwy. 113 to Dixon.

The Dixon Lambtown festival is a pleasant one-day street fair, where Dixon's North 1st Street is closed off and pedestrians reign supreme. The city park is the site of the lamb cook-off, where enticing aromas float through the air as some 20 volunteers and vendors vie for various awards. Public tasting and official judging take place in the late afternoon. You can also do some wine tasting.

In the streets, local growers sell fresh produce, and art and crafts relevant to the festival's theme are also on sale. Activities include spinning and weaving demonstrations, live radio broadcasts, 5K and 10K runs, and other programs. In the evening you can dance in the street to the lively tunes of a popular country/western band. This is a thoroughly enjoyable rural festival, attracting a pleasant crowd of both locals and out-of-town visitors. —M.J. and D.J.

Feather River Railroad Days
Portola   (916) 832-5444

Fourth weekend in August (Friday-Sunday). 10,000. 9 years. Free. Railroad museum area. I-80 to Truckee. Take Hwy. 89 north to Hwy. 70 east to Portola.

Set in the beautiful mountain country of the Sierra Nevadas, this three-day event pays tribute to Portola's railroad-town heritage. It's geared toward railroad fans, with train rides for everyone and a model railroad exhibit. On Friday, there's dinner and golfing at Feather River Inn followed by a dance in the park. There's also a large parade, an arts and crafts show, and a dance Saturday night. Special events include a karate demonstration, horseshoe tournament, petting zoo, and a variety show. Sunday morning is an interfaith service.

California Festivals   August

Everyone knows how mountain air makes you hungry, so there's no need to be shy when you visit the many food booths to snack on barbecued steak, hamburgers, hot dogs, tacos, pies, cakes, beer, wine, and soft drinks. And what festival would be complete without music: folk, country/western, and more. Any requests?

Gilroy Hispanic Cultural Festival
Gilroy   (408) 848-5780

Last weekend in August (Sat-Sun). 35,000. Five years. $5 adults, $1 children 6-12 years, 5 and under free. Christmas Hill Park. From Highway 101 go to Gilroy, take 10th street exit and follow signs to the festival.

You are sure to get the real thing at this festival dedicated to building Latino cultural pride. You'll hear music in the air everywhere — Mexican mariachi bands, Guatemalan marimbas, Peruvian harps— and the beat is exclusively Latin. Past year's headliners have included such luminaries as Vicki Carr, Jose Feliciano, Lalo Guerrero, Culture Clash, Pete Escovedo and his band, the Ray Camacho Band, Luis Valdez' Teatro Campesino and Tierra.

Festival organizers have food tasters to guarantee that flavors and foods are authentic Hispanic ones, and vendors that don't measure up are turned away. Try Chilean fish marinated in famous Chilean sauces, the famous Paella from Spain, or Peruvian tortes, to name just a few. Over 30 food booths can satisfy every Hispano-American taste.

Take the kids over to "Para Los Ninos," where they can take a whack at the colorful pinatas filled with traditional candies and candles. Nearby, they can try their hand at creating an image on a collective mural or fashioning a clay sculpture.

Arts and crafts from traditional pinatas to original pre-Colombian ceramic sculptures can be found, along with exhibitions by local Hispanic artists and guest artists with international reputations.

The shaded tent for Mexican bingo (loteria) is the perfect place for seniors to rest while they try to win prizes and strolling Mariachis or Nortenos play their favorite songs.

Wear a traditional Hispanic costume to the festival and you may win the $300 first prize money for best costume.

California Festivals   August

Gladiola Festival
Union City   (415) 471-3232
              (415) 471-6877

First Saturday and Sunday in August. 8,000. 8 years. Free. Charles F. Kennedy Park and Community Center. I- 880, take the Alvarado/ Niles East exit, go left on Decoto Rd.

For gardeners and spectators alike, this festival offers some great scenery, from the professional arrangements in the various competitions to the displays set up by the organizers of the event. Union City is the second largest producer of gladiolas in the U.S., so you can imagine there might be a few of these flowers on hand.

But the festival also offers two day's worth of continuous entertainment, including music from the last three decades, living history exhibits and craft persons, food booths selling gyros, ribs, and traditional Mexican dishes; and a wide variety of arts and crafts.

Gourmet Food and Wine Tasting Festival
Torrance   (213) 540-5858

First Saturday in August. 1,200. 4 years. Advance tickets $30, $35 at the door. American Honda Motor Co. headquarters. Take 405 Freeway, exit on Western Ave, Right on Torrance Blvd., right on Van Ness Ave., 700 Van Ness Ave.

This festival is designed to foster friendship and harmony in the community with the theme "Friendship in Bloom... an evening of socializing and friendship within the community of Torrance." This festival brings together the business, civic and private sectors of the Torrance community along with the surrounding communities of the South Bay, in an elegant atmosphere, for wine and gourmet food sampling, fine music by the Torrance Symphony Orchestra as well as a silent auction.

Over 35 of the South Bay's most prominent restaurants and over 40 California and international wineries are showcased. Along with a myriad of fine food and wines, this elegant coat-and-tie festival also includes a special guest performance by Zenshuji Zendeko, a group of Japanese drummers.

California Festivals   August

Gravenstein Apple Fair
Sebastopol   (707) 544-4728

Early August. 20,000. 19 years. Adults $3.50, Children $1. Ragle Park. Hwy. 101 to Santa Rosa. West on Hwy. 12 to Sebastopol.

A friendly country fest dubbed "The sweetest little fair in Sonoma County," this festival has one of the best settings going: a pretty, oak-shaded park in Sebastopol, where more apples of the Gravenstein persuasion are grown than who knows where. It also has some of the best food, arts and crafts, activities, and demonstrations you're likely to find at any festival.

The major emphasis is on, of course, apples and their by-products. You can sample apple juice, slushes, pies, fritters, and ice cream; participate in the apple peel-off, pie-eating contest, or trivia game; or just take in some of the beautiful apple-growing country around Sebastopol. As for other entertainment, two separate stages feature plenty of bluegrass and country/western music, and the seating is very "country," too: long wooden planks placed over hay bales.

The festival site is set up in several sections, such as the Children's Corner, which features jugglers, puppeteers, and storytellers. Another section, called "Life on the Farm," features bee-keeping, goat-milking, and sheep-shearing demonstrations; rabbits, oxen, and llamas to admire; and displays of herbs, flowers, and Bonzai gardens.

In addition to all this apple madness, you can enjoy Greek food, Mexican food, barbecue, and conventional fast foods and drinks and visit the many fine arts and crafts booths where local artists sell their creations.—M.J. and D.J.

Hayward Art and Wine Festival
Hayward   (510) 881-5400

Second weekend in August. 50,000. 12 years. Free. B St. Plaza. I-580 east to the Hayward/Foothill exit. Go one mile to B St. Or Hwy. 580 west to the Stroughbridge exit, first right then turn left at Castro Valley Blvd., left on Foothill, 1 mile east to B St. Hwy 880 to 238, EastFoothill off, 1 mile to B St.

You don't have to drive all the way to the wine country to sample fine California wines. The Hayward Art and Wine Festival is a good way to spend an enjoyable summer afternoon sampling wines from local vineyards. You can also stroll through the downtown area as artists and craftpersons display their works.

Although there are dozens of arts and crafts displays throughout the state, I can honestly say that in Hayward I saw some unique items I have

California Festivals — August

never seen elsewhere. Serveral artists from Europe and Africa featured some beautiful etchings and paper art. It just goes to show that not every art show is the same!

The festival also includes food booths, some games for the kids, and entertainment. The Hawaiian dancers were great, especially when they "selected" people from the audience to learn the hula. Shake those hips! Other entertainment featured rock and roll groups, gymnastic students, karate students, and even belly dancers. Who says Hayward doesn't have any unusual local talent?

The selection of food is very diverse, including Cajun shrimp, jambalaya, pizza, full Chinese dinners, and samples of Korean, Mexican, Italian, Thai, and Filipino foods. —L.F.

Hayward Zucchini Festival
Hayward   (510) 881-5400

Third weekend in August (Saturday and Sunday). 45,000. 10 years. Adults $3, seniors and children $1. Kennedy Park (19501 Hesperian Blvd.). I-880 to A St. exit. West on A St. to Hesperian Blvd., north on Hesperian.

"Cook them Zukes!" That's the way they talk in Hayward during the annual Zucchini Festival, a local event since 1983. The folks in Hayward have found dozens of new ways to cook this green cylindrical vegetable, as well as designing zucchini alternatives to apple-bobbing and other festival games. Of course there is a zucchini-growing contest and a carving contest, with prizes awarded for the largest, the shapliest (I personally liked the one that looked like a bathing beauty—dressed in a bikini, no less), and the most unusual. You can feast on zucchini bread, zucchini tempura, zucchini nachos, or zucchini fingers. Other foods include Mexican sweet bread, mango chutney, Jambalaya L'Acadien (Cajun dirty rice), suja with apricot,

King and Queen Zucchini reign for the weekend. (Photo by Jim Chapman)

California Festivals   August

meat-on-a-skewer, calamari, perogies, and dozens of other delicacies.

Entertainment is provided on three separate stages throughout the day, featuring contemporary rock, gospel, belly dancers, renditions of Broadway classics, comedians, and more. One of the most popular events is the body-building contest on Saturday, open to both men and women.

The zucchini recipe contest always features many new ways to cook the big zuke, as do the cooking demonstrations by guest chefs. Many nonprofit groups sponsor food booths, game booths, or information booths, and there is a large arts and crafts section. This festival is Hayward's largest community cooperative event and is definitely a great way to celebrate the zucchini! —L.F.

International Calamari Festival
Santa Cruz   (408) 427 3554

The entire month of August. 10,000. 12 years. Cost varies, depending upon event. India Joze at the Santa Cruz Art Center. Take Hwy 17 South from San Jose to Hwy 1 North. Turn left at the second signal. First right is Center Street. India Joze is on the first block on the right in the San Cruz Art Center.

True calamari aficianados take note. This is the festival for you. Or rather, this is a month-long exploration of all the ways people from around the world enjoy preparing and eating calamari or squid. Nearby Monterey Bay has one of the largest squid populations on the planet. And the month of August is high season for catching these creatures. Expect everything to be especially fresh and tasty.

Local restaurant India Joze is both the site for and sponsor of this event and stages weekly special menus from around the world featuring squid. For example, one week spotlights Mediterranean cuisine. The variety of preparation in Asia necessitates special weekly sessions for South Asia, South East Asia and Near East Asia. Latin American and African cuisines are covered, too. In all, more than 80 dishes are prepared.

If you are keen on learning to prepare calamari on your own, you can attend daily classes that teach the history and cultural background of the respective regions featured each week.

On Tuesday nights you can go to a special Calamari Tasting Room, where these treats are served Dim Sum style. Jazz accompanies dinner on most nights.

California Festivals   August

International Percussion Explosion
Oakland   (510) 763-3962

Fourth Saturday in August. 2,500. 4 years. Free. Bandstand in Lake Merrit Park. I-580 to Lake Merrit Park or Grand Ave. exits. Go west to Lake Merrit Park.

Drums and other percussion instruments are unique in that every cultural group uses some form of them. This is especially true on the African continent where drums have been used for everything from entertainment to sending messages. In fact, in Ghana a particular drum is referred to as the "talking drum." As Africans were dispersed throughout the Americas during the slave trade, they took their intricate drumming techniques with them. Although drums were outlawed in some countries, their rhythms were never truly extinguished.

The annual International Percussion Explosion brings together drummers from all over the African diaspora for an afternoon of music and dance. Drummers and groups from the U.S., Cuba, Trinidad, Brazil, Haiti, Ghana, Senegal, Nigeria, and the Congo participate. The infectious rhythms of groups like the Mandingo Drummers, the Harmonics Steel Band, the Ladzepko Brothers, and Batacucaje create a celebratory atmosphere that is contagious. As Kwaku Ladzepko, executive director of the Mandeleo Institute (which sponsors the event) said,

The beats the thing at this multi-cultural festival. (Photo by Scott Hess)

147

California Festivals   August

"Something very dramatic happens. We don't have any audience, everyone participates, dancing! Even the kids in Childrens' Fairyland (across the fence from the bandstand) were dancing." Besides fantastic drumming, some of the groups also feature singers and dancing. Batucaje, a Brazilian group, performs *capoeira*, a Brazilian martial art done to music. African, Caribbean, and Brazilian food and drinks are also available. --G.B.

La Habra Corn Festival
La Habra   (213) 691-3482

First Friday and Saturday in August. 60,000. 43 years. Free. El Centro Park. North of Imperial Hwy on Cypress Street between La Habra Blvd. and Whittier Blvd.

Back in 1949, the Lions Club was discussing different fund-raising ideas when one member said, "What about corn?" Over 40 years later, the Lion's Club still ships in corn on the cob from Chino and puts on a tremendous festival that is like a country fair and a carnival all rolled into one.

According to festival organizers, they boil over 25,000 ears of corn each year. People come from far and wide for the corn and swear that it is the best they have ever tasted. When pressed about the "secret" recipe, festival chairman Chuck Overbey said, "There is no secret. The truth is, when you boil a lot of corn like we do in the same water, the flavor stays in the corn rather than the water."

But this festival offers much more than just corn. The Saturday morning parade lasts a full three hours and is the biggest summer parade in Southern California, with visiting celebrities, marching bands, horse groups, antique vehicles, floats and more. Also, you can enjoy continuous music including Latino, country & western and bluegrass.

The best part of the festival is that it gives people in the area a reason to get together. For many people it is their one-day-a-year reunion, made even better by the chance to enjoy some delicious corn.

Lake Tahoe Starlight Jazz Festival
South Lake Tahoe   (916) 542-4166

Last weekend in August through the second weekend in September. 100,000. 4 years. Varies per concert. Sites throughout the city. Call ahead for directions.

The rekindling of a tradition dating from the 1920s is the spirit behind this festival. Legends of jazz and blues make Lake Tahoe evenings come

California Festivals — August

alive with great music, just as they did 70 years ago, when the wealthy families of San Francisco summered there and enjoyed jazz on the lake shore. For three weekends (a different artist plays each weekend), you'll be entertained by such groups as The Dirty Dozen Brass Band and Zachary Richards topped off with rhythms and blues legend Johnny Otis. Each of these evening performances, held in an outdoor amphitheater on the edge of the scenic Taylor Creek meadow so you can enjoy music under the stars with towering Mount Tallac as a backdrop, is prefaced by wine tasting from a local restaurant and food samplings from top restaurants on the South Shore.

In addition to the major concerts at the Forest Service Amphitheater, live jazz is featured in the showrooms and cabarets of South Shore hotels, casinos, nightclubs, and restaurants.

Nisei Week Japanese Festival
Los Angeles   (213) 687-7193

Middle of August. 50,000. 51 years. Free. Little Tokyo in Los Angeles. Harbor FWY exit 4th St. east on 4th St. to San Pedro St. turn left and go north to Little Tokyo. Little Tokyo is between 1st and 3rd Streets.

This annual cultural festival, held during the second week of August, offers a wide variety of special events, cultural and community exhibits, and sporting competitions throughout Los Angeles' "Little Tokyo." You'll see exhibits of flower arranging, Bonsai, doll making, Japanese art, calligraphy, ceramics, needlecraft, Japanese swords, tea ceremonies, painting, photography, and textile dyeing. Sporting competitions include aikido, jiu-jitsu, bicycling, bowling, volleyball, golf, karate, kendo, tennis, and running. Special events include a coronation ball, dance performances, a carnival, a street dance, a luncheon, the prince and princess pageant, a fashion show, and a street art festival. There is also a grand parade, and the week culminates with a carnival and street dancing on the last Sunday.

If the Japanese culture interests you, this festival is a wonderful opportunity to enjoy it.

Los Angeles' Little Tokyo is the site of a full week's worth of Japanese cultural, community, and sporting events during the Nisei Week Japanese Festival. (Photo by Toyo Miyatake)

California Festivals August

Oakland Chinatown Street Festival
Oakland   (510) 893-8979

Fourth weekend in August (Saturday and Sunday). 90,000. 3 years. Free. Oakland's Chinatown. Chinatown is located in downtown Oakland, near the Park Oakland Hotel on 12th St.

This festival continues to draw larger crowds and attract greater community involvement each year. The streets of Oakland's Chinatown district are closed to traffic for the festival. Local organizations provide information booths, some game booths, and food booths. Local restaurants and vendors also provide a variety of Chinese and other ethnic foods. The two stages have continuous entertainment, featuring disco, rock and roll, ethnic dances, Chinese opera, and comedy acts.   In years to come, the festival is certain to continue to grow and become a major celebration of Chinese culture in Oakland. — L.F.

You'll have plenty of opportunity to make new friends in Oakland's Chinatown. (Photo courtesy of Oaklands Chinatown Chamber of Commerce)

Old Adobe Fiesta
Petaluma   (707) 778-0150

Second Sunday in August. 15,000. 30 years. Free. Petaluma Adobe State Historical Park. Hwy. 101 to E. Washington St. exit; go east to Old Adobe Rd. and turn right. 1 mile to park. Free Bus Transportation from Downtown Petaluma.

California Festivals — August

This is a small festival, held on the grounds of the Petaluma Adobe State Historic Park and across the road in a grove of Eucalyptus trees. It is also very fun and educational!

The sprawling two-story adobe house, built between 1836 and 1846, was the occasional residence of General Mariano Guadalupe Vallejo and the operational headquarters for his 66,000-acre, 100-square-mile Mexican land grant ranch. About half the original house still stands and contains authentic furniture and equipment. The festival's craft demonstrations (featuring crafts necessary to the maintenance of a large ranch in the 1840s) are held in the spacious courtyard and on the huge wraparound second-floor veranda. Artisans freely explain the processes of brickmaking, blacksmithing, corn grinding, bread baking, weaving, and the making of candles, lace, quilts, etc., and visitors may make their own candles. Park rangers are present to give information on the Adobe's history.

Across the road, under the trees, are some food booths, games (including a beard-growing contest and a costume contest—many festival attendees wear period clothing), a large stage featuring a lively Mexican band, and a dance floor. The food is primarily Mexican.

With Petaluma's close proximity to San Francisco (about an hour's drive north), a visit to this festival can be a quick and pleasant day trip from the City. —M.J. and D.J.

Old Spanish Days Fiesta
Santa Barbara   (805) 962-8101

First week of August (Wednesday-Sunday). 10,000. 67 years. Mostly free. Downtown Santa Barbara and Northside area. Two hours north of Los Angeles on Hwy. 101, Pacific Coast Hwy.

Santa Barbara's largest and oldest annual festival has been celebrating its early Spanish and Mexican heritage for 65 years with five days of colorful activities for the entire family.

This is some festival, attracting 200,000 people each day and featuring a wide variety of food, music, entertainment, and crafts. The scene is set with two authentic Mexican marketplaces, "El Mercado Del Norte" and "El Mercado de la Guerra Plaza," which feature Spanish, Mexican, and early

You'll think you're on the streets of Old Mexico at Santa Barbara's Old Spanish Days Fiesta. (Photo by Len Wood)

California Festivals   August

Californian foods as well as gaily decorated booths of arts and crafts by native artisans, free entertainment, and special Fiesta Days memorabilia.

The atmosphere continues with the parades—"El Desfile Historico" (the historical parade) and "El Desfile De Los Ninos" (the children's parade)—both traveling throughout downtown Santa Barbara. The rodeo and stock horse show capture another piece of California history with bronc riding, Brahma bull riding, wild cow milking, and roping.

One of the true traditions of the fiesta is the "Nights of Gaiety," where colorfully costumed dancers, singers, and musicians entertain audiences under the stars in the sunken gardens of the County Courthouse. Other activities include a carnival, costume shows and contests, an arts and crafts show, tours of the Fiesta Carriage Museum and the courthouse, community breakfasts, a steak luncheon, ethnic performances at the Lobero Theatre, and "big-name" shows at the County Bowl.

No wonder this event has been ranked one of the five best regional festivals in the U.S.

Pacific States Craft Fair
San Francisco   (914) 883-6100

Second or third week of August (open to the public only on Friday-Sunday). 22,000. 16 years. $5. Fort Mason. Van Ness Ave. to Bay St. to Fort Mason.

Three hundred of the nation's outstanding craft artists, selected from 1,300 applicants by a jury of prominent experts, exhibit and market their handmade artwork created from clay, glass, metal, wood, leather, fiber, paper, and mixed media at the Pacific States Craft Fair, held annually at Fort Mason in San Francisco.

The distinctive works presented at the show range from orginal museum-quality pieces for the serious collector to personal adornments or uncommon yet functional items for the home. You will find such items as textiles woven into sculptured figures, glass blown and cast into unusual shapes, handpainted tapestries, porcelain vessels finished with contemporary designs, and wood turned and chiseled into unique forms.

This craft fair is a must for those who enjoy arts and crafts because it is one of the major national shows sponsored by the American Craft Council. It is also a major show for wholesale buyers. The show is open to the public only on Friday, Saturday, and Sunday; wholesalers have an opportunity to attend earlier in the week. You are certain to find the newest techniques featured at the show since buyers from all along the West Coast will be looking for unique creations.

The Fort Mason site is ideal for the festival. Two buildings are provided for the show: one featuring crafts that are fashion-oriented, and the other featuring items that are home- or office-oriented. Food booths sell wine and smoothies to drink and gyros, Greek salads, sausage sandwiches, and barbecued chicken to eat. The admission fee of $5 lets you know that this is a serious art show geared to adults who truly appreciate arts and crafts. If this is an interest or hobby of yours, you will definitely enjoy the show. If you are looking for unique items for your home or office, you will find many creative objects on display and for sale. —L.F.

Palo Alto Celebrates the Arts
Palo Alto   (415) 346-4446

Fourth weekend in August (Saturday and Sunday). 100,000. 11 years. Free. University Ave. between Webster St. and High St. Hwy. 101 or I-280 to Palo Alto, take the University Ave. exit.

This annual city celebration of visual and performing arts attracts some 100,000 people to its shops and outdoor cafes along University Ave. Street performers entertain visitors while they browse among the exhibits of excellent arts and crafts from some of the finest artists and craftspeople in California. But this festival also features continuous entertainment, fine wines, gourmet foods from many local restaurants, and a tea dance contest. On the central stage you'll find a full-scale big band dance orchestra, as well as more contemporary jazz, folk, and rock music.

Park Street Art and Wine Faire
Alameda   (510) 523-1392

First weekend in August (Saturday and Sunday). 25,000. 7 years. Free. Park St., Alameda. Off Nimitz Fwy. (I-880), use 23rd Ave. or 29th Ave. to come over the Park St. bridge.

For two days during August, six blocks of Alameda's Park St. is blocked off, with four blocks of arts and crafts booths, food booths, wine, beer, and entertainment. Two stages feature continuous entertainment, including jazz, swing, bluegrass, rock, and dancers. "Fun Alley" is a series of game booths for the kids, including a dunking booth. Food booths offer a variety of ethnic dishes.

Each year this community event gains popularity, focusing attention on Alameda's historic downtown business area and lovely turn-of-the-century Victorian homes.

Petaluma River Festival
Petaluma (707) 762-2785, (707) 762-5331

Third Saturday in August. 25,000. 7 years. $1-$2 for adults, less for children. Petaluma River Turning Basin (downtown). Exit Hwy. 101 (39 miles north of San Francisco) at E. Washington to Petaluma Blvd. N. In historic downtown area.

This street fair beside the Petaluma River celebrates the city's early days when the river was of great commercial significance. It was begun as an effort to turn people's attention back to the river for recreation and as an appreciation of the river as a natural resource.

The festival features the usual arts and crafts booths, music (rock, folk, and Dixieland), and fast food and drinks. Its most unique offerings are the boats on display, some of which run regularly scheduled 45-minute river cruises on a sternwheeler and a "walking beam engine" steamboat (they'll explain it to you). In addition, you can have your picture taken with Petaluma's "real live" mermaid!

The day begins at 7 a.m. with foot races and a pancake breakfast and lasts until dusk. Besides the boat tours and rides, there are also raft and boat races. Visitors to this festival could plan to attend Petaluma's Old Adobe Fiesta the second Sunday of August and make a fun, educational, historical week of it in this beautiful town just north of San Francisco. — M.J. and D.J.

It's full stream ahead in Petaluma. (Photo by Scott Hess)

California Festivals   August

Reggae on the River
Garberville   (707) 923-3368

First weekend in August. 10,000. 8 years. $25 per day, $10 for children 2-12 years. No on site ticket sales. Limited on site camping. French's Camp in Piercy. Nine miles south of Garberville on Hwy. 101 in Humboldt County.

Burning Spear and the Burning Band, Third World, Freddy McGreggor, Lucky Dube, David Lindley, Judy Mowatt, Hugh Masekela, Messenja, Sister Carol, Pato Banton—do these groups sound familiar to you? If your answer is "yes," you are most likely a reggae music fan, and you will probably enjoy the Reggae On the River Festival, the largest outdoor reggae festival on the West Coast.

Sponsored by the Mateel Community Center, the festival began six years ago when the Mateel building was destroyed by fire. Members decided to sponsor a reggae music festival as a way to raise money to rebuild and expand the center. Since that time the festival has become a very popular event for the people who live in Humboldt County and enjoy life away from the big cities.

The Mateel is a focal point for people who enjoy music, culture, and the arts in this rural community. The festival takes place at French's Camp, directly off Hwy. 101 in Piercy (just south of Garberville). The setting itself is picturesque—on the banks of the Eel River with its many swimming holes, framed by majestic redwood trees. You can bring your picnic and swimming gear and plan to spend the day enjoying the outdoors listening to the music, or wander the grounds admiring the arts and crafts displays. Picnic baskets are welcome (no glass, however), but food is also available at the site. No alcoholic beverages are permitted to be carried in, but there is a wine and beer tent at the festival. No dogs are allowed.

The festival combines the best current international reggae music with the finest local and California-based bands and brings together a cross section of people, many of whom are turned on to reggae music for the first time. The success of the festival is due to the spirit of volunteerism that exists among the members and staff of the Mateel Center. This festival is unique, and if you enjoy reggae music, you will undoubtedly enjoy yourself here. —L.F.

Reggae fans enjoy a day in the sun listening to some of their favorite artists at Garberville's Reggae on the River. (Photo by Kim Sallaway)

California Festivals — August

Renaissance Pleasure Faire
Novato (415) 892-0937
(800) 52-FAIRE

Labor Day weekend to first weekend in October (weekends and holidays only). 120,000. 25 years. $14.50 adults, $7.50-$11.50 children, students, seniors. military. Black Point Forest. Hwy. 101 north of San Francisco to Hwy. 37 east to the park.

The Renaissance Pleasure Faire is a pleasure indeed. From the moment you walk in you know this is not your average festival. You have been transported to a place and time when jousting, dancing, and merriment were a way of life and food and drink paramount.

The Faire is actually a complete Elizabethan village tucked back in the hills of Blackpoint Forest. Once inside, you'll be swept up in the bustling activity and fun of life in the 16th century. You'll be invited to try your hand at crossbow firing, juggling, fencing, and cannon firing, as well as simple games of wit such as chess and backgammon.

For the more sedate there's a wide variety of unusual and exquisite crafts to choose from. In many instances you can watch the craftsmen at work and sometimes try it yourself. If you're in need of a new drinking horn, dulcimer, mace, or mask, this is the place to be. You can also find extraordinary jewelry, perfumes, spices, weaving, pottery, pewter, and much, much more.

The food of the Renaissance Pleasure Faire is truly tantalizing. You'll be amazed by the giant turkey legs and artichokes, as well as fresh baked bread, scones, and gingerbread, plus cornish pasties, piroshki, and steak on a stake. One thing you definitely should not miss is the Toad-in-a-Hole...absolutely the best you'll ever taste!

Whatever your desire, the Renaissance Pleasure Faire has plenty to offer. There are several stages and other areas to watch Shakesperean plays, comics and jugglers or listen to storytellers and bawdy songs.

In reality, the whole village is a stage. As you wander the "streets" you'll see peasants washing their clothes, dancing and laughing villagers eating giant turkey legs and drinking ale from pewter mugs tied conven-

God save the queen! More than 3,000 costumed participants and their 20th century guests gather at Novato's Blackpoint Forest for several weekends of revelry and merry-making during the Renaissance Pleasure Faire. (Photo courtesy of the Living History Centre)

iently to their clothing, and plenty of royalty and servants. Many Fairegoers dress the part for the day, but if you'd rather not, that's o.k. (You can rent or buy costumes right there if you change your mind.)

If you want a splendid way to spend a weekend day, the Renaissance Pleasure Faire will surely fit the bill. It's really a special treat. —K.L.

Round Valley Blackberry Festival
Covelo   (707) 983-8124
(707) 983-6380

First weekend in August (Saturday and Sunday). 4,000. Free. Main St. in downtown Covelo. Hwy. 101 10 miles north of Willits. Go east on Hwy. 162, 28 miles to Round Valley. Festival grounds are in downtown Covelo on Main St.

Scenic Round Valley, located in the northeast corner of Mendocino County in Northern California, is the home of the Round Valley Blackberry Festival. The festival is held annually in early August at the historic Old Mill near downtown Covelo and honors, as might be guessed from its name, the wonderful blackberry. Many exciting activities, delicious foods, colorful country entertainment, and various arts and crafts booths are offered.

The types of food available at the festival include blackberry delicacies— ice cream, pies, punch, slushes, jams, and cobblers; Native American food, such as Indian tacos; Chinese cuisine; Mexican food; and a Western barbecue (Saturday evening only).

Varied activities are organized to entertain festival goers: a pancake breakfast both days, 5K and 10K footraces open to both runners and walkers, wine tasting featuring a variety of Mendocino County wines, bingo, and friendly horseshoe games.

At the top of the entertainment list is the fiddle competition for all skill levels. Other entertainment includes a country/western dance, a coed softball tournament, an antique engine display, the Blackberry Jammers, and an appearance by "Mickey the Clown." You can also visit an authentic cowboy campsite and an old farm equipment display.

The arts and crafts booths feature spinning and weaving items plus a demonstration of spinning techniques, a unique stained glass display, colorful quilts, sheepskin crafts, and a ceramics display. In addition, a Farmer's Market offers organically grown fruits and vegetables picked daily in Round Valley. —B.C.

California Festivals — August

Salsa Tasting and Music Festival
Fresno   (209) 454-2424

Last weekend in August (Saturday and Sunday). 55,000. 6 years. Taster tickets are $3. Fulton Mall. From Hwy. 99, take the Fresno downtown exit. Downtown Fulton Mall is located just half a mile from Hwy. 99.

The history of this festival is almost as interesting as its star. In ancient Mexico, the Aztecs would pay homage to the chile god "Chantico." All provinces were obligated to produce tons of chiles for the great Aztec lords. Great celebrations followed.

Well, this festival certainly pays homage to the salsa gods. You'll find the very best in Mexican food and spicy salsas, as well as the hottest in live salsa music featuring Lula and Afro Brasil from Southern California and Riofrom Sacramento. Local entertainers include Cana, Mad Dog, the Mighty Statons, plus Tex/Mex favorite Redwine from Visalia, a salsa hat and salsa dance contests, a children's carnival, crafts, face painting and, of course, a salsa-making competition with two categories: restaurant/professional and family/individual. In addition, salsa food products and chips are provided free to visitors.

It's a two-day Brazilian Mardi Gras, in the heart of California's Central Valley.

Shakespeare at Sand Harbor
North Tahoe   (916) 583-9048

Month of August, excluding Mondays. 15,000. 13 years. $13-11 seniors or members of the Arts Council. Lake Tahoe State Park. Hwy. 80 to Truckee, then Hwy. 89 south or Hwy. 267 south to Hwy. 28. Follow Hwy. 28 east 5 miles past Incline Village, Nevada.

For 15 summer nights, you can enjoy the best of Shakespeare (and other playwrights) under the stars on the shores of beautiful Lake Tahoe. Produced by the North Tahoe

The pines of Lake Tahoe are the perfect setting for Shakespeare. (Photo courtesy of North Lake Tahoe Fine Arts council)

Fine Arts Council, a bi-state, nonprofit community organization dedicated to the development of the arts in this area, the plays are performed by members of the California Theater Center. Three plays are repeated over the run of the festival. Past performances have included *The Tempest, A Midsummer Night's Dream* and *The Lion in Winter*.

Most people bring picnic dinners to enjoy while the performances take place, and cold drinks are served. Some 12,000-15,000 people attend, making this the largest event of the summer season at Lake Tahoe.

Somethin's Brewing: A Fine Beer Tasting
Santa Rosa   (707) 579-1500

Last Friday in August. 1,200. 6 years. Sonoma County Museum members $16, nonmembers $18; $20 at the door. Veteran's Memorial Building. From Hwy. 101, take Hwy. 12 east to Veteran's Memorial Building, about 1 mile from Hwy. 101.

Microbreweries are becoming major business ventures for many entrepreneurs all over the country, and Northern California is at the forefront. Thirty microbreweries from throughout the area pour over 100 distinctive brews while several local restaurants serve a variety of finger foods (cheeses, French bread, pretzels, chips, salsa, etc.) at this brief festival that highlights Sonoma County's long-standing history as a hop-growing and beer-producing area. Educational exhibits present information about brewing techniques and collections of antique beer memorabilia. The entire event lasts only three hours and three minutes (from 5:05-8:08 p.m.), so you'd better get there early if you want to taste all the beer. Featured breweries include North Coast Brewing Co., Mendocino Brewing Co., Hogshead Brewpub, Triple Rock Brewery, Sierra Nevada Brewing Co., Anchor Brewing Co., Humboldt Brewery, Pete's Brewing Co., and Calistoga Pub/Napa Valley Brewing Co. A decorated biergarten adds to the atmosphere.

Entrance entitles you to a free souvenir pilsner glass, along with a chance in the raffle that features $1,000 in prizes and one door prize. Live music will keep you entertained, as will those attending as the tasting progresses.

California Festivals   August

Sonoma Summer Arts Festival
Sonoma   (707) 938-5879

Last weekend in August to third week in September (Every Saturday-Sunday). 3,000. 3 years. Admission varies with event. Andrews Hall. From Hwy 80 take Hwy 12 West into Sonoma. Turn right at historic Sonoma Plaza. Andrews Hall is two blocks on the left.

For a month of weekends you can get a dose of culture in Sonoma. This is a multi-disciplinary event including theater, dance, music, visual arts and lectures united with a single theme. Last year's theme was Americana and the featured event was the musical "Quilters". Coinciding with the play was a quilt show, bluegrass concert, old-time hoedown, BBQ and slide show. Each year features a different theme and much quality entertainment.

Sunset Junction Street Fair
Los Angeles   (213) 661-7771

Second weekend in August (Saturday-Sunday). 100,000. 11 years. Free. Sunset Blvd. from the 3700 to 4100 block. From Highway 101 freeway, take Vermont Ave. north; turn right onto Santa Monica Blvd. to its endpoint at Sunset Junction.

Created in 1980 to ease tension among the residents of Los Angeles' most diverse community, the sunset Junction Street Fair is now this city's largest free community street festival. Where else can you find gang members, gays and lesbians, and all races and ethnic groups working together to develop a community fair?

It's a big party with over 100,000 packed into the Silverlake district. The fair includes everything - carnival rides, petting zoo, two stages with continuous entertainment, ethnic dance, disco, Punch and Judy Show, beer gardens and more than 100 food and arts and crafts booths. This event is organized and produced totally as a volunteer, grassroots effort and has become one of the best examples of the strength of community in urban Los Angeles.

Swedish Crayfish Festival
Kingsburg   (209) 897-2925

Third weekend of August. 5,000. 4 years. Free. Except for crayfish dinner. Held on Draper St. Exit Conejo off Hwy. 99.

The Swedish settled in Kingsburg in 1888 and brought with them many of their homeland customs, among them this traditional Swedish festival featuring native food, decorations, costumes, music, and children's games. It is pretty much a family affair, with clowns, balloons, and musicians for the kids and lots of great food. In addition to the tasty crayfish, there is also 40 food booths of all kinds, and approximately 130 arts and crafts booths, all featuring handcrafted items.

This festival has a few added twists to the traditional Swedish crayfish festival. One of the more interesting events at this two-day celebration is the Crayfish Derby, where crayfish are lined up for a five-foot race. Not only are the little critters stubborn, you just never know which direction they'll run, making this a pretty challenging endeavor for all involved. There's also a crayfish-eating contest.

Tehachapi Mountain Festival
Tehachapi   (805) 822-4180,

Third weekend in August (Friday-Sunday). 40,000. 28 years. Free except for rodeo—$8-10. Rodeo grounds. Other activities at the Coy Burnett Stadium on Tehachapi Blvd. From Hwy. 99, go east on Hwy. 58 to Tehachapi. From I-5, take Hwy. 14 through Lancaster to Hwy. 58 west.

This festival features western family fun, including a PRCA Rodeo with a Rodeo Queen competition, parade, arts and crafts fair, cow chip throwing contest, 10K run, western dance, games, and food galore: tri-tip sandwiches, hamburgers, hot dogs, chili, fresh fruit, popcorn, cotton candy, and soft drinks.

One of the "highlights" of this event is the world champion cow chip thrower, who has entertained crowds at this festival for several years. It is three fun filled days in the cool Techachapi Mountains.

California Festivals   August

The Great Potato Harvest Festival
Somerset   (209) 245-3248

Second Saturday of August. Limited to 100. 3 years. $20. Fitzpatrick Winery. Take Hwy 16 from Plymouth and go 15 miles, then turn right on Fairplay Road and go 3 miles to Fitzpatrick Winery.

Every vegetable must have its day. Why not the good old potato? No matter if you call them papas, badadas, patatas, potatoes, pomme de terre, spuds, or taters you'll enjoy them at Fitzpatrick's Winery & Lodge once a year. (Make your reservations early since they only have room for 100.) The festival organizers present a buffet of potato dishes from around the world, from appetizers to desserts. While munching on your tater you'll be entertained with some fun ethnic folk music.

Wildwood Days
Rio Dell   (707) 764-3436

First weekend in August (Friday-Sunday). 1,000. 23 years. Free except barbecue, which is $6.50 for adults and $3.50 for children. Downtown Rio Dell. Hwy. 101 to Rio Dell.

Held in the mountain community of Rio Dell in Humboldt County, this three-day community celebration features a "peddler's faire" (an arts and crafts show), a parade, a logging show, a pancake breakfast, a barbecue, raft races, softball tournaments, tennis tournaments, bingo, 2- and 8-mile runs, a firemen's rodeo, a white elephant auction, pony rides, and fire engine rides, clowns, face painters, and games for the kids. In addition, several local bands perform throughout the weekend, and there's lots of good food, including barbecued beef, Mexican dishes, hot dogs, chili, chowder, and baked goods.

This small festival began as a logging show for the local loggers and has grown into the community's biggest yearly event.

California Festivals   September

A la carte, a la park
San Francisco   (415) 383-9378

Labor Day weekend (Saturday-Monday). 60,000. 7 years. $5.00 plus taste tickets—.50¢ to $5. Sharon Meadow, Golden Gate Park. JFK Dr. across from McLaren Lodge in Golden Gate Park

At A la carte, a la park, you can visit 50 restaurants at once—with no reservations and no tipping. In addition to sampling some of San Francisco's best food, you can see top-name musical entertainment and master chef presentations. The three-day Labor Day event makes for a giant family picnic in Golden Gate Park.

Make no mistake about it, this is a "food frenzy." The restaurants are grouped under five pavilions—American Classics, Continental Cuisine, California Cuisine, Flavors of Asia, Latin/Middle Eastern/Indian, and the Sweets of San Francisco. You pay from 50 cents to $5 a dish and create your own picnic smorgasbord. The food choices are unlimited—seafood ceviche, coxinaha de Gallinha (chicken croquette), crab cakes, tandoori chicken, Imperial shrimp, potato latkes,

It's a connoisseurs feeding frenzy every Labor-Day weekend at Golden Gate Park. (Courtesy of Ala Carte, Ala Park)

California Festivals — September

chicken brochettes with peanut salsa, jambalaya, plus hundreds more dishes. And once you have your food and drinks, you can lay a blanket down and listen to music (mostly jazz) or watch a benefit presentation by the San Francisco Shakespeare Festival.

Just remember to wear loose-fitting clothes—you'll be plenty full after this event.   —C.L.

Apple Festival
Templeton   (805) 238-5634

Last Saturday in September. 6,000. 6 years. Free. Templeton Park. Hwy. 101 south of Paso Robles, take Vineyard turn off, go east to Main street. Turn left to 6th Street.

Over 40 northern Californian apple growers take one afternoon to display and sell their products to residents and visitors of Templeton. Each farmer sets up a booth with his farm's apples, and you can sample over 25 different varieties of apples, along with cider, dried apples, apple butter, apple syrup, and apple pie (there is a small fee for some of these). Other food includes barbecue, hot dogs, hamburgers, cookies, and popcorn.

Other entertainment includes games for the kids, a BBQ, musical entertainment, pie contests, and prize giveaways every half hour.

Atwater Fall Festival
Atwater   (209) 358-4251

Third weekend in September (Saturday and Sunday). 20,000. 15 years. Free. Ralston Park. Take Hwy. 99, exit at any Atwater sign. Take Atwater Blvd. to Third St.   Ralston Park located on Third between Fir and Grove.

For 15 years this fall festival has put the spotlight on the art of handcrafts, with over 100 craft and food vendors from all over the state. You can browse through booths of woodcrafts, crochet, baskets, silk flowers, ceramics, and paintings while sampling a wide variety of ethnic foods. Special events include the 5-mile run and a 2.5-mile run through town.

California Festivals   September

Balloons Over the Valley Hot-Air Balloon Festival
Modesto   (209) 577-5757

Third weekend in September (Saturday and Sunday). 30,000. 8 years. Adults $5, children 14 and under $2. Advance tickets: Adults $3 general, children $1. Modesto airport. Hwy. 99 to Modesto. Take the Mitchell Rd. exit. Follow signs to airport.

The festival kicks off with more than 500 hot-air balloons inflating and sailing off in a rainbow of color at sunrise (excellent photo opportunities!). After watching the balloons take off, you might want to have breakfast—try the full omelet breakfast served in the airplane hangar, an experience you won't have too often in this lifetime! Other foods are also available throughout the day.

Local musicians and a Navy band provide entertainment while you browse through the arts and crafts exhibits or shop for T-shirts, pins, programs, posters, and other souvenirs. You'll also see unique displays and demonstrations of aircraft, from hot-air balloons of the past to high technology in aviation today, including remote-control model planes and military aircraft. For the kid's there's games and face painting.

This salute to aviation history is recognized as a national air show leader; four similar shows in the United States are modeled after this event. If you are interested in an inside look at aviation history, this festival is for you!

Over 500 hot-air balloons fill the sky at dawn to kick off Modesto's Balloons Over the Valley Hot-Air Balloon Festival. (Photo courtesy of the Balloons Over the Valley Festival)

California Festivals					September

Bay Area Cajun and Zydeco Festival
San Rafael   (415) 386-8677

Last weekend in September (Saturday-Sunday). 10,000. 5 years. $15 adults, $12 Seniors, $12.50 advance purchase. Marin County Fairgrounds. From Hwy 101 take the Marine Center exit near San Rafael.

Dancing is what a Cajun-Zydeco Festival is all about. House dances called "fais do-dos" (meaning "put the kids to sleep") have evolved into people of all ages gathering together in a dance hall where they dance the weekend away on the festival's specially-built dance floor. And if that rhythm doesn't take you over, there are dance workshops both days so you can learn to waltz, cajun two-step, jitterbug, Zydeco or do the "Harlem Shuffle." Cajuns are direct descendants of the French Acadians (shorted to "Cadians" and then to "Cajuns") who were driven from Nova Scotia 200 years ago. Their distinctive culture has developed in the isolation of the Louisiana bayous, swamps and prairies.

Cajun and Zydeco music features the fiddle and accordion accompanied by a triangle or spoons for keeping time. The musical influences include country and western, Afro-American, bluegrass and swing. Zydeco refers to the Black Creole counterpart of Cajun music, incorporating R&B, jazz, blues, and soul. Much of its distinctive Afro Caribbean sound comes from an instrument called the Frottoir—a corrugated metal vest the wearer plays with spoons, or other metal scrapers. Such groups as Michael Doucet & Beausoleil or C.J. Chenier & the Red Hot Louisiana Band, Wayne Toups & ZydeCajun, to name a few, appear at this festival each year.

But you can't go home without feasting on the creole and cajun home-cooked cuisine and traditional American barbecue. Experience savory gumbos, authentic jambalaya, red beans and rice, shrimp, etoufee, boiled crawfish, boudin, barbecued turtle, alligator, blackened shrimp, catfish and such desserts as pecan pie, bread pudding with whiskey sauce and beignets— the famous, flaky, deep-fried French Quarter delicacy—all topped off with dark-roast Louisiana coffee.

Bay-to-Burgers
San Francisco   (415) 564-5689

First Sunday after Labor Day. 100. 4 years. Free. Ferry Bldg. parking lot. From the Bay Bridge take the Fremont exit, turn right on Howard until you hit Embarcadero, then turn left and continue to the Ferry Building.

California Festivals   September

This festival was dreamed up as a less strenuous rival to the famous Bay-to-Breakers foot race that draws tens of thousands. Don't confuse this event with any kind of race though. In fact, those who ride slow and complain a lot are encouraged to return. Here station-wagon loads of fun lovers bring their bikes from all over the Bay Area and rendevous at the Ferry Building parking lot. From there the loose assortment of couples, families and friends heads off along the waterfront, stopping from time to time to listen to Page Milliken, the event's imaginative creator and spiritual leader, tell stories about old San Francisco and its legendary characters. Original participants were friends and family members of the Milliken's but the event has grown now to include people from all over. Stops include a tiny shop in the back of Pier 39 where everyone buys Churros (a famous Mexican sweet that makes your hands sticky). Then the group pedals off to the Marina Green, a pleasant rest stop where you can lay on the grass and watch people fly colorful kites. Next comes Fort Funston, a brick bulwark at the foot of Golden Gate bridge. Old timers just rest while the neophytes take the tour of the Fort where soldiers in authentic costumes man the ancient guns and pose for pictures. Everyone pushes their bikes up the path and rides across the Golden Gate Bridge, coasting downhill to Sausalito to a waterfront restaurant where burgers and beer are consumed in heroic amounts. Late in the afternoon everyone takes the Sausalito Ferry back to San Francisco and their cars.

Big Bear Lake Oktoberfest
Big Bear Lake   (714) 866-5634

Labor Day weekend through the end of October (weekends only). 40,000. 21 years. $5. Big Bear Convention Center. II-10 to I-215 east. Exit on Highland, go left to Hwy. 330, then Hwy. 18 to Big Bear Lake.

Every weekend for two months you can visit Europe right here in California at this German-style festival celebrating the fall harvest. Bavarian dancing and music (polkas, of course!) highlight the festivities, along with authentic German bratwurst, knockwurst, sauerkraut, and, of course, plenty of beer! There are also sing-a-longs, log-sawing contests, yodeling contests, beer-drinking contests, and 25 carnival booths. Experience some of Bavaria's most popular traditions—without having to travel half way around the world.

California Festivals — September

Big Time Indian Days
Pine Grove   (209) 223-0350

Fourth weekend in September (Saturday and Sunday). 2,000. 15 years. $3 per vehicle. Indian Grinding Rock State Park, 14881 Pine Grove-Volcano Rd. I-5 to Stockton. Take Hwy. 4 east to Hwy. 99. Go north on Hwy. 99 to Hwy. 88. Follow Hwy. 88 to Pine Grove.

Big Time Indian Days is a fall celebration of American Indian culture. Tribes from all over the state gather together for two days to participate in ceremonial dances, games, and artwork. A showing of Indian artwork can be seen at the Regional Indian Museum, and authentic Indian crafts can be bought from the many display booths. Saturday's highlight is a deep-pit barbecue; other native foods are available both days. All events are open to the public.

Bigfoot Daze
Willow Creek   (916) 629-3314

Labor Day weekend (Saturday through Monday). 4,000. 26 years. Dance $5. Downtown and Veterans Park. Hwy. 101 to Hwy. 299 to Willow Creek.

Known as the "Gateway to Bigfoot Country," Willow Creek has been the site of this salute to the shy beast for nearly 25 years. Held Labor Day weekend, it's the last big fling before each new school year, and the emphasis is on family entertainment. There's a parade, a softball tournament, a golf tournament, a horseshoe tournament, a talent show, co-ed mud wrestling, a country/western dance, other musical entertainment, and a variety of arts and crafts booths. All proceeds go to the Willow Creek Parks and Recreation program.

Brownsville Mountain Fair
Brownsville   (916) 692-0311

Third weekend in September (Saturday-Sunday). 10,000. 17 years. $2 adults, $1 seniors, children under 6, free. Ponderosa Park. Take Hwy 20 from Marysville to Grass Valley, turn left at Marysville Road (Browns Valley) and follow to Brownsville.

Artists come from all over Northern California to display their creations at this mountain festival that features an interesting mixture of artwork, ethnic foods, logging exhibits, music and unusual activities for kids. Take the petting zoo, for example. You'll find emus, tame snakes, Egyptian geese, miniature horses and donkeys and rabbits. Or let the kids smear their hands in paint and put their hand prints along the wall of the children's pavillion. It's allowed, even encouraged. Then they can sign their names. Or have them enter the sand sculpture contest or try cookie decorating.

Food booths feature unique cuisine, including East Indian, Hmong Tribesman, Scottish, Soul, Native American (such as egg corn soup), Mexican and Chinese.

California Prune Festival
Yuba City   (916) 743-6501

Weekend following Labor Day. 25,000. 3 years. Adults $5, Senior and Children $3, children under 6 free. Yuba-Sutter Fairgrounds. I-5 or Hwy. 99 to Hwy. 20 to Yuba City.

Prunes. What can you say about prunes? Well, the folks at the California Prune Festival, launched in 1988 and attended by around 25,000 people, figure they have a lot to say about the wonders of prunes. And apparently, given the quality of this festival, they're right.

The festival is centered around the "Prune Station," a gourmet food alley featuring unusual foods prepared from prune recipes. The adjacent "Prune Pavilion," an educational display, depicts the history, planting, growing, harvesting, and processing of prunes. A Farmer's Market highlights other commodities, such as fresh fruits and vegetables and prepared rice and beans. If your tastes go more toward the exotic, the "Tastes of the Valley" exhibit offers authentic international foods, art forms, music, costumes, and dance. There is also a prune cook-off, with top cooks from Bakersfield to the Oregon border. Winning recipes are used in each year's official *Prune Festival Cookbook*.

The variety of food is astounding (Filipino, Indian, Mexican, Greek, Chinese, Japanese, and Laosian, plus good ol' ribs, hot dogs, and hamburgers), and an abundance of shaded tables and benches make for enjoyable eating (try the "Rip-Roaring Prune Chili"!). Wine tasting is also available, with vintners from some of the surrounding counties offering their finest.

The musical entertainment is as rich as the food. Several top Dixieland Bands perform alternately on two stages, while on a third stage continuous performers delight the "Taste of the Valley" audience with their cultural sounds. A fourth stage is dedicated to the classic sounds of the 50's and

60's. A treat for all ages, they keep the audience rocking and bopping all day.

In addition to arts and crafts for sale, some 30 artists demonstrate everything from quilting, bronze and clay sculpturing to watercolor techniques and woodcarving.— M.J. and D.J.

Capitola Art and Wine Festival
Capitola   (408) 688-7377
(408) 475-6522

Third weekend in September (Saturday and Sunday). 20,000. 7 years. Free. Capitola Esplanade. Hwy. 1 to Park Ave. exit. The beach shuttle is available into town.

This two-day autumn festival, set along the beautiful Monterey Bay, is billed as "a celebration of three Pacific Rim passions: art, wine, and the beach!" Over 150 juried artists from all over the state share their works, along with the fruits of several local wineries. The food is provided by several area restaurants and includes smoked salmon, bite-sized Mexican delicacies, and delicious desserts. There's something for every member of the family: a children's theater with puppet and clown performances, two stages of musical entertainment (featuring rock and roll, classical, and big band), and the chance to purchase much of the artwork that's displayed, along with festival wines, T-shirts, and posters.

Capitola National Begonia Festival
Capitola   (408) 476-3566

Begins the Sunday of Labor Day weekend and ends the following Sunday. 15,000. 39 years. Free. Capitola Village, Soquel Creek Lagoon. Take Hwy. 1 south to Capitola, take Bay Ave. turnoff (Capitola-Soquel) to village—public parking lot on Capitola Ave. and McGregor (there's a shuttle bus).

The climax of this two-weekend festival—begun as a way to use the blossoms discarded by local growers—a nautical parade featuring floats covered with begonia blossoms that drift down the creek. Local groups and businesses interpret each year's theme with creative parade entries. Other events include a sand sculpture contest, fishing derby, and rowboat races.

You can dine at any of the wide variety of restaurants around Capitola, or picnic along some of California's beautiful coastline. Many campsites are available in the area as well, but plan ahead—it's a busy weekend!

Castroville Artichoke Festival
Castroville   (408) 633-2465

Third weekend in September (Saturday and Sunday). 50,000. 32 years. Adults $2. Children free Community Center. Hwy. 1 to Hwy. 183 to Castroville.

This two-day tribute to the artichoke—set in (where else?) the "Artichoke Center of the World"—is one of the oldest agricultural festivals in California. Activities include a parade, firefighters' muster, artichoke eating contest, horseshoe tournament, arts and crafts fair, carnival games, and artichokes, artichokes, artichokes!

In addition to a pancake breakfast that begins the weekend, other food includes artichoke and ethnic specialties, and there's plenty of musical entertainment, from bluegrass and country to big band and rock and roll. And for the kids, there's clowns, face painting and games. Better come hungry!

No mistaking what Castroville is famous for. (Photo courtesy of Castroville Artichoke Festival)

Concord Fall Fest
Concord   (510) 346-4446

Labor Day weekend (Saturday-Monday). 100,000. 9 years. Free. Todos Santos Park on Willow Pass Rd. I-680 to Willow Pass Rd. exit. Go one mile.

This Labor Day weekend celebration in one of the Bay Area's warmer climes features an arts and crafts exhibit, chili cook-off, 10K run, wine tasting, celebrity grape stomp, face painters, and continuous musical entertainment by local musicians, from jazz to country/western (dancing's allowed!). It's a community event, so you'll find special entertainment for

California Festivals — September

the kids too, and lots of good food, including Indian, Mexican, Greek, Chinese, and Japanese cuisine.

Cotton Harvest Festival
Buttonwillow   (805) 764-5406

Third Saturday in September. 1,000. 23 years. Free. Buttonwillow County Park. Parade begins at the school (400 McKittrick Hwy.) and ends at the park (McKittrick and Meadow St.).

Set in Buttonwillow, the heart of California's cotton country, this festival celebrates cotton harvest time for this community. In addition to such special events as the crowning of the cotton princess and an awards ceremony for parade entries, there's the parade itself, a soccer game, carnival booths, a barbecue, and live music. Besides the barbecue—cooked in special underground pits—other edibles include hot dogs, nachos, cotton, snow cones, and homebaked cupcakes and cookies. Proceeds benefit local clubs and organizations.

Danish Days
Solvang   (805) 688-3317

Third weekend in September (Saturday and Sunday). 25,000. 55 years. Free. Solvang Village. Hwy. 101 to Solvang/Lompoc exit. Three miles east.

What better place for a celebration of Danish roots and traditions than in Solvang, a predominantly Danish community founded in 1911 as the site for a folk colony. Learn to dance traditional Danish folk dances while you munch on such specialities as aebleskiver (Danish pancake balls) and medisterpolse (sausage). And what Danish festival would be complete without roving folk dancers, village singers, a village band, and, of course, a smorgasbord?

Delicato Charity Grape Stomp
Manteca   (209) 239-1215

Sunday of Labor Day weekend. 7,000. 9 years. Adults $2.50, children and seniors $1.50. Delicato Vineyards. On Hwy. 99, 1/4 mile south of French Camp Rd. (between Manteca and Stockton).

California Festivals   September

Vintage television aficionados will probably remember the old "I Love Lucy" episode in which Lucy, while in Europe, gets involved in a grape-stomping endeavor. Naturally, she botches the thing somehow and the whole grape stomp turns into one big purple mess (which you knew even though the show was in black and white).

If you've always thought it might be fun to stomp grapes like Lucy, the opportunity awaits you at the annual Delicato Charity Grape Stomp. You can participate in the grape stomp as an individual contestant, as a couple, or as a four-person corporate team. Each stomper or pair of stompers is given 90 seconds to "crush" as much juice as they can from a 25-pound lug of grapes that has been dumped into a large half-barrel. The stompers wear old tennis shoes for safety and to enhance their stomping effectiveness. The juice is then measured and the winners proceed to the final stomping event to determine the ultimate champion in each category. (Don't worry—Delicato Vineyards DOES NOT use this juice to make their wine!).

It isn't necessary to train for months to take part in the grape stomp or to have your own grape stomping attire—shoes and clothes are available at the site. 90 seconds of grape stomping, especially when the temperature soars near the 100-degree mark, is tougher than it sounds—take it from one who found out by stomping! But it's great fun for people of all ages. In fact, you might be surprised to find out that your kids can stomp better than you can!

The festival also includes continuous entertainment—mostly country and bluegrass. Concession stands featuring mostly Italian foods (including pasta, garlic bread, pizza, and sausage) are staffed by local charitable organizations. Naturally, wine tasting is a big part of the event, and you can take a tour of Delicato, one of the largest vineyards in Northern California. There is also a large selection of arts and

Stomp 'til you drop. (Photo by Glenn Kahl)

crafts and a display of antique and vintage cars.

Delicato Vineyards is a good location for the festival. There is plenty of room so that as the festival grows, there is space available for additional arts and crafts booths, food stands, etc. The folks at Delicato Vineyards are more than willing to do their best to make sure everything goes well during this fun-filled, one-day event that raises money for many local charities. — L.F.

Denver Dan's Apple Bake-Off
Camino   (916) 644-2893

Mid-September (Saturday). 2,000. 4 years. Free. Denver Dan's. From Highway 50 take the Camino exit, turn left onto Barkley Road and go to the end. Turn left onto Larsen and continue to Denver Dan's.

Denver Dan, a self-described "poor old apple farmer", kicks off the apple growing season every year with a big bake-off. But more than that this festival is a great day of bluegrass music, apple bobbing and a ton of apple eating in every way, shape and form.

Still, the highlight is the apple bake-off. Contestants from all over the country are judged in three categories: pies, cakes (including cheesecakes) and other desserts. These delicious apple treats are judged on appearance, taste, texture and presentation. The winners receive cash prizes as well as the honor of being included in the Apple Hill Growers Cookbook.

Those without the necessary baking skills can have fun participating in the apple-crisp eating contest and bobbing for apples on a string.

Whatever your plans for the day stop by Denver Dan's for a relaxing day in the country. You are encouraged to bring a picnic and pick some apples. They'll even provide a pole to pluck the high ones off the tops of the trees.

Dinuba Raisin Festival
Dinuba   (209) 591-2707

Third weekend in September (Thursday-Saturday). 15,000. 29 years. Free. Rose Ann Vuich Park. Hwy. 99 to Mt. View exit, travel east 14 miles to park. Hwy. 198 to Dinuba/Road 80 exit, travel north 20 miles to city.

This festival began 25 years ago as a salute to this town's once-primary industry. Though the community's economic structure may have shifted a bit, the three-day event is still going strong. Featured are a parade, a carnival, a barbecue, a pancake breakfast, and games of all kinds for the whole family. Besides the barbecue, you'll also find a variety of Mexican, Chinese, and Armenian foods. There's a variety of music as well, from easy listening and light rock to gospel and Spanish.

The wrinkles may have faded, but the fun goes on.

Egyptian Festival
Hayward   (510) 889-1641

Last weekend in September (Friday-Sunday). 4,000. 3 years. $1 adults, free for children and seniors. St. Antonius Coptic Orthodox Church. From Hwy 880 take the Jackson exit, turn east and watch for the signs.

If you've ever dreamed of visiting Egypt, here's your chance to sample some authentic Egyptian food and get to know the people and the culture. The Egyptian Festival, put on by members of St. Antonius Coptic Orthodox Church, features home-cooked delicacies such as shish-kebab, kofta, shawerma with sauce, stuffed grape leaves, filo dough cheese puffs and mesaka (eggplant). Other specialities include an Egyptian bean dish called foul medames along with falafel, yogurt salad and tahini salad. For dessert try baklava, konafa, bassboussa, kahk, and lokomadis. And prepare to do some shopping since they set up a covered bazaar with many items imported from Egypt especially for this event: tapestries and antique sculptures, handmade copper and brass plates and trays, papyrus artwork, silver and costume jewelry, colorful galabias (dresses with pharaohnic designs), and Egyptian cotton shirts and tote bags.

Other highlights include historic films and lectures of ancient and modern Egypt and continuous tours of the church. You can also have your name written in ancient hieroglyphics and mounted for framing. For more Egyptian atmosphere you can purchase books, postcards, music tapes, souvenirs and icons to take home with you.

Fall Festival
Castro Valley   (415) 537-5300

Second weekend in September (Saturday and Sunday). 65,000. 19 years. Free. Castro Village. I-580 to Castro Valley.

Castro Valley's Fall Festival is a community-oriented arts and wine fair that offers unique crafts, a diversity of ethnic foods (Thai, Vietnamese, Mexican, American, etc.), and continuous free entertainment, with over 120 food and service booths and 150 arts and crafts booths. Among the many crafts you'll find are pottery, metal sculptures, woodworking, colorful arrangements of dried and silk flowers, handmade jewelry, shadow boxes, and music boxes. Some of the fine artwork includes original paintings in acrylics, pastels, and watercolors.

A variety of fine wines from local vintners is available for tasting, and each year features a different commemorative glass that many people collect. Three stages contain the continuous live music, from soft rock and pop to country/western, jazz, folk, blues and gospel.

Field and Fair Day
Lodi   (209) 333-7863

Labor Day. 20,000. 13 years. Adults $3, seniors $2, children $1, children under 5 Free Hutchins Street Square, corner of Oak St. and Hutchins St. From I-5 or Hwy. 99, take Hwy. 12, go north on Hutchins St.

Begun 12 years ago to illustrate the need to save an abandoned high school site and convert it into a community center, this volunteer community fair features competitive games, races, exhibits, hot-air balloons, and live entertainment. The day begins with 15 hot-air balloons lifting off at 6:30 a.m., a pancake breakfast, a 5K/10K run, and semi-pro/citizen bicycle race (the Central Valley's flat highways are perfect for this event). Other activities throughout the day include Bingo, National Guard Air Show, pig races (you can sponsor a pig or a race), a baking contest, a chili cook-off, a lip-sync contest, arts and crafts booths, and eating—you can choose from 35 different food booths. For the kids there's games, a petting zoo, face painting, foot races and theater shows every half hour. All proceeds from this one-day event are donated to the building fund for Hutchins Street Square.

Fiesta de las Artes
Hermosa Beach   (213) 376-0951

Labor Day weekend. 200,000. 22 years. Free. Pier and Hermosa Ave. Hwy. 405 7 miles south of Los Angeles International Airport. Take Artesia Blvd. exit. Go to the intersection of Pier and Hermosa.

This three-day outdoor festival, which takes place both Memorial Day weekend (see May) and Labor Day weekend, has a lot of the best of most festivals. Over 350 booths feature unique handmade arts and crafts and fine art. Over 40 booths, assembled in the Food Pavilion, offer a diversity of international foods. In addition, this festival hosts the collegiate playoffs for the prestigious Playboy Jazz Festival.

Located just one block from the beach, this festival of course offers many outdoor activities as well, such as a 10K race and volleyball games. In addition to the jazz competition, other entertainment includes harp and dulcimer bands, saw playing, jugglers, and mimes. And if the 100,000+ crowd gets to be too much, you can slip off to the beach to catch some sun, cool off with a dip in the ocean, or join in that ultimate spectator sport: people watching.

Fiestas Patrias Celebrations
San Jose   (408) 258-0663

Closest Sunday to September 16. 100,000. 8 years. Free. Downtown San Jose. From Hwy. 101 take the Alum Rock exit west. From I-280 take Guadalupe St. south.

This festival takes place on two different days, one in May and one in September, and honors Cinco De Mayo and Mexican Independence Day. It features a large parade (150 units) in the morning, food and crafts booths, a Mexican art and cultural exhibit, and lots of live music, including mariachis and Folkloric dances.

If you're a Mexican-food lover, you may want to spend the day tasting the variety of traditional Mexican and contemporary Chicano foods, including fajitas, tamales, fried chicken, corn on the cob, hot dogs, chili burgers, and ice cream. If you're more interested in education than eating, be sure to check out the art and culture exhibits; they offer a look into Mexican life both long ago and today. Whatever your pleasure, don't miss the parade or the music, both colorful and full of life.

Grape Bowl Festival
Sanger   (209) 875-4575

Third weekend in September (Thursday-Sunday). 5,000. 39 years. Free. North and Academy Avenues. Hwy. 99 to Jensen Ave. exit. East 12 miles to Sanger.

The end of the grape harvest spells relief for the people of Sanger, and every year since 1925 they've celebrated with the Grape Bowl Festival. You might think there's some big football game or something, but this festival's Grape Bowl is actually a silver bowl filled with grapes that is given to "Mr. and Mrs. Farmer"—the outstanding farmers in the area each year. The recipients are also honored at the Mr. and Mrs. Farmer dinner.

California Festivals

September

Other special events during this agricultural festival include the Grape Bowl Queen coronation, a giant carnival, a fireman's muster, arts and crafts, and food booths serving traditional Mexican dishes and other ethnic fare. The music includes country/western, jazz, contemporary, rock, and mariachi bands.

Greek Festival
Cardiff   (619) 942-0920

Second weekend in September (Saturday-Sunday). 15,000. 12 years. Adults $2, children under 12 free. St. Constantine and St. Helen Greek Orthodox Church. I-5 to Manchester Ave. East one-half mile.

The Greek Festival is the ultimate travel preview for those who long to visit Greece. A $2 ticket provides entry to a Greek bazaar and market. There are performances of folk dances that alternate with instruction in the festive steps. Not only are the dances fun, they are a great workout! And with all that dancing, there's no need to feel guilty about eating the syrupy baklavah or buttery kourabiethes cookies. Visitors can also take home souvenirs, such as Greek records, clothing, jewelry, and, of course, the traditional Greek fishing caps. And the children aren't forgotten—there's a variety of game booths and pony rides to entertain them.

The deli offers produce and Greek food items such as olives and feta cheese. A full-course Greek meal is also sold. The combination dinner features a Greek salad with olives and feta cheese, souvlakia (shish kebab), spanakopita (spinach pie), pastichio (Greek lasagne), domathes (stuffed grape leaves), and pilaf rice.

Visitors to the Greek Festival should definitely try the rich coffee. Greek coffee is made from pulverized grounds that are blended with sugar to produce a sweet, dessertlike treat. The Greeks recommend recycling the sediment by reading the coffee grounds. This is accomplished by turning the cup upside down and then righting it. According to one cookbook, "Knowing your guest, the message can be almost anything."

At this festival, one thing the grounds may reveal is if the coffee drinker is a raffle winner. Each year, a Mercedes Benz is raffled off. The prize may not be Greek, but who can fault a country that created baklava and the dances to burn off its calories? —L.S.

Greek Food Festival
Modesto   (209) 522-7694

Third weekend in September (Saturday-Sunday). 6,000. 28 years. $10-$12. Greek Orthodox Church. Hwy. 99 to Briggsmore Ave. exit, take Briggsmore Ave east, turn left on McHenry Ave., then right on Tokay Ave.

Visit a Greek cafe and marketplace right in California's Central Valley at the Modesto Greek Food Festival, a celebration of Greek food, music, dancing, and culture. The Greek Pavilion serves an authentic Greek meal (including chicken, rice, vegetables, and pastries) while a band plays Greek music and five different dancing troupes in folk costumes perform traditional dances—Zorba style! The festival also features an "Agora," a Greek marketplace where you can purchase books, records, clothing, food products, etc., from the old country.

You may not find islands of white sandy beaches surrounded by translucent blue oceans, but this festival features the rest of the best Greece has to offer.

Greenfield Broccoli Festival
Greenfield   (408) 674-5240
(408) 674-3061

Labor Day weekend (Saturday and Sunday). 15,000. 8 years. Adults $4, children 6-17 $1.50, children under 6 free. Greenfield Oak Park. Hwy. 101 to Greenfield.

Once a year, the community of Greenfield pays homage to Monterey County's number two agricultural commodity when it hosts the Broccoli Festival, a two-day bash dedicated to a nutritious vegetable and the spirit of community fun. The festival features an abundance of broccoli-related dishes and other refreshments on "Food Alley," as well as live music (country/western, 50s and 60s, rock, jazz, Dixieland, and Mexican), arts and crafts, entertainment for the kids (including a carnival, clowns, puppets, and live animals), a 10K run, a chicken barbecue, and a parade on Saturday. The area around Greenfield offers wine tasting; camping; lakes for boating, water skiing, fishing, swimming, and picnicking; and national forests.

The organizers say their goal with this festival is to offer festival-goers a day (or two) of "easy-going fun and friendship—Greenfield-style." They want visitors to "enjoy the music, dance your shoes off, feast on broccoli, and bask in the sunshine."

California Festivals   September

Gunfighters' Rendevous
Coulterville   (209) 878-3074

Fourth weekend in September (Saturday and Sunday).   2,500. 66 years. Free. Historic Main St. Hwy. 49 to Hwy. 132.

They show up at high noon, guns on their hips, cowboy hats on their heads, spurs on their heels. They're professional gunfighters, lookin' for a showdown.

Actually, they're professional actors and stunt men, steeped in the lore and ways of the 1800s, who visit the Old West town of Coulterville each September to perform carefully planned and staged stunt shows featuring action, gunfights, and excitement. In between shows and gunfights, authentically costumed gunfighters and dancehall girls walk the streets, and a live band performs. You can also stroll through town and enjoy the arts and crafts booths, plus lots of food and beverages to satisfy all taste buds. A raffle is held both days for a variety of prizes.

Coulterville is a small, historical gold-mining town in the Mother Lode foothills of the Sierras. Its Main Street is registered in the National Register of Historic Places and is a treat for photo and history enthusiasts.

Jazz on the Waterfront
Stockton   (209) 825-7905

Last weekend in September (Friday-Sunday). 1,200. 12 years. $45 for all events ($40 before Sept. 1), All 5 sites at Best Western Stockton Inn, 4219 Waterloo Rd. (at Hwy. 99), Stockton.

Some 21 bands from around the U.S. play traditional New Orleans and Dixieland music during this three-day jazz jubilee. The bands will play in the ballroom, cabaret, convention meeting rooms, and around the pool at the beautiful Best Western Stockton Inn. Dance floors will be available at most sites for your dancing pleasure.

Special events include a Saturday afternoon concert featuring New Orleans Jazz, a Sunday morning Spiritual Celebration, and a Sunday afternoon concert featuring West Coast Jazz.

Good food, plus drinks will be served at the Stockton Inn throughout this jazz event. RVers can park in a special area in the huge parking lot. Badges are limited.

California Festivals   September

Lakeside Chili Cook-Off
Lakeside   (619) 444-0464

Last Sunday in September. 15,000. 12 years. $2. Rodeo Grounds, Mapleview Ave. Hwy. 67 to stop lights, right on Mapleview Ave., then one block to rodeo grounds.

Pull out the secret family recipe for this one-day chili cook-off in Lakeside, just east of San Diego. Some 50 people compete (are there really that many ways to cook chili?) for the $1,000 grand prize, awarded by a panel of celebrity judges. If you want to enter, you must bring all your own ingredients and cooking utensils.

For some reason, this festival also pays tribute to Phyllis Diller, with Phyllis Diller Chili and a Phyllis Diller and "Fang" look-alike contest. Other events include a carnival, games for the kids, horseshoe contests, gun fights, a Western dance the night before the cook-off, and food booths.

Linda Vista Multicultural Fair
San Diego   (619) 565-8259

Fourth Saturday in September. 8,000. 7 years. Free. Linda Vista Rd. between Comstock St. and Ulric St. I-805 to Mesa College Dr., turn left on Linda Vista Rd., head to Ulric intersection (Linda Vista Plaza).

Linda Vista has been an ethnic melting pot for so long that a resident once quipped someone from outer space could land there and it would be days before people noticed. After all, 22 different languages and dialects are spoken in Linda Vista, according to Janet Kaye, director of the Linda Vista Multicultural Fair.

The day begins at 8am with a 5k run followed by a parade. Then it's time to explore the booths along Linda Vista Rd. The display of crafts includes the intricate Hmong needlecraft. Other booths contain information about community groups. Fair food can include the doughy Philippine lumpia, Vietnamese chicken, and Mexican burritos. Visitors may also find foods that originated in Africa, Italy, Spain, and Laos.

The diversity continues with the day-long entertainment. A skateboard demonstration by the Boys Club may be followed by a performance of a troupe from the Buddhist temple. The dance performances include tiny dancers in Indo-Chinese costumes, jigs by the Pride of Erin Celtic dancers, and hula performers. Music ranges from performances by local high school bands to an appearance by Santa Claus (that's Santa Claus the rock and roll band, not St. Nick).

Linda Vista's salute to its many cultures ends with a fireworks display. The dazzling finale can be seen from the Linda Vista Plaza, a shopping center with a past: Then-First Lady Eleanor Roosevelt cut the opening-day ribbon at the plaza, one of the nations' first shopping centers. —L.S.

Lodi Grape Festival & National Wine Show
Lodi   (209) 369-2771

Third week of September (Thursday-Sunday). 95,000. 54 years. Adults $4.50, children 6-12 $1.50, children 5 and under free. 413 E. Lockeford St. North on Hwy. 99, take the Lodi exit. South on Hwy. 99, take the Turner Rd. exit.

It's not too hard to figure out what this festival is all about: grapes. They grow 'em, pick 'em, squish 'em, eat 'em, drink 'em—just about everything you could ever imagine doing with a grape, they do at this celebration of the grape harvest. In fact, they probably do a few things you wouldn't imagine, including building 8' x 12' grape murals out of individual grapes and creating the world's largest indoor display of grapes.

Overall, though, this is a traditional fair, with a carnival, photo exhibits, floriculture, hand crafts, art exhibitions, home art displays, and more. There is also wine tasting, though, which most fairs don't offer, and a wide variety of music, including jazz, gospel, country, and rock.

Los Angeles Classic Jazz Festival
Los Angeles   (213) 391-1357 or (818) 340-1516

Labor Day weekend. 8,000. 8 years. $60 for all events. Single days $15-$20. L.A. Airport Marriott and Hilton Hotels. Take Hwy 405 to Century Blvd. and go west to the Marriott/Hilton hotels.

If you enjoy jazz, head to Los Angeles Labor Day weekend for the Classic Jazz Festival. You'll be treated to a four-day jazz extravaganza — 250 musicians, 35 bands, 11 stages and four dance floors. The organizers have covered a lot of ground with big bands as well as small groups featured. One of the highlights is seeing different combinations of jazz "all stars" do an improv set. Whether you enjoy Chicago jazz, New Orleans Jazz, Big Band, Swing, blues or Dixieland you'll have a great time at this swinging festival, whre visitors feel free to dance in the streets.

California Festivals September

Millbrae Art & Wine Festival
Millbrae   (415) 697-7324

Labor Day weekend (Saturday and Sunday). 100,000. 21 years. Free. On Broadway in Millbrae. Go west from Hwy. 101 on Millbrae Ave. Turn right on Broadway.

If you're in the San Francisco Bay Area for Labor Day and would like to get out of the city for an afternoon, a trip down to the Millbrae Art & Wine Festival might be just the answer. This event features six blocks of booths offering a wide variety of arts and crafts from over 250 artists. There are also several food booths, offering American and international food plus wine, beer, and champagne (there's also wine tasting). The kids can keep themselves entertained in the children's area while you browse, and a variety of live music fills the air.

Monterey Jazz Festival
Monterey   (408) 373-3366

Third full weekend in September (Friday-Sunday). 35,000. 34 years. Varies. Monterey Fairgrounds. Hwy. 101 or Hwy. 68 to Hwy. 1 to Monterey. Follow signs to fairgrounds.

This is the granddaddy of all the jazz festivals, the oldest continuously presented jazz festival in the U.S. It's pretty famous, too, having had songs written about it, discovering some of the greats (remember Jimi Hendrix?), and attracting the best musicians in the business. But its 30+ years have brought a few changes—it's not the funky, intimate jazz happening it used to be, but a slick, corporate-sponsored, three-day musical extravaganza.

Still, where else can you see the likes of Ray Charles, Buddy Guy, B.B. King, Etta James, Woody Herman, and Bobby McFerrin in one setting, for an all-shows price of no more than $80, with the profits going toward jazz education? In addition to the performances, the festival also hosts the California High School Jazz Competition and showcases its winners at concerts throughout the weekend.

Some jazz enthusiasts may need little more than the music to get them through the weekend, but for those of you who need food and drink also you'll find plenty of both around the festival grounds. And Monterey is a vacationer's paradise, with many fine restaurants, lodging, and sights to see.

California Festivals   September

Mountain View Chamber of Commerce Art and Wine Festival
Mountain View   (415) 968-8378

Weekend after Labor Day (Saturday and Sunday). 120,000. 20 years. Free. Downtown Mountain View. Hwy. 101 to Moffett Blvd. Go toward downtown. Moffett turns into Castro. (You can also take the train from San Francisco or San Jose.)

Talk about an art festival—this festival attracts over 400 artists and craftspeople to the two-day event, and it just might take you two days to get around to seeing all of their displays. As for wine, they've got that too, with several wineries from all over California offering wine tasting. This festival also features a 5K run (with T-shirts, awards, and prizes), jugglers, mimes, face painters, beer booths (three kinds of beer), food booths (with Polish sausage, teriyaki chicken, steak sandwiches, shish kebabs, hamburgers, nachos, churros, gyros, and ice cream), and all kinds of commemorative souvenirs, including T-shirts, mugs, glasses, and posters.

If this festival doesn't keep you busy for a weekend, nothing will.

North Lake Tahoe Chocolate Festival
Northstar   (916) 546-7804

First Saturday in September. 1,000. 3 years. $12 advance. $15 at door. Northstar Ski Resort. I-80 to Hwy. 267. 5 miles outside of Truckee. Follow signs.

At the North Lake Tahoe Chocolate Festival, local chefs repare chocolate treats and enter them in the recipe contest, and all festival attendees can taste the luscious desserts to their hearts' (and stomachs') content. Each chef must prepare one sample for the judges and another for tasting by the crowd. A single ticket entitles the bearer to five dessert samples or a taste of wine. Additional tasting tickets may be purchased for $1, and tickets entitle each guest to participate in the raffles. This festival also features live music and gourmet coffee.

If you're a chocolate or wine connoisseur and need another reason to travel to beautiful Lake Tahoe for a summer weekend, then this festival is your ticket.

Newman Fall Festival
Newman   (209) 862-2222

Labor Day weekend (Wednesday-Sunday). 5,000. 21 years. Free. Wine and cheese sampling $7. Newman City Park. Off of I-5 take the Newman exit east. Go 5 miles to Hwy. 33. Go south on Hwy. 33 one mile.

You may never have heard of this small community located 100 miles southeast of San Francisco or thought of visiting there, but they sure would like you to. What started as a harvest kick-off in the Newman area has grown into a full-blown, community fiesta that packs more events into four days than you can imagine.

Things begin Wednesday night with a fashion show featuring the candidates of the Ms. Newman beauty pageant. Friday night features a wine and cheese tasting reception, with a wide variety of California wines from 12 wineries and locally made cheeses from four cheese manufacturers.

But Saturday and Sunday are the big days, with bathtub races (the tubs must be cast iron and many are specially designed and aerodynamic, with some contestants spending up to $4,000 to design the fastest tub), a parade, tennis tournament, carnival rides, tractor pull, barbecue, horseshoe tournament, lip-sync competition, West Coast arm-wrestling championship, Polynesian dancers, mariachi bands, and booths of food and crafts in the park. In addition, the Diamond Walnut Association sponsors a bake-off, where all entries must be made with walnuts.

Besides the wine and cheese reception and barbecue, other food includes Mexican dishes, linguica, Polish and Italian sausages, Japanese dishes, hamburgers, ice cream, cotton candy, and bowls of fresh fruit. You can sip frozen margaritas, wine coolers, beer, or sodas. Locally grown produce is also for sale, as well as packages of walnuts, almonds, and dried fruit.

It's B.Y.O.B. (Bring Your Own Bathtub) at the Newman Fall Festival bathtub races. (Photo courtesy of the Newman Fall Festival)

California Festivals   September

Newark Days Celebration
Newark   (415) 793-5683

Second weekend after Labor Day weekend (Friday-Sunday). 70,000. 36 years. Free. Newark Community Center. From Hwy 880 take the Thorton Ave exit west to Cedar Blvd. Turn left on Cedar, go one mile.

Tots to seniors can find plenty to do for three days at the Newark Days Celebration. Kids enjoy Make-A-Circus where they learn to juggle and clown around and cool off by playing in the ice and snow shipped in to make a winter wonderland in the middle of September. Families enjoy watching over a hundred horses involved in the California State Horsemen's Association Championship parade, as well as listening to storytellers and watching fire eaters and jugglers. And you can't miss the contests for cutest pet and most unusual pet. It's continuous music and fun each September on 20 beautiful acres at the Newark Community Center and Park.

New York Landing Seafood Festival
Pittsburg   (510) 432-7301

Second weekend in September (Saturday and Sunday). 75,000. 57 years. $2. Waterfront area. I-680 to Hwy. 4. Go right. Take Railroad Ave. exit. Go left toward the waterfront.

If you're in search of a "whale of a time for a few clams," you can enjoy gourmet seafood dishes prepared by some of the Bay Area's foremost up-and-coming chefs at this festival devoted "solely" (sorry) to seafood and its preparation. Over 60 chefs from restaurants around the Bay Area compete in this festival, which was begun six years ago to "set a standard for seafood cooking" and to recognize that Pittsburg (which used to be known as New York Landing) was once the fishing capital of the San Francisco Bay Area.

Judges and visitors alike pick the winner of the gourmet seafood competition at the New York Landing Seafood Festival, featuring chefs from some of San Francisco's finest restaurants. Shark fin soup anyone? (Photo courtesy of the Pittsburg Post Dispatch)

Dishes are judged by the California Culinary Academy of San Francisco, and portions are sold to the public for 75 cents to $2. Some of the things you'll find include barbecued oysters on the halfshell, seafood pasta, calamari, clam chowder, blackened redfish, shark, seafood gumbo, and sushi. There's also live entertainment, including gospel singers, 50s and 60s music, easy rock, western dancing demonstrations, and street artists.

It's a halibut good time.

Old-Fashioned Ice Cream Social and Tasting
San Francisco   (415) 553-2200

A Saturday in September. 2,000. 10 years. Adults $12, children 10 and under $7. Concourse Exhibition Center, 8th St. and Brannan St. Hwy. 101 in San Francisco to 9th St. exit. Left lane of exit feeds onto 8th St. Continue left onto 8th. Two blocks down is Brannan. Concourse is on southeast corner of 8th and Brannan.

Forget Baskin and Robbins' 31 flavors--this afternoon-long event features 200 flavors from 50 different ice cream vendors. It's a dessert-lover's heaven, with all the ice cream, sorbet, gelato, frozen yogurt, dipped bars,

Beware of ice cream thieves at the Old-Fashioned Ice Cream Social & Tasting. (Photo courtesy of KQED)

ices, sundaes, and shakes you could ever hope to taste right at your fingertips (or should that be "on the tip of your tongue"?). Bring the whole family and see if you can decide who has the best ice cream: Ben & Jerry's, Breyer's, Bud's, Dreyer's, Haagen-Dazs, Steve's, or Big Alice's (to name a few). You can also compare Dove Bars, It's Its, Rondos, and Nestle Ice Cream Bars. And for the calorie-conscious (what are they doing here anyway?), there's Tofulite, Tofutti, Yoplait Soft Frozen Yogurt, and Weight Watchers Ice Milk.

While all this old-fashioned fun may be entertaining enough for some people, there's also live music, face painting, and balloons. And if you need to clear your palate in between licks, there's plenty of sparkling water and coffee.

Pacific Coast Fog Fest
Pacifica   (415) 346-4446

Last weekend in September (Saturday and Sunday). 75,000. 7 years. Free. Palmetto Ave. between Shell and Santa Rosa. I-280 to Hwy. 1. Take the second exit (Francisco Paloma) in Pacifica.

Although past festivals have at times been unseasonably fog-free, the Pacific Coast Fog Fest usually goes off with nary a hitch—though more bikinis and shorts are sometimes in sight than windbreakers and jeans. This two-day event—begun as an attempt to change Pacifica's image as a foggy city—actually celebrates the city's "mascot" with arts and crafts, a Discover Pacifica parade, a Family Fun Fest, gourmet seafood (including barbecued oysters on the half shell), outdoor cafes, exceptional music (jazz, folk, and contemporary), and a variety of unusual contests: oyster shucking, foggy photos, Fog Cutter drink recipes, and a fog bank guessing game.

The annual fog trophy—awarded to the area's foggiest city—moves from coastal town to coastal town each year. Residents of each year's winning community say they feel "rather foggy" about the dubious honor.

Peach Festival and Annual Rickshaw Race
Willow Creek   (916) 629-3324

Labor Day weekend (Saturday and Sunday). 2,000. 6 years. $7.50 for luau. Don Cave Visitors Center and Park. Hwy. 299 to Willow Creek. Intersection of Hwy. 96 and Hwy. 299.

California Festivals	September

Way back in the 1850s, the town of Willow Creek was known as China Flats. Whether that has anything to do with the annual rickshaw races we're not sure, but several years ago this community held the first such race, and it's grown now into a two-day festival that also highlights some local agriculture (an interesting combination, to say the least).

The rickshaws must be homemade, so you can imagine the originality of some of the vehicles. In addition to the races, there are food and craft booths (featuring, of course, peach jams, jellies, pies, smoothies, and daiquiries), and, to top it all off, a luau and dance (we told you this was an interesting combination!).

Poway Days
Poway   (619) 748-6600

Last week of September. 20,000. 29 years. Varies according to day and event. Poway. I-15 to Poway Rd. to Bowron Rd. south.

This week-long series of western events draws people from throughout San Diego County, and the three-day rodeo—the festival's main attraction—features some of the rodeo circuit's top riders. Other events include a big parade, evening concerts by such performers as the Drifters and the Coasters, and a fireworks show after the concerts. Food booths offer beer, bratwurst, hamburgers, soda, and more.

The whole community pitches in, volunteering their time and energy for this fund-raiser to make Poway Days a success.

Russian River Jazz Festival
Guernerville   (707) 865-3940

Weekend after Labor Day (Saturday and Sunday). 10,000. 15 years. Varies from $21-30 per day. Johnson's Beach, Guerneville. From the San Francisco area take Hwy. 101 north to Santa Rosa, exit at Russian River Resort Area and River Rd. Take a right on River Rd. Festival is about 17 miles up River Rd.

Located on Johnson's Beach in Guerneville, this festival presents two full days of jazz in a unique setting of beach, river, and redwoods. Pack a picnic (although food and drinks are available at the site), beach chairs, blankets, swim suits, towels, and jackets (for the evening breeze) and settle in for some fine entertainment. There's not a bad seat in the house, whether you're on the beach or in the water, and everybody joins in the celebration. As one reviewer said of a past festival, "Even the little old lady who'd been quietly knitting all day put down her needles and boogied."

Of course, with some of the performers they manage to get for this event, it's not hard to see why. Past headliners have included Chick Corea with John Patitucci, Bobby Hutcherson with Steve Turre, Richie Cole, Bobby "Blue" Bland, James Moody, Elaine Elias, Benny Barth's Bay Area Grand Masters of Jazz, and many local musicians. And with a setting like Guerneville, it's not hard to see why so many of the greats are willing to perform here. In fact, this event is now acclaimed as one of the best jazz festivals in the U.S.

Sonoma County is a heck of a place to visit, and you probably wouldn't even mind living there once you've been there. The area is renowned for its wineries, and the many bed and breakfast inns are quite popular as weekend retreats for folks from San Francisco. There are also many fine restaurants, as well as some of the most beautiful coastal redwood scenery in northern California. Add to all this a weekend of some of the finest jazz around, and you've got yourself quite a little vacation.

Santa Clara Art and Wine Festival
Santa Clara   (408) 984-3257

Second weekend in September (Saturday and Sunday). 35,000. 10 years. Free. Central Park, Santa Clara. I-280 north; take the Saratoga Ave. exit toward Santa Clara; turn left on Keily Blvd. The festival is located approximately two miles north, in Central Park.

Held in the city's spacious and beautiful Central Park, this free outdoor art and wine festival features premium wines from some of California's finest wineries, tempting American and international foods, 180 arts and crafts booths (some with audience participation), continuous entertainment, a petting zoo, and a special "Kid's Kingdom." Entertainment includes performances of jazz, easy rock, fusion, and country/western. All proceeds from this event go to the Crippled Children's Society, Agnews Hospital, and the Santa Clara Police Activities League, and other local charities.

Santa Rosalia Festival
Monterey   (408) 372-7272

Sunday after Labor Day. 6,000. 22 years. Free. Custom House Plaza. Hwy. 101 to Hwy. 1 to Monterey.

The day begins with the traditional Italian blessing of the fishing fleet. A procession carries a statue of Santa Rosalia to the wharf, the fleet is blessed, and an outdoor mass is led by the Bishop of Monterey. The rest of the day is filled with dancing and music and food, including such Italian specialities as squid, sausage, macaroni, pizza, and cannoli. The day's entertainment is Italian as well and includes Italian tarantella dancers, plus performances by other groups. Game booths are also set up around the plaza, making this day something the whole family can enjoy—regardless of your nationality.

Sausalito Art Festival
Sausalito   (415) 332-0505

Labor Day weekend (Saturday-Monday). 60,000. 40 years. Adults $5, Children and Seniors $2. Marinship Park and the Bay Model. 2100 Bridgeway. Take the Sausalito exit off of Hwy. 101, just north of San Francisco and the Golden Gate Bridge.

When they say art festival they mean art festival, and this community's tribute to its strong artistic heritage is just that. Over 160 artists set up booths around the park, and you can browse to your art lover's content. There are also booths of delicious food, including gyros, hot links, baked potatoes, ice cream, funnel cakes, beer, wine, etc., live entertainment, including jazz, Brazilian, "world beat," classical, and rock bands, and a children's area.

Sausalito itself is always worth a visit. With its beautiful homes, wonderful vista points, quaint shops, and unique bayside restaurants, a day trip from San Francisco can be quite romantic—especially if you take the ferry.

Seafood Festival
Crescent City   (707) 464-3174

Labor Day weekend (Saturday-Sunday). 10,000. 8 years. Free. Crescent City Harbor Commercial Boat Basin. Hwy. 101, 20 miles south of the Oregon border.

If you like seafood, Crescent City isn't too far to go to get some of the freshest—and finest—at this two-day festival, the largest in Del Norte County. Once they bless the fishing fleet on Saturday morning, you can spend the rest of the day (and Sunday) wandering around the city's beautiful harbor among the many displays, enjoying the live entertainment, and eating seafood to your stomach's content.

There's ceviche (fish "cooked" in lime juice and spices), fish kebabs, barbecued oysters, clam chowder, shrimp cocktail, grilled fish dinners, fish and chips, shrimp won-tons, deep-fried albacore tuna, garlic bread, snow cones, popcorn, doughboys, hot dogs, and more.

In addition to all this great food, there are many displays of freshly caught fish, boats and sea crafts, fishing gear (such as net mending, cable splicing, and pot knitting), life rafts and safety, and Coast Guard air-sea rescues. There's also a regatta, many children's activities, tours of a Coast Guard cutter and rescue helicopter, a 10K beach run, a triathalon, a street dance, horseshoes, volleyball, Yurok Indian dancing and singing demonstrations, a tug-of-war, games for the kids, face painting, clowns, a petting zoo, live entertainment and the annual Survival Suit race, where contestants look like a bunch of orange Gumbies! (We don't make this stuff up!)

Serbian Festival
San Diego   (619) 534-5049

Last weekend in September (Saturday and Sunday). 2,000. 20 years. Adults $2, children under 12 free. St. George's Serbian Orthodox Church. I-5 to Clairemont Dr. exit east. Go left on Denver St.

St. George's Serbian Festival is a fun, educational event that provides an opportunity to learn about the big, white building near San Diego's Mission Bay and the people who worship there.

The festival is held on the church grounds, and guided tours of the building are provided four times daily. During these tours you'll learn that the three blue and gold domes outside represent the Christian trinity, that the church is modeled after those built in Serbia (a republic of Yugoslavia) and is an example of Serbian-Byzantine architecture, and that the building was constructed in 1967-1968. It is also the only Serbian church in this country to be completely decorated inside with mosaic tiles. The church interior is an artistic delight.

Outside, the emphasis is on feasting and dancing. Serbian fare includes raznjici (grilled marinated meat), sarma (cabbage rolls), and strong, thick coffee—similar to Turkish coffee but not as sweet. Festival visitors like to fill a tray with desserts such as baklava and chocolate cookies, then take it back to a table to share with family, friends, even strangers.

Serbian cookbooks are offered at the American flea market. The sale brings together rummage sale-type items, antiques, and European imports, such as linens and handicrafts.

Entertainment is provided by folklore groups dressed in Serbian costumes. Visitors are urged to join in the singing and dancing—the performers help visitors learn the steps of the Serbian kolos. Music is performed by Tamburitza orchestras with their stringed instruments. The music is Slavic, with an Oriental influence. The tempo is upbeat. The Old World and New World combine delightfully when dancing outdoors to a Serbian song while the sun sets over Mission Bay. —L.S.

Sixteenth of September Fiesta
Calexico   (619) 357-1166
(619) 357-1365

September 16. 5,000. 19 years. Free. Rockwood Plaza. I-8 south to Hwy. 111. South to Calexico. Go to 6th St. Go four blocks and turn left.

You can probably guess by the name of the city that this festival has some Mexican roots (as does the city itself). In fact, it is a traditional celebration of Mexican Independence Day, with booths of native food and crafts, entertainment, and lots of traditional music. You'll see and hear folklore dancers and singers, mariachi bands, Mexican chorale groups, trios, and Latin rock dance music. There are also clowns, games, and face painting for the kids, plus the crowning of the Miss 16th of September queen. The food includes such Mexican/American fare as tacos, tamales, and deep-pit barbecued beef. The day is capped with that Independence Day tradition that seems to transcend nationality—a fireworks extravaganza.

Taste of San Mateo
San Mateo   (415) 341-5679

Fourth Sunday in September. 4,000. 6 years. $30 per person—all you can eat. Bay Meadows Racecourse. Hwy. 101 to Hwy. 92 west to San Mateo. Take El Camino Real South exit to 25th Ave. Turn left.

It may not be the Kentucky Derby, but they set up tents full of food and drink in the infield of Bay Meadows racecourse for a day of gourmet food and wine tasting at "Taste of San Mateo." For $30 per person, you can eat till you pop, with restaurants and wineries from all over the area serving everything from Chinese and Japanese delicacies to Mexican and Continental cuisine. Some tables are devoted entirely to pastries! Live bands serenade you while you dine, with a delightful mixture of easy listening and Dixieland jazz. Special events include a champagne competition, ice carving demonstrations, and, of course, horse racing.

Tuolumne County Wild West Film Fest and Rodeo
Sonora   (209) 533-4420

Late September. 4,000. 3 years. Free. Sonora. Washington and Green Streets, Downtown.

When Hollywood filmmakers began to get away from shooting even such panoramic classics as *Gone With the Wind* on sets and started shooting on location, one of the first areas they discovered was the countryside around Tuolumne Country. Though Westerns were some of the first to use this natural scenery, almost every type of scenery in the U.S. can be recreated in this area, and in the past 70 years over 400 feature films and TV productions have been filmed here.

Because of this heritage, the folks in Sonora decided it was time to pay tribute to the Old West Film Fest and Rodeo. This young festival has featured such classics as *The Virginian, High Noon, Duel in the Sun, The Lone Ranger, My Little Chickadee, Sawyer and Finn, Hopalong Cassidy*, the Marx Brothers *Go West*, and *One-Eyed Jacks*.

Movies run from 10 a.m. to 5 p.m. daily, but in between there's lots of other Western entertainment to keep you occupied, including a western movie memorabilia museum, live entertainment, celebrity autographs, a western arts and craft fair, and a western BBQ.

The event begins Friday with a gala reception and dinner with celebrity awards. Saturday's excitement includes a rodeo, barn dance, and BBQ at the Motherlode Fairgrounds. Sunday brings in all kinds of western fun.

Vacaville Onion Festival
Vacaville   (707) 448-4613

Weekend following Labor Day (Saturday and Sunday). 25,000. 9 years. Adults $5, senior citizens $2, children under 3 free. Pena Adobe Park. I-80 halfway between Sacramento and San Francisco, take Pena Adobe exit.

If you've ever driven on I-80 on your way to or from the San Francisco area and suddenly smelled a distinctively onion aroma, you were passing through Vacaville. As their motto says, this festival "takes your breath away." It's two days of food, arts and crafts, and continuous entertainment.

The Cuisine Center features the festival's famous onion rings, onion shish kebabs, fried onion pitas, chicken stir-fry (it MUST have onions in it!), and more oniney (and other) creations. There are also cooking demonstrations (many featuring onions, of course), a Kiddie Korner with games and activities for the kids, an onion recipe cook-off,and the "Wheel of Fortu-onion" (that's really what they call it), where for $.50 a spin participants can win a free admission to the festival, money off food items, and more. The two entertainment stages feature mostly local bands playing 50s music, rock, and country. There are strolling entertainers as well.

But the highlight is the onion eating contest, where contestants see how many raw onions (and these are some of the strongest tasting onions in the world) they can get through in a certain period of time. The organizers say it's even been suggested they try to get this contest into the *Guinness Book of World Records*.

Valley of the Moon Vintage Festival
Sonoma   (707) 996-2109

Last full weekend in September (Friday-Sunday). 20,000. 94 years. Tickets for wine tasting are $5. Sonoma Plaza. From Hwy. 101, take Hwy. 37 to Hwy. 121 to Hwy 12. Follow signs to Sonoma's plaza.

This vintage festival, the oldest wine festival in the state, honors the wine grape harvest in the Sonoma Valley and celebrates Sonoma's colorful history. Weekend events focus on this union of wine and history, including a reenactment of the 1846 Bear Flag Revolt; the 1863 double wedding uniting two prominent winemaking families—the Vallejos and Harszthys; and an old fashioned grape stomp competition.

Wine tasting takes place from noon to 5 pm on the Plaza under colorful tents and canopies. With a commemorative wine glass in hand, stroll the Plaza enjoying free, non-stop live music, performing artists, games and events for children, or cooking-with-wine demonstrations. Parades, a fireman's waterfight, and an art show fill out the weekend for this popular festival. A wide variety of festival food can be purchased from community nonprofit groups.

Walnut Festival
Walnut Creek   (510) 935-6766

Third full weekend in September (Thursday-Sunday). 40,000. 54 years. Adults $3, children 6-12 and seniors $2, children under 6 free. Heather Farms Park. I-680 north or Hwy. 24 east, take Ygnacio Valley exit. Go two miles to the festival. From I-680 south or Hwy. 24 west take North Main exit; go 1/2 mile to Ygnacio Valley Rd., then 1 1/2 miles to the festival.

California Festivals   September

Despite this city's name, folks who live in the Bay Area may not think of Walnut Creek as having agricultural roots, but way back when, Walnut Creek was primarily a farming community. This festival started out as a grape festival, but as suburban developments began to replace walnut orchards (there—that's the Walnut Creek we know), the name was changed to the Walnut Festival.

Anymore it's pretty much a community event, with four days of fun, including a carnival, food and game booths, arts and crafts, commercial exhibitors, a children's area, strolling minstrels (plus other music), and stage entertainment for all ages. Special activities include a lip sync contest, a celebrity nut-cracking contest, 5K and 10K runs, and a children's parade. Food booths offer a variety of ethnic and American dishes.

Wasco Festival of Roses
Wasco   (805) 758-2746

First weekend after Labor Day (Thursday-Sunday). 20,000. 22 years. Free. Barker Park. Hwy. 99 to Hwy. 46 exit.

If you like roses, this festival is a "can't miss!" The blooming of the roses is a spectacular sight, and there are a lot of them in Wasco, a community in Central California that once was little more than desert. Today, over 75% of all roses grown in the U.S. are grown in Wasco, whose climate and soil make it the perfect rose-growing area.

The American Rose Society sponsors an outstanding rose show from the gardens of Kern County and elsewhere around the state. A featured rose is honored each year, as is the Rose Queen. For 50 cents you can take a bus tour of the rose fields ablaze in all the colors of the rainbow. The outdoor fair features several artists and food vendors on the shaded lawns of Barker Park. There is also a tennis tournament and a "mini Rose Bowl," featuring the local high school football team, golf tournament, carnival, and tractor pull.

The weekend also includes a pancake breakfast, 5K and 10K fun runs, a parade, a deep-pit barbecue with plenty of live country/western music, a dinner and barn dance. Other food includes Thai dishes and tri-tip sandwiches.

Wild Game Barbecue
San Luis Obispo   (805) 543-1323

Sometime in September (call for date). 2,500. 26 years. Free. Cuesta Park (north of the city). Off Hwy. 101 at the end of Monterey.

California Festivals　　　　　　　　　September

Come on, don't be shy—a little rattlesnake never hurt anyone. That's what you'll have to tell yourself over and over at San Luis Obispo's Wild Game Barbecue, where you'll have a chance to sample not only rattlesnake but wild boar, venison, elk, bear, albacore tuna, buffalo, antelope, mountain lion, wild turkey, and bobcat. And you better eat quick, 'cause the hungry crowd usually chows down a half-ton of wild meat in just three hours.

It all began nearly 26 years ago when a state game warden in the area suggested that local hunters donate surplus game for a community barbecue to give people an idea of how settlers in the Old West ate. Environmentalists in the crowd may have a hard time stomaching the thought of some of these dishes, but if you're a wild game lover you'll think you died and went to heaven at this very unusual barbecue.

WINESONG!
Fort Bragg　　(707) 964-5185

First Saturday after Labor Day. 1,000. 7 years. $40. Mendocino Coast Botanical Gardens, 18220 N. Hwy 1. Hwy. 101 to Hwy. 128 to Hwy. 1, or Hwy. 101 to Willits to Hwy. 20 to Hwy.1.

Wine aficionados should flock to Fort Bragg's WINESONG! this September, where you can bid on some of the finest wines from California, Oregon, Australia, and Europe. Over 75 wineries participate in the one-day auction and winetasting festival, with over 175 auction lots from Jekel, Edna Valley, St. Francis, Roederer U.S., and Domaine Chandon, to name just a few. Other wineries include special lots from their private libraries, and private donors often contribute unusual and eclectic wines. Also included in the auction are luxury vacation getaway both domestic and foreign and special gourmet dinning in private winery tours.

In addition, over 30 restaurants and caterers from the area serve delicious hors d'oeuvres, such as Mendocino chocolate, mousse, cookies, fish kebabs, and Creole dishes. And approximately 20 musicians play classical and jazz throughout the day. The wine and food tasting begins at 11 a.m. and runs until 2 p.m., when the auction begins. The auction concludes at 5:00 p.m.

Fort Bragg is a lovely coastal community north of San Francisco, and the setting for WINESONG!—the Mendocino Coast Botanical Gardens—is said to be nothing less than spectacular.

California Festivals   September

Zucchini Festival
San Andreas   (209) 754-6477

Third Sunday in September. 2,000. 5 years. Free. Utica Park. Adjacent to Hwy 49 in Angels Camp.

Have you ever seen a 29 1/2" zucchini? You're bound to stumble across one at the Zucchini Festival in Angels Camp during their annual "Zucchinimania." The day includes plenty of childrens games and such fun events as a zucchini derby better known as "zucchini on wheels." They've built a zucchini ramp that kids race around in cars built with — you guessed it—zucchini! Apparently, the kids have figured out the secret to building a faster zucchini-mobile as they add weights to hollowed out parts of the zucchini.

But this festival also features zucchini in a variety of forms that it was meant for: easting. You can sample zucchini cooked every way imaginable including: fried, in pancakes, chocolate-covered and in a variety of baked goods. And, of course, there are contests for the longest, heaviest and most unique zucchini—which always yields some interesting, and often astounding results.

California Festivals   October

Apple Valley Days
Apple Valley   (619) 247-3202

Next to last week in October (Wednesday-Sunday). 4,000. 41 years. Free. Hwy. 18 and Apple Valley Inn Rd. From I-15 take the D St. exit east to Apple Valley. D St. turns into Hwy. 18. Follow Hwy. 18 to festival.

Every festival has its own interesting beginnings. This one was born 40 years ago over a couple of drinks in a local bar and originally was known as "Powwow Days," with several local Indian tribes involved. It has since become a community-wide event that takes place all over Apple Valley.

It's pretty typical as far as country fairs go, with a pancake breakfast, big carnival, parade, rodeo, arts and crafts show, and food concessions offering hot dogs, hamburgers, and other basic fair food. But there's also a Halloween celebration, making this one festival that really does seem to offer something for everyone.

Beach Street Revival
Santa Cruz   (408) 438-1957

Second weekend in October (Friday-Sunday). 10,000. 14 years. $5. 2601 East Lare Ave. Watsonville (Santa Cruz County Fairgrounds) From the north: Hwy 101 south to Hecker Pass Rd.(Gilroy) south to 2601 East Lare Ave. (Hecker Pass Rd. turns into East Lare Ave.) From the south: Hwy 1 to Green Valley Rd. north to Holohun Rd. east to East Lare Ave. north to 2601

This three-day 50s and 60s nostalgia event was the first of its kind in the United States. And what better place for it than Santa Cruz, one of the most enjoyable beach towns on the California coast. You'll see and hear more than a few "blasts from the past" at the car show (featuring all types of cars from 1900-1969: classic, custom-built, and street rod), the bikini contest, and the dances on Friday and Saturday nights.

Listen to such favorites as Johnny Barow, DADDY-O, and Shaboom as you munch on hamburgers, French fries, calamari, chili, ribs, hot dogs, Thai food, smoothies, and more. There is even a public poker car cruise, where you can challenge some of the best cars in the area. For all you cool cats out there, it's a little bit of history and a whole lot of fun.

Brussels Sprout and Italian Heritage Festival
Santa Cruz   (408) 423-5590

Second weekend in October (Saturday and Sunday). 18,000. 11 years. Free. Boardwalk. Take Hwy. 1 or Hwy. 17 into Santa Cruz, then follow the signs to the main beach. Santa Cruz is located 35 miles south of San Jose, 40 miles north of Monterey.

This much-maligned vegetable earns new respect along the Santa Cruz Beach Boardwalk, with food items such as sprout water taffy, sprout pizza, and sprout ice cream. For sprout-haters, there is the traditional Sprout Toss and the Sprout Putt Recent festivals have honored the area's Italian population as well, many of whom grow sprouts, artichokes and other local produce stars.

Other salutes to the mighty sprout include sprout juggling, a 5-foot Mr. Sprout, and sprout face-painting. Santa Cruz is the proud "Sprout Capitol of the World," growing 90% of the nation's annual 36,000 tons of sprouts.

Mr. Sprout and Popeye greet young fans at the annual Brussels Sprout Festival. (Photo courtesy of the Santa Cruz Seaside Co.)

Calico Days
Barstow   (619) 254-2122

Second weekend in October (Saturday and Sunday). 10,000. 24 years. Adults $5, juniors $2, children 5 and under free, camping $9. Calico Ghost Town. On I-15, 10 miles north of Barstow, take the Ghost Town Rd. exit.

This 1880s boomtown celebration, set in an actual ghost town, relives Calico's glory days with over 47 boomtown events including a steak fry and costume party Friday night, a parade honoring the wild west Saturday, National Gunfight Stunt Championships (like the shoot-out at the OK Corral!), and a country and bluegrass concert. Sunday trail rides, a burro race, He-Man Triathalon, and the gunfight stunt ffinals. Other 1880's style contests are held all week long.

Other special attractions include an Old West character hall of fame and an old-fashioned confectionary where you can purchase candy of all kinds. Restaurants can be found throughout town, and you'll hear plenty of bluegrass and country music.

Cover me, partner. (Photo by Kimberley L. Sickel)

California Avocado Festival
Carpinteria   (805) 684-0038

First weekend in October. 100,000. 5 years. Free. Downtown Carpinteria, Linden Ave. From Hwy. 101, take the Casitas Pass Rd., follow signs to free parking. Shuttle service available. (Located about 1 1/2 hours north of Los Angeles, 10 minutes south of Santa Barbara).

California Festivals — October

During the first weekend each October (this often encompasses the last day or two of September as well), the avocado is king in the seaside city of Carpinteria. This two-day festival is "a joyous salute to an important local crop, with an appetizing array of foods, treasures, and other pleasures"-- and the world's largest guacamole event on Sunday. You can sample dozens of avocado-based foods both tried and new, including avocado ice cream (always a quick sell-out), avocado brownies, avocado cream pie, tamales and tacos filled with sliced avocados, and, of course, lots of guacamole.

Arts and crafts booths feature handmade items such as jewelry, clothing, and other gifts from around the state. There is also a Farmer's Market with area fruits, vegetables, plants, and many varieties of flowers. The kids will enjoy the many games and craft projects while the adults listen to live music, both professional and "home-grown." There is also a morning fun run for charity, complete with prizes. Also included is Avocado Bingo, a fabulous flower show, and an Avocado County jail.

There are lots of reasons to attend this festival, but most of all because it's fun. Each year promises to be bigger and full of more of everything. It is a colorful, versatile salute to a healthy, yummy fruit. —S.M.

Calistoga Beer and Sausage Fest
Calistoga   (707) 942-6333

Second Saturday in October. 1,000. 8 years. $15 (includes commemorative beer stein). Calistoga Fairgrounds. From Vallejo, Oakland, and San Francisco, take I-80 north to Hwy. 29 to the top of the Napa Valley. Follow signs to Napa Valley/Calistoga Fairgrounds. Or take Hwy. 37 from Vallejo or Hwy. 121 from Sonoma to Hwy. 29.

What two ingredients typify an Oktoberfest better than beer and sausage? These two tasty treats are the stars of the afternoon at the Calistoga Beer and Sausage Fest. You can taste a variety of brews from many of California's microbreweries (many of these beers are not available in stores, so this is a chance to try them out), as well as several types of sausages, such as chicken apple and bratwurst. You can eat 'em plain, with gourmet mustard, on a French roll—however you like. Also for sale are pret-

What you see is what you get at Calistoga's Beer and Sausage Fest. (Photo courtesy of Calistoga Chamber of Commerce)

zels, German desserts, and nonalcoholic beverages such as mineral water (this is, after all, Calistoga). In addition to the sausage and beer, you can watch the home brewer's and beer bread contests. Participants are encouraged to dress in German costumes and dance to lively polka bands.

Calistoga is also the home of many health spas and mud baths, and just an all-around beautiful and relaxing place to hang out for a weekend.

Campbell Highland Games
Campbell   (408) 378-6252

Second Saturday in October. 3,500. 13 years. Adults $7, children $5. Campbell Community Center Stadium. Take Hwy. 17 (I-880) to the Hamilton exit, take a right on Hamilton; left on Winchester Blvd. It's on the corner of Winchester Blvd and Campbell Ave.

This festival is a tribute to California's Scottish population and Campbell's Scottish heritage, brought here more than a century ago by the city's founder, Benjamin Campbell. You'll find almost every Scottish tradition, including skirling bagpipes; Olympic-like athletic events like the caber toss and javelin throw; ethnic dances; such food staples as meat pies, fish and chips, bangers; and, of course, lots of beer. There's also a parade, dancing and bagpipe competitions, and lots of booths featuring native crafts.

Clam Festival
Pismo Beach   (805) 773-4382

Third weekend in October (Saturday and Sunday). 20,000. 45 years. Free. Various locations throughout Pismo Beach. Hwy. 101 to Pismo Beach exit.

They've been celebrating the clams at Pismo Beach for over 40 years now, with a parade, arts and crafts, food booths, volleyball, and lots of local entertainment, including musicians playing country/western and jazz at sites all over town. You can sit back and enjoy the entertainment or compete in the clam-digging contest, clam chowder cook-off, or, for the more daring, the clam queen contest.

As you've probably already guessed, the featured food for the weekend is clams, so you'll find lots of clam chowder, barbecued clams, and clam cakes. There's other food too, but if you're a clam lover, you'd better get there early.

California Festivals   October

Colony Days Celebration
Atascadero   (805) 466-2044

Third Saturday in October. 10,000. 19 years. Free. Sunken Gardens Area. Located at the intersection of Hwy. 101 and Hwy. 41.

Colony Days is a one-day historical salute to the founding of Atascadero in 1913, with costumes, concerts, dancing, entertainment, a 10K run, and 100 arts, crafts, food, and game booths. One of the day's highlights is the "Wild and Wet" firemen's bucket brigade—a contest in which local firemen challenge other teams to see who can fill two big barrels full of water first—using buckets of water .
The food booths offer a wide variety, from American to Cajun to Mexican, and the music should suit all tastes too: jazz, marches, western, and more.A two-hour parade caps this day of looking back at the Colony of Atascadero.

Columbus Day Celebration
San Francisco   (415) 434-1492

Week of Columbus Day. 200,000. 120 years. Free. San Francisco North Beach area. From Hwy. 101, take the Broadway exit, follow Broadway to Columbus.

This week-long celebration of the founding of America by Christopher Columbus is the largest and oldest of its kind outside of New York City. The festival has much historical significance, especially for the city's Italian-American community, and is located in San Francisco's noted Italian district: North Beach.
Events include a chidrens art fair, a banquet and ball, a parade, and a cycling competitions. Of special note is the Queen Isabella pageant, where young women of Italian ancestry compete for the crown of Queen Isabella and her court; the winner is coronated at City Hall by the mayor of San Francisco.
And of course there's food—good and good for you! Whether you're Italian or not, you can imagine how tasty it is—just like Mama used to make!

California Festivals   October

Cotati Indian Festival
Cotati   (707) 795-5478

Second Sunday in October. 1,200. 14 years. Free. Downtown Cotati. Hwy. 101, between San Francisco and Santa Rosa.

Cotati was named for Indian chief Cotati of the Miwok Indian tribe. And this festival honors these Native Americans as well as other tribes such as the Qquadorians, Aztecs, and Pomos. There's lots of Native American culture and special activities, including native dancers and the selection of the princess, and several booths selling native arts and crafts and foods

Ceres Western Art Show and Sale
Ceres   (209) 537-3246

First weekend in October (Friday-Sunday). 5,000. 9 years. $5. St. Jude's Center. Take the Mitchell Road off ramp from Hwy 99 to 3825 Mitchell Road.

The town of Ceres spends three days each fall promoting the legacy of the American working cowboy with some splendid art. The event is kicked off Friday night with a champagne reception (donation $25) for the artists where you can view all the artwork and meet the festival's 30 guest artists, who come from all over the Western United States. The sale begins on Saturday accompanied by great entertainment all day including quartets, old-time fiddlers and a jazz ensemble. And what Western festival wouldn't

Kids get to see artists at work. (Photo courtesy of Ceres Western Art Show)

be complete without some square dancing and a tri-tip sandwich? It's also fun to take a hay wagon from the art show to the big BBQ. All proceeds from the sale benefit the high school scholarship trust fund.

Desert Festival
Borrego Springs   (619) 344-5555

Last weekend in October (Friday-Sunday). 3,000. 27 years. Free. Center of town. 80 miles northeast of San Diego, 90 miles south of Palm Springs.

Autumn in the California desert is one of the most beautiful times of year there, and this festival is a salute to the passing of another summer season in the desert.

Each day of the festival begins early (there's a pancake breakfast on Sunday) and includes an arts and crafts show, a parade, a barbecue, a talent show, dances for everyone, and the crowning of Miss Borrego Springs and the Honorary Mayor. For the kids there's games, clowns, face painting, and a petting zoo. Booths feature popcorn, ice cream, baked goods, barbecue, and beer, and you'll hear a wide variety of music.

East West Orchid Show
Los Angeles   (213) 485-1177

Fourth weekend in October (Friday-Sunday). 3,000. 5 years. Free. The New Otani Hotel & Garden and the Weller Court Shopping Center at 2nd St. and San Pedro St. in Little Tokyo. From the Hollywood Fwy. Southbound, exit at Los Angeles St. and turn left on 2nd St.

The East West Orchid Show features more than 40 themed floral displays by Southern Californian orchid societies and thousands of orchid plants from more than 30 growers from around the country. Activities include ongoing seminars, lectures and demonstrations, offered both days. More than 3,000 exotic orchids including big, richly colored cateyas, lush Phalaenopsis (or Butterfly Orchid), Ha-

Cymbidium Abundance Orchids, one of more than 3,000 orchids on display. (Photo courtesy of East West Orchid Show)

waiian Dendrobiums and Paphiopedilum-Maudiae hybrids: vinicolors; and colratums are exhibited in elaborate, themed displays throughout the hotel and Weller Court.

Escondido Harvest Festival
Escondido   (619) 743-8207

Third Sunday in October. 10,000. 7 years. Free. Grape Day Park, North Broadway and Woodward Ave. I-15 to Valley Parkway, head east and turn left on Broadway.

Escondido is the Spanish word for "hidden," and time has hidden some of the rural roots of this town founded in 1888—but that hasn't stopped residents from celebrating the fall harvest and remembering the past each year with the Escondido Harvest Festival. The one-day event is free and serves as a fundraiser for the Escondido Historical Society.

Old-timers remember when grapes grew throughout the valley. The harvest was celebrated for nearly a half-century during Grape Day. The celebration stopped in the 1950s and was revived as the Harvest Festival in 1985. Naturally, the festival is held in Grape Day Park, located just this side of Heritage Walk Park. The emphasis is on local entertainment and history. Expect to hear at least one of the bands from the city's three high schools. Folk singers, cloggers, and clowns also perform. The festival also includes demonstrations of folk crafts, such as lace making, spinning, and weaving. Quilters show their needlework, and the local doll club exhibits its collection and demonstrates restoration techniques.

Escondido is the home of one of the only working blacksmith shops in the nation, Tom Bandy and Son, which opened in 1908 and now restores carriages and wagons. A representative from the shop demonstrates smithing. There is also a blacksmith display in the history museum, one of four buildings on Heritage Walk. Its neighbors are the original library, a barn, a Victorian house, and the 1888 Santa Fe depot. Admission is free, but donations are accepted.

Festival food is on the modern side. Baked goods, hot dogs, and other refreshments are sold. Visitors can also tour Escondido for samples of its contemporary harvest, including grapes. Stop by Ferrara Winery, in business since 1930. —L.S.

California Festivals   October

Exeter Fall Festival
Exeter   (209) 592-2919

Second weekend in October (Saturday-Sunday). 10,000. 55 years. Free. City Park. Hwy. 99 to Hwy. 198. Hwy. 198 east to Hwy. 65 (Kaweah exit). Go 2 miles south to Exeter.

For over 50 years, they've been celebrating the 1888 founding of this community named after Exeter, England, at this festival held each October. The festivities begins with a Queen's luncheon, a parade culminating Sunday with a street dance. In between, there's a carnival, an arts and crafts show, and lots of local entertainment, including country/western music, gospel singers, dancers, soloists, fiddlers, and rock and roll. In addition, you can enter tournaments for cow chip throwing, and horseshoes. Food booths feature deep-pit barbecue, hamburgers, hot dogs, corn on the cob, ice cream, pies, and beer.

Fall Fest—Desert Hot Springs
Desert Hot Springs   (619) 329-6403

Third weekend in October. 10,000. 7 years. Admission varies. Downtown Desert Hot Springs. I-10 to Palm Dr. exit. North on Palm Dr. 3 miles to the heart of the city. Main intersection of Palm and Pierson.

Enjoy the rejuvenating mineral waters of the hot springs for which this city is named during this week-long festival. The festival is located in downtown Desert Hot Springs, where you'll find exhibitor booths (including arts and crafts), food booths (featuring international cuisine), and lots of activities all weekend. There is also a wide variety of musical entertainment.

Fall Festival of Wines
Gardena Valley   (213) 217-9574

Sunday before Columbus Day. 700. 8 years. $22.50, $25 at the door (group rate: 8 for $160). 60 and over $15. Torrance Marriott Hotel, 3635 Fashion Way, Torrance. I-405 to Torrance, take the Hawthorne Blvd. exit and head south on Hawthorne to Marriott. Torrance Blvd. Go east, Hotel is on the right.

California Festivals — October

Over 30 California and Washington wineries pour their finest wines and Southern California restaurants and food purveyors offer international appetizers during this one-day, afternoon-only event benefiting the Gardena Senior Citizens Day Care Center.

The appetizers include cheeses and pates, plus Mexican, Italian, and Japanese specialities. You'll be serenaded by classical guitars, and you can enter special drawings to win bottles of wine or free visits to some of the area's fine restaurants.

Fall Fun Fest
Seaside   (408) 899-6270

First weekend in October (Saturday-Sunday). 7,500. 6 years. Free. Canyon Del Rey Blvd. Get off Hwy. 1 at Del Ray Oaks exit, make left at off ramp stop sign, proceed straight, through Del Monte Blvd.

At the Fall Fun Fest teams of five—one rider and four pushers—must maneuver factory-built beds mounted on wheels and otherwise beautified and glamorized over the 175-yard race course, including a U-turn, to the checkered flag. While this sounds pretty simple, you never know when your bed might lose a wheel, your rider might lose control, or your pushers just can't run fast enough to beat the average time of 30 seconds it takes the winning teams to qualify for the finals.

In addition to the races, there's also a kiddie carnival, classic car show, fire department displays and demonstrations, plus international foods, and arts and crafts. Featured entertainment on Saturday will be Daddy-O, a San Francisco-based band playing 50s and 60s tunes. Special attractions include dance demonstrations, pie eating contests, jazz and blues bands and a pancake breakfast to initiate Sunday's festivities.

Fiesta Italiana
Santa Barbara   (805) 687-7197

Second weekend in October. 20,000. 11 years. Free. Oak Park. Southbound: Take the Las Positas exit off Hwy. 101; left on Las Positas; right onto Tallant; right onto Samarkand; left onto Calle Real; left onto Junipero. Northbound: Pueblo exit; right onto Junipero.

Celebrate the Italian heritage and spirit in a beautiful, relaxing atmosphere created by good food, good people, good music, and the beauty of Oak Park. You'll find some of the best Italy has to offer, including traditional foods (calamari, polenta and cheese, pastas and sauces, calzone, and sausage sandwiches), ice cream and popcorn, music (an orchestra featuring European dance music). Italian product displays, clowns, and strolling minstrels.

Festival of Cultures
Merced   (209) 385-6894

Third Saturday in October. 4,000. 8 years. Free. Merced County Fairgrounds. Take Hwy. 99 to Hwy. 59 south. Go approximately 1 mile to fairgrounds.

This one-day community event honors the various ethnic cultures and people that reside within Merced County—and there are a lot of them. The different ethnic groups brought together at this festival to share their culture and history include Italian, Nicaraguan, Kenyan, Japanese, Peruvian, Palestinian, Filipino, Hungarian, Jewish, Korean, Basque, Hawaiian, Norwegian, Scottish, Asian, Black American, and Mexican American. The event includes a wide diversity of music, crafts, arts, food, entertainment from all the cultures represented, and school children draw murals depicting their cultures.

Fishermen's Fiesta
San Pedro   (213) 832-7272

First weekend in October (Friday-Sunday). 30,000. 10 years. Free. Fisherman's Wharf. I-110 to Harbor Blvd. exit. Turn right to Sixth St. Turn left and then right on Sampson Way. Follow Sampson Way to fiesta grounds.

Fishermen are known for their superstitions, and the blessing of the fleet seems to be one of the biggest rituals in the business. In San Pedro, they not only bless the fleet, they celebrate for two days afterward—but this party is for the whole family.

Some 30,000 people turn out for this three-day event, which includes a cioppino (fish stew) contest, and lots of family-oriented entertainment. You won't find just seafood—they also serve hamburgers, hot dogs, and Mexican and Italian specialities.

This festival began after World War II and grew into one of the major festivals in the U.S., attracting 200,000 people annually. It died out in 1972 but was revived in 1981 and continues to be a popular event in the Los Angeles area.

Frontier Days
Canyon Country   (805) 252-4402

First weekend in October (Thursday-Sunday). 30,000. 27 years. Adults $5, Children and Seniors $4. Frontier Days Fairgrounds. I-5 to Valencia Blvd. Valencia becomes Soledad Canyon. Follow Soledad Canyon to Lost Canyon. Go right under the bridge.

For four days each October the community of Canyon Country (doesn't the name just say "Western?") in the Los Angeles area celebrates its heritage with Frontier Days. For the last quarter century, this festival has featured a rodeo, parade, carnival, midway games, a pet parade, and, of course, lots of live country/western music. Food and drink booths sell the usual carnival fare, including hamburgers, hot dogs, corn on the cob, Mexican food, and Oriental dishes. There are also special games for the kids.

If you can find your way down Lost Canyon to Canyon Country, you can enjoy a little of the Old West, right here in California.

Goleta Valley Days Festival
Goleta   (805) 967-4618

Second weekend in October. 15,000. 14 years. Most events free. Eight miles north of Santa Barbara. Hwy. 101 to the Fairview exit.

It may be a small-town affair, but 15,000 people make their way to Goleta every year for this Valley Days festival. It all begins with an 8k Classic Run/Walk at Goleta Beach.

Saturday, the Santa Barbara Municipal Airport holds their Airport Day with many exciting displays of vintage and new aircrafts. Sunday features the Fiddler's Convention at the historic Stow House, which includes a tri-tip barbeque and continuous bluegrass entertainment.

Other events during the following week including a photo contest, golf tournament, Queen's coronation and western hoedown. The festival continues on Saturday with a parade, chili cook-off, arts/crafts, a food faire and a community concert. Sunday climaxes the festival with a Depot Day at the Goleta Railroad Depot Museum.

California Festivals   October

Grape Harvest Festival
Rancho Cucamonga   (714) 987-1012

First or second weekend in October (Thursday-Sunday). 50,000. 52 years. $6 adults, kids 12 and under free. Cucamonga Guasti Regional Park. From I-10 take Archibald Ave one block north.

They've been stomping grapes at the Grape Harvest Festival for over 50 years. Music is also a tradition with continuous entertainment featuring 50s and 60s groups as well as country and western. Don't miss the pie-eating contest, arts and crafts, carnival rides, food court, wine tasting and beer garden.

Great Halloween Pumpkin Festival
San Francisco   (415) 346-4446

Weekend closest to Halloween (Saturday-Sunday). 50,000. 6 years. Free. Clement St. between 3rd Ave. and 8th Ave. Hwy. 101 to Geary Blvd. Right on Geary to 3rd Ave.

This Halloween party features an urban pumpkin patch, hay rides, parades, pumpkin carving and pumpkin pie eating contests, an arts and crafts exhibition, continuous entertainment, and the champs of the World Pumpkin Weigh-Off. Kids in costumes parade down Clement Street and go trick-or-treating in the stores of participating merchants. Besides such pumpkin treats as pie, ice cream, and bread, garden cafes offer a variety of gourmet food and wine—even pumpkin wine! You'll hear jazz, folk, and contemporary music and be entertained by some of San Francisco's infamous street performers.

All these activities combie to create a festive weekend and bring a little country to the city of San Francisco.

Half Moon Bay Art and Pumpkin Festival
Half Moon Bay   (415) 726-9652

Weekend after Columbus Day in October (Saturday and Sunday). 300,000. 21 years. Free. Main St., Half Moon Bay. Hwy 1 to Half Moon Bay.

California Festivals — October

With the abundance of pumpkin patches that dot the coastline in and around Half Moon Bay, a pumpkin festival seemed a natural extension for families who came pumpkin picking each year. Since its inception in 1971, this festival has grown, and grown, and grown—much like the size of the winner of each year's Great Pumpkin Weigh-Off! Some locals say they actually leave town or stay in their homes during the two-day extravaganza because so many people (300,000!) jam the small community of Half Moon Bay (population 7,500!) that it's pretty much impossible to do anything but party with the visitors. And forget about parking.

Festival goers can browse through the 250 arts and crafts booths; sample such food and beverages as artichokes, turkey sandwiches, calamari, apple cider, pumpkin bread, pumpkin crepes, pumpkin ice cream, and pumpkin strudel from the 30 or so concession booths; and enjoy a wide variety of entertainment, including live music (bluegrass, jazz, and country/western), puppet shows, mimes, magicians, jugglers, clowns, face painters, and professional pumpkin carving demonstrations. Kids can participate in the costume contest, and there's a masquerade ball for the adults. You might want to sign up for the 1/2 mile fun run or 10K Pumpkin Festival Run before entering the pie-eating contest. There's also a pumpkin-carving contest, and, of course, the Great Pumpkin Parade (Charlie Brown, where are you?).

The perfect pumpkin awaits you at the Half Moon Bay Art and Pumpkin Festival. (Photo courtesy of the Half Moon Bay Art and Pumpkin Festival)

Hangtown Dixieland Jazz Jubilee
Placerville   (916) 621-5885
(800) 457-6279

Third Sunday in October. 2,500. 66 years. $12 in advance; $15 day of the event. Various locations throughout downtown Placerville. I-80 to Hwy. 50 to the first stoplight in Placerville. Main Street.

If you like Dixieland jazz and you're anywhere near Placerville this October, you might want to check out the Hangtown Dixieland Jazz

California Festivals October

Jubilee. Started by the Chamber of Commerce, this festival now features ten Dixieland jazz bands performing at locations throughout downtown Placerville, some in local restaurants, others at Fountain Plaza. You'll find a variety of food at the restaurants, but the music remains the same—good ol' Dixieland jazz, in a beautiful setting.

Harbor Days
Oceanside (619) 721-1101

First weekend in October (Saturday and Sunday). 50,000. 10 years. Free. Oceanside Harbor. I-5 to the Camp Pendleton exit for free parking and shuttle to the festival.

Oceanside's beautiful harbor and marina are the setting for two days of activities that honor the development of this small-craft harbor—the only such harbor refuge between Newport Beach and San Diego.

A number of aquatic events take place, including a Hobie Cat regatta, boat races, jet ski races, water skiing competitions, bathtub races, and sand sculpting. Other events include foot races along the beach, a car and boat show, a beauty pageant, a Marine Corps display, arts and crafts sale, and plenty of live entertainment (jazz, country/western, Dixieland, and clogging shows). Food booths serve hot dogs, hamburgers, Mexican and Oriental dishes, popcorn, nachos, and ice cream.

Harvest Craft Fair and Halloween Celebration
Rocklin (916) 632-4100

The Saturday before Halloween. 5,000. 6 years. Free. Rocklin Community Center. From I-80 go to Rocklin Road. Drive west until you cross Pacific/Taylor to Fifth Street, then turn left to 5480 Fifth St.

This October, head to Rocklin to get into the Halloween spirit at this one-day event that's great for the kids. Toddlers to 5th graders are invited to dress up in their scariest Halloween get-up and join in the costume contest. Local elementary school classrooms and youth groups from the area are encouraged to build scarecrows for the annual scarecrow contest. (We understand that the 1st-grade class has a history of using the same recycled scarecrow each year!) There is even a pumpkin pie contest and a pumpkin bread contest. Between all the pumpkin activities you can browse through a variety of quality craft items including stuffed animals, woodwork, ceramics, pottery and needlepoint and wildflower crafts.

California Festivals											October

Harvest Festival
Carmel   (408) 624-8886

October (call for exact date). 1,000. 9 years. Free. The Barnyard, Hwy. 1 and Carmel Valley Rd. Carmel is located on Hwy. 1, just below Monterey.

This popular community event offers activities and entertainment for all ages, including authentic hay rides, trick or treating, vaudeville entertainment, and live music (country/western). Anyone can enter the pumpkin-carving contest, with categories ranging from preschool to adult to "artiste," and all participants receive free cookies and cider. Any child wearing a costume can go trick-or-treating among participating shops and restaurants in this shopping center. If you get hungry, you'll find hamburgers, hot dogs, beer, and soft drinks, plus a variety of food at the many restaurants. Bring the whole family for a day of free family fun.

Italian-American Cultural Festival
San Jose   (408) 293-7122

First weekend in October (Saturday and Sunday). 120,000. 15 years. Free. Santa Clara County Fairgrounds. Hwy. 101 to San Jose, follow signs to fairgrounds.

An Italian village is recreated with decorated booths, painted carts, tarantella dancers, authentic food, wine, souvenir glasses, and three stages of continuous musical entertainment, ranging from opera to pop. There are also bocci ball exhibitions, a Saturday night street dance, and a Sunday morning open-air mass. Whether you're Italian or not, you can taste a bit of the old country during this two-day celebration of European culture.

Johnny Appleseed Day
Paradise   (916) 877-9356

First Saturday in October. 20,000. 50+. Free. Town recreation center—Skyway Rd. Rte. 99 to Chico, then 12 miles up the Skyway to Paradise.

Nothing says "Fall" quite like an apple festival, and whether or not Johnny Appleseed actually made his way as far west as Paradise, they still take the opportunity to celebrate apples, the coming of Fall, and the best of the Paradise Ridge area. Over 220 booths feature food, arts and crafts, commercial and club exhibits, games for the kids and face painters. There's also a 3.5-mile Apple Ridge Run and door prizes.

The day begins at 7 a.m. with a pancake breakfast, and exhibits open two hours later. Local entertainers perform throughout the day and include combos, singers, choirs, and dance groups. The emphasis in the food area is on apples, with apple pies, cakes, ice cream, etc.; for the discerning palate, the winners of the recipe contests auction off their creations. There is also an apple pie and ice cream social in the afternoon, in case you haven't eaten quite enough apples or sugar by that time.

Rumor has it that past visitors to this festival have subsequently moved to Paradise, which isn't really surprising if you like pine trees, hill country, and friendly people.

Julian Fall Apple Harvest Festival
Julian   (619) 765-1857

Every weekend in the Fall. 3,000. 62 years. Free. Various locations throughout Julian. I-405 to the city of Oceanside. Go east on Hwy. 78 to Julian. Or take I-15 to Escondido to Hwy. 78. Julian is 60 miles from Oceanside, 40 miles from Escondido.

Julian was founded by former Confederate soldiers who were looking to strike it rich in gold. After mining in the hills of eastern San Diego County, the prospectors soon learned that the climate could bring about another type of gold—in the form of apples.

When the gold mines ran out, the people of this small town brought in apple trees, and with them an apple festival. The first Apple Day was held in 1909, and while the town and the event have grown since then, it's still easy to imagine the streets of this hamlet during the pioneer days.

Each year thousands of people use the Fall Apple Harvest Festival as an excuse to take the beautiful drive up to Julian. The town has some very nice, quaint restaurants, and the drug store still houses an old-fashioned soda fountain, complete with a marble countertop.

During the apple festival the streets are alive with people, and the smell of freshly baked apple pie is everywhere. The Julian restaurants and three bakeries on Main Street specialize in hot apple pie every day.

Different community organizations get together during the weekend to entertain the visitors. During every weekend of October the Triangle Club present an old-fashioned melodrama (admission under $5) and local artists and craftspeople sell their goods. A horse-drawn carriage takes riders into the countryside, and the Pioneer Museum displays the clothes,

California Festivals October

tools, and day-to-day items used in the early days of the community. Tours of Eagle Mine are also conducted.

Julian boasts that it has 50 places to spend the night, including hotels and bed-and-breakfast inns. Come October, you might just have to find out for yourself. —G.W.

Konocti Winery Harvest Festival
Kelseyville   (707) 279-8861

Second weekend in October (Saturday and Sunday). 3,000. 11 years. Free. Konocti Winery. Hwy. 29 at Thomas Dr., midway between Kelseyville and Lakeport. Hwy. 101 to Hwy. 175 east to Hwy. 29.

This small-town celebration of the grape harvest includes sales on selected wines, 50 arts and crafts booths (featuring mostly local artists), a grape-stomping competition, three-mile and 10K "Vineyard Runs," and lots of live entertainment. Music ranges from old-time fiddling, country, bluegrass, and blues to a special appearance by the University of California Alumni Big Band. If you get hungry, you can munch on Cajun hot dogs, hamburgers, and pita bread sandwiches, and on Sunday you can help out the local 4H club by attending the chicken barbecue.

La Mesa Oktoberfest
La Mesa   (619) 465-7700

First weekend in October (Friday-Sunday). 100,000. 16 years. Free. Downtown La Mesa. I-8 east to Spring St. south to La Mesa Blvd.

La Mesa is the home of the largest German-style Oktoberfest in the western United States, attracting a crowd of about 100,000 during the three-day event. Downtown La Mesa, with its red cobblestone streets, is the perfect location for an Oktoberfest, and each year the community gets into the spirit of the festival with hundreds of booths and events. Visitors can walk through more than 200 booths displaying handcrafted items. The stores along the streets are open as well for window-shopping and browsing.

An open-air beer garden features a live oompah-pah band, costumed dancers performing polka steps, and several German-style contests. Among the unique events are log-sawing, nail pounding, and apple peeling contests. But along with the entertainment is, of course, the traditional pastime of drinking beer and eating German food (including bratwurst, potato salad and sauerkraut), and there's always lots of both on hand to help folks lose their inhibitions and join in the singing and dancing. —G.W.

Lake Tahoe Kokanee Salmon Festival
South Lake Tahoe   (916) 573-2600

First weekend in October (Saturday and Sunday). 11,000. 2 years. Free. From I-80 take Hwy 50 to South Lake Tahoe, Hwy. 89 north to USFS Lake Tahoe Visitors Center (2 miles north of town).

Celebrating the annual spawning run of the Kokanee salmon and the fall colors of Lake Tahoe, this festival focuses on environmental awareness for families. Forest service rangers and wildlife experts explain the life cycle of the Kokanee salmon and other wonders of nature as thousands of the bright red fish swim up Taylor Creek to lay their eggs. You can easily see the fish from the stream banks or get even closer in the underground stream-profile chamber that allows visitors to watch the Kokanee underwater. Other activities include a fun run, a salmon cooking contest, salmon feed, nature walks, environmental educational displays, children's "fishing" booth, storytellers, fishing demonstrations, cooking lessons, costumed characters and more.

Manteca Pumpkin Fair
Manteca   (800) 872-6546

First weekend in October (Friday-Sunday). 50,000. 7 years. $6 adults, $2 children 6-12, free for children 5 and under. Manteca Industrial Park. From I-5 or Hwy 99 take the Hwy 120 bypass to Oakwood Lake Resort in Manteca via the Airport Way exit.

Rumor has it that most of the pumpkins found at the more famous Half Moon Bay Pumpkin festival are actually grown in Manteca and trucked in. Manteca calls itself "The Pumpkin Capital of the World" and claims to grow over 5,000 pumpkins each year. Fortunately, the state's big enough for both festivals.

Manteca's Pumpkin Festival is also big on name entertainment with such draws as the Tower of Power, The Guess Who and Charlie Daniels in years past. (The entertainment is included in the admission price.) There are free events too, including train rides and pumpkin contests where festivalgoers can compete in wheelbarrow races, seed spitting and pie eating contests.

The fair is combined with the annual Arts & Crafts Show featuring hundreds of handcrafted items, and over 50 food booths. Saturday features the Manteca 100 Auto Show with the finest in street rod, street machine, Corvette, Mustang, Camaro and mini-truck competitions. Other attractions include a shaded pavilion area for dancing and drinking, free jet ski shows performed on nearby Oakwood Lake lagoon, a haunted house, pony rides, petting zoo, pumpkin carving and National Guard displays.

Morro Bay Harbor Festival
Morro Bay   (802) 231-0592

First weekend in October (Saturday-Sunday). 20,000. 10 years. $2 general admission, $1 seniors and students, children under 12 free. Harbor Area. From Hwy. 1 get off at Morro Bay Blvd. Come all the way down to the Embarcadero, at intersection of Embarcadero & Beach St.

The Harbor Festival, with its dramatic waterfront setting, celebrates one of the few natural harbors and active fishing villages on the west coast by showcasing seafood, the fishing industry, and the diversity of Morro Bay marine life and coastal lifestyles. The the two-day event is a winetasting and seafood sampling fair.
But this festival offers a lot more than just a beautiful setting, good wine, and great food. There are also many booths of arts and crafts, entertainment (jazz, big band, country and rock), a fishing derby, jugglers, clowns, puppeters, a Farmer's Market, bay cruises, boat races and a variety of marinetime and marine life exhibits.
Whether you're a fisherman, a sailor, or landlubber, this festival is a great way to enjoy Morro Bay.

Nut Tree Pumpkin Patch and Great Scarecrow Contest
Vacaville   (707) 448-6411

Weekends throughout October. 13 years. Adults $3, Seniors $2. Children under 12 Free. Next to the Nut Tree Restaurant. Take I-80 east from San Francisco. The Nut Tree is just east of Vacaville and west of Davis at the Monte Vista exit.

The Nut Tree Pumpkin Patch and Great Scarecrow Contest captures the feel of an old-fashioned harvest festival even though it's situated right next to a major highway. Whether you stop for an hour's rest while traveling

California Festivals   October

down I-80 or plan to make a day of it, this festival is fun and unique. The scarecrow contest is the first of it's kind and offers over $6,000 in prizes. Over 300 entries promise results that are often hilarious. What crow wouldn't stay away from a cornfield guarded by Alf, the alien of TV fame? The scarecrows are set up in a maze of cornstalks in a 10-acre open field, and each bend of the path brings a surprise.

The festival also features live music by a variety of bands, and hamburgers and other foods are sold. There's an area in which kids can play and a pumpkin patch where you can select just the right pumpkin for a jack o' lantern. Gourds, Indian corn, and other produce are sold in open stalls. There's also a booth selling fresh pumpkin breads and pies. If you've never tried pumpkin ice cream, you can sample this seasonal treat at another booth. Rounding out the nostalgic air of this festival is a display of old farm equipment used when Solano County was mainly an agricultural area. Also included is a petting farm, pony rides, puppet shows, and pumpkin carving.

Oktoberfest
Montrose   (818) 249-7171

First Saturday of October. 40,000. 14 years. Free. 2300 and 2400 blocks of Honolulu St. in Montrose. Glendale Freeway intersects the Foothill Freeway (I-210). Montrose is north of Glendale.

What would October be without an Oktoberfest or two to remind us what we're missing over in Germany during this month-long harvest celebration? Though the Montrose Oktoberfest is only one day long, they do their best to recreate a Bavarian village in the downtown area of this foothill community. There's German music, of course, and dancers, and such German classics as knockwurst, sauerkraut, potato salad, rye bread, pretzels, strudel, and brownies (are they German?) are served up by locals dressed in traditional Bavarian garb. Beer, non-alcoholic beer, wine and soft drinks are also available. For fun, there's a variety show, bingo games, and special rides and games for the kids.

Pioneer Days
Artesia   (213) 924-6397

First Saturday in October. 7,000. 34 years. Free. Artesia Park, 18750 Clarkdale Ave. About 1 mile from I-605 and Hwy. 91. Park borders on South St. between Pioneer Blvd. and Norwalk Blvd.

California Festivals	October

This one-day event is an extension of the old Dairyland Fair, which attracted numerous dairymen and farmers from miles around back when this used to be farmin' country. Now it's a community-oriented festival that pays respect to Artesia's roots and gives everyone a fun day in the park. There's a parade, of course, plus a country-style fair with food and vendor booths, as well as an auction featuring items donated by local merchants and plenty of other entertainment. The atmosphere is definitely western, with festival workers sporting western garb, a beard contest (for the longest, fullest, and most unusual), and a western costume contest. In addition to the various food booths (featuring hot dogs, hamburgers, etc.), there's deep-pit barbecue from noon to 4 p.m., serving 1,500 pounds of beef.

Pioneer Days
Twenty-Nine Palms   (619) 367-3445

Third weekend in October (Thursday-Sunday). 10,000. 8 years. Fee for PCRA rodeo, dances. Amboy Rd. 2 miles east of Adobe Rd. Take I-10 to Hwy. 62 east, left at Adobe Rd., right on Amboy Rd., 2 miles east.

Nothing says "pioneer" quite like an outhouse race and a rodeo, now does it? And that's just part of what you'll find at Twenty-Nine Palms' Pioneer Days.

The rodeo, sponsored by the Professional Rodeo Cowboys Association, features men and women competing in team roping, bareback riding, calf roping, steer wrestling, barrel racing, bull riding, and saddle bronc riding. The outhouse race pits straining teams of men and women against one another, hauling outhouses Roman-chariot-style through a course, with a "charioteer" riding shotgun (so to speak). The legs contest (which once appeared on the TV show "Real People") has men competing to see who has the nicest legs.

Friday and Saturday nights feature dancing to country and rock music. And this festival wouldn't be complete without a carnival, a parade, an arm-wrestling contest, and a beard-growing contest. Local organizations sponsor food concessions, serving the typical hot dogs, hamburgers, Oriental food, beer, and soda.

California Festivals   October

Reedley Fiesta
Reedley   (209) 638-3548

Second weekend in October (Friday-Saturday). 10,000. 21 years. Free. Hwy. 99 to Manning Ave. exit. Go 12 miles east to downtown "G" Street at Pioneer Park.

Often referred to as the "fruit basket of the world," Reedley holds this post-harvest celebration each October to honor its agricultural heritage. This community festival features a parade, an art show, a frog-jumping contest, beard-growing contests. Food booths sell all kinds of ethnic food, including German, Japanese, Armenian, and Thai. Other booths feature arts and crafts and games.

Renaissance of Kings Cultural Arts Faire
Hanford   (209) 585-2527

First weekend in October (Saturday and Sunday). 12,000. 11 years. Free. Civic Auditorium Grounds. I-5 or Hwy. 99 to Hwy. 198 to Hanford. From the north, take hwy. 99 to hwy. 43 to 10th ave. to Hanford.

Every Fall, the town of Hanford in the San Joaquin Valley transforms itself into the Old English village of "Hanfordshire," where the year is 1521 and young King Henry VIII and his court join the celebrating villagers in their merry reveling. Festivities include a village harvest process, knightly combat, public plays and dances, and courtly ceremonies. Tongue-in-cheek scenes and tomfoolery bring forth merriment, and music and song fill the air--as do the smells of foods born in the spirit of the Renaissance (we're talking turkey legs, Scotch eggs, potato pies, scones, ale, wine, etc.)

The visitor is tempted by games and handicrafts in the marketplace as well as good food and drink during this two-day affair, and the organizers do their best to recreate the scene not only with authentic buildings and booths but with performers who dress in traditional garb and wander the village streets acting out such parts as Liz Darling, the village scum, and Angelica Allspice, the spice merchant's daughter. Musicians, dancers, and singers from all over the state regal visitors with performances, and some of the musical instruments you'll hear include recorders, sackbuts, krummhorns, viols, dulcimers, and a hurdy gurdy.

If you've ever been to a Renaissance festival (especially Novato's Renaissance Pleasure Fair), you'll feel right at home at this festival, for they share many of the same characteristics (and characters). But one thing that makes this festival unique is it's "soap opera" storylines that carry on from year to year, with the characters growing and changing with the festival itself.

Riverbank's Cheese and Wine Exposition
Riverbank   (209) 869-4541

Second weekend in October (Saturday and Sunday). 105,000. 15 years. Wine tasting sessions $15. Santa Fe St. (downtown). Hwy. 99 to Hwy. 108, 6 miles north of Modesto.

Spend a country weekend at this European-style cheese and wine fair in the Central Valley. You can taste, savor, and enrich your knowledge of wines from some of the state's select wineries. Between tastings (which last an hour each—admission entitles you to one tasting and a souvenir wine glass), you can enjoy a variety of cheeses from California companies—and the cheese and crackers are complimentary.

In addition, 275 art, craft, and antique booths are set up along Santa Fe St. in downtown Riverbank. Wandering minstrels and on-stage entertainment (including bluegrass, Dixieland, country, and 50s-60s nostalgia music) add to the fun and excitement of this street fair.

Established in 1977, this free street festival also features tours of the cheese factories, 2-mile and 10K runs, bike races, and booths at the street fair that serve a wide variety of food, from hot dogs to steamed oysters.

Silverado Days
Buena Park   (714) 826-5666

Third week in October (Thursday-Sunday). 130,000. 60 years. Free. William Peak Park. Fwy 91, Knott off ramp, south half mile, turn left on El Dorado.

Begun in 1932 when Buena Park businessmen started a Hometown Days promotion, this annual community fair was expanded and renamed Silverado Days in 1957. A western atmosphere takes over this Los Angeles suburb for four days each October, with game and food booths (offering ethnic and standard fair food), crafts, a carnival with games and rides, the Grand Parade, a chili cook-off, hog calling, arm wrestling, a car raffle, baby contest, a men's "best legs" contest, a mutt show, live music, and more.

There's a wide variety of entertainment, too, including square dancing, boxing, 50s and 60s dance music, western and flatland cloggers, a talent search, a beauty pageant, a children's poster coloring contest, and the Silverado Ball.

Springville Apple Festival
Springville   (209) 539-3218

Third weekend in October (Saturday-Sunday). 30,000. 11 years. Free. Downtown Springville. South of Fresno and north of Bakersfield. Hwy. 99 to Hwy. 65 to Porterville, Hwy. 190 to Springville.

Nestled in the foothills of the Sierra Nevadas in Southern California, the community of Springville is the surprising home of many apple orchards and the Springville Apple Festival. Apple-related goodies of all kinds are available, including apple turnovers, sundaes, shakes, strudel, cobbler, crisp, cookies, cakes, donuts, sauce, yogurt, butter, juice, cider, and pizza (pizza?). Each day begins with a pancake breakfast—featuring apple pancakes and apple syrup, of course. In addition, several orchards display and sell their apples, and you can tour many of the apple ranches.

But this festival isn't just about apples; it began in 1980 as a way to promote family-oriented entertainment and has grown tremendously ever since. Activities include a 5K and 10K cross country race, quilt show, square dance, drawing contest for the kids, and lots of live music (jazz, western, and more). Around 100 booths feature a wide variety of handcrafted items.

Springville is considered the "gateway to the golden trout wilderness," so you can just imagine the array of outdoor activities available in this area. You'll find plenty of camping, hiking, swimming, fishing, picnicking, and boating, even this time of year.

Stagecoach Days
Banning   (714) 849-4695

Weekdays surrounding the first weekend in October. 10,000. 35 years. Free. Town and A.C. Dysart Equestrian Park. I-10 between San Bernardino and Palm Springs on 22nd St.

What kind of festival is Stagecoach Days? You guessed it: Western. From its rodeo to its parade to its mock shoot-outs and traveling jail, this series of activities is loaded with western fun. Located between San

Bernardino and Palm Springs, Banning was one of the last stagecoach stops in Southern California, and this festival commemorates those days.

In addition to the activities already mentioned, there's also a carnival, a horse show, a car show, a whiskerino contest, a grandmothers contest, a quick-draw demonstration, a costume promenade, a street dance, a spaghetti feed, and a barbecue. Other foods include American, Mexican, Thai, Indian, and western dishes. And the music? Guess.

Twenty Mule Team Days
Boron   (619) 762-5070

First weekend in October (Saturday and Sunday). 4,000. 28 years. Free. Homeland Park on Boron Ave. at John St. Hwy. 58 to Boron Ave. exit. Boron is 30 miles east of Mojave and 39 miles west of Barstow.

Can't you just picture an old wagon train, led by Lorne Greene or somebody, galloping through the desert? Well, desert is what you'll find in Boron, and if you like it, this festival is the place to be. Twenty Mule Team Days is associated with 20 Mule Team Borax, which is sponsored by U.S. Borax, the largest employer in Boron.

In the early days, this two-day event was considered a homecoming festival, and many former residents still return for the festivities, which include a parade, game booths, horseshoe pitching, a pet parade, a beautiful baby contest, a battle of the bands, and more. Food booths offer hamburgers, hot dogs, chili, corn, soft drinks, beer, and wine coolers. The band competition features rock, country/western, and even a classical band in a fight to the finish. Other special events include an honorary mayor's contest, old-timer's contest, and museum tours.

Village Venture Street Faire
Claremont   (714) 621-9644

Last Saturday in October. 20,000. 10 years. Free. Claremont Village area. Take Hwy 10 to Indian Hill Blvd. exit. Continue on Indian Hill Blvd., turn right on Second Street and left on Yale St. Village Venture is located between First Street and Bonita Ave.

Scarecrows and goblins appear one day a year in the tiny village of Claremont. Beginning mid-morning, tiny ghosts, witches, fairies and other such ghouls parade through town during the Children's Halloween Parade. Local merchants hand out bags of candy for all the goblins. A new highlight of the faire is the "Scarecrow of the Year"contest, where local merchants, organizations and individuals create some unique looking scarecrows and the community votes on the best adult and children's scarecrow.

The faire has a reputation for quality handcrafted arts and crafts—no flea market stuff here! And the food is tempting as well. You can sample Italian sausage sandwiches, Indian fry bread, chicken shish-kebob and veggie curry. This family-oriented event is something everyone looks forward to each fall.

Waterford Western Heritage Day
Waterford   (209) 874-9525

First Saturday in October. 5,000. 25 years. Free. Community Park at C St. 12 miles east of Modesto. From Hwy. 99, take Hwy. 132 to Waterford.

This small western town returns to its roots for a day each October, reliving the Old West with a parade, a flea market, a craft fair, a block party, a street dance, wagon rides, and a variety of entertainment throughout the day. You can enjoy Mexican and American foods, hear plenty of country/western and jazz music, and take a walk through the past and this town's heritage with a visit to Waterford during this festival.

Western Days
San Dimas   (714) 592-3818

Second weekend in October (Thursday-Sunday). 10,000. 9 years. Free except for Casino Night ($7). Bonita Ave., downtown San Dimas. I-210 to Arrow Hwy. exit. Go to Bonita Ave. east. Bonita Ave. ends at the festival grounds.

Western Days is a full weekend of music, food, crafts, and the "Puddingstone Falls Casino." A dance Friday night kicks things off, followed by a parade Saturday morning and "Casino Night" Saturday night. There are also western dancers and strolling entertainers (with the emphasis on western music, of course). An arts and crafts fair, a carnival, outdoor games for all ages, and lots of good food can be found both days, with the food booths serving up American, Italian, Thai, Chinese, and Mexican dishes.

If you feel lucky this October, be sure not to miss Western Days for some old-fashioned western fun and a couple of hands of poker.

California Festivals   October

Whaleboat Regatta
Vallejo   (707) 648-4200

First weekend in October (Saturday-Sunday). 16,000. 18 years. Free. Vallejo waterfront. From I-80, take the Tennessee St. exit. Head west on Tennessee, turn left on Mare Island Way. Continue on to the festival—it's on the right side of the street.

Sponsored by the California Maritime Academy, this two-day festival features a series of exciting boat races, with each boat manned by a crew of eight people. Held in Mare Island Channel, along Vallejo's lovely waterfront, the races start in the morning so it's chilly, but the excitement will probably warm you up. Preliminary races are on Saturday; finals are on Sunday.

If the boat races aren't entertaining enough, you can wander among the many arts and crafts booths, which feature juried, handmade items.

Ye Olde English Renaissance Faire
San Marcos   (619) 744-1270

Second weekend in October (Saturday and Sunday). 15,000. 8 years. Adults $7, children 7-12 $3, children 5 and under free. Rancho Santa Fe Park. West off I-15 on Hwy. 78, exit Rancho Santa Fe Rd., go south to LaCosta Meadows Dr., turn left.

Knights in armor, damsels in distress, wild and brazen gypsies, hawking merchants, clever jugglers, pranksters and mimes, medieval mayhem societies, Scottish clans, country and courtly dancers, a queen, a princess, peasants galore—all await you at this festival that takes a step back in time to a 16th century English village at harvest time.

Parades celebrate the arrival of Good Queen Guinevere as she makes her way through this recreated village, traveling among merchants selling jewelry, clothing, crafts, and such tasty treats as tarts, turkey legs, ribs, ales, beers, crepes, fruit, fruit ices, and popcorn. You'll

You'll see colorful costumes and characters at San Marcos' Ye Olde English Faire. (Photo courtesy of the San Marcos Chamber of Commerce)

be entertained not only by performers in traditional dress who seem to believe they really are the characters they portray, but also by mock battles, stage and street performances of Shakespeare, puppeteers, and Old English games you can participate in. You can also have your fortune told or your palm read by one of the local "gypsies."

This two-day family-oriented event brings a touch of fantasy to an otherwise ordinary October weekend.

Auburn Craft and Christmas Marketplace
Auburn   (209) 533-3473

Second weekend in November (Saturday and Sunday). 10,000. 5 years. $2. Auburn Fairgrounds. I-80 to Auburn exit.

You can get a jump on Christmas and avoid the crowds at the mall, plus find unique, handcrafted gifts at the Auburn Craft and Christmas marketplace. You'll see lively entertainment in a festive Christmas setting of brightly decorated halls and be treated to a variety of live music: bluegrass, swing, folk, Irish, and, of course, Christmas carols.

Nearly 10,000 visit this two-day affair, enjoying Christmas cheer and the best in baked goods and seasonal drinks. Other food includes Mexican and Thai cuisine, Polish sausages, corn on the cob, and soft pretzels. The kids can get their faces painted, and the whole family will enjoy the carolers, jugglers, merry elves, and twinkling trees. And if you've been dreaming of a white Christmas, well, the mountains are just a few miles up the road.

Brawley Cattle Call
Brawley   (619) 344-3160

Second weekend in November (Friday-Sunday). 30,000. 35 years. Rodeo $7. Rodeo Arena. I-8 east to Hwy. 86. Go north directly into Brawley.

"Round 'em up, move 'em out!" may not be quite the cattle call you'll hear in Brawley, but you sure will see more great rodeo action than at almost any other festival around. This three-day event is a tribute to the cattle industry in Imperial County, and it may just turn you into a born-again cowboy.

California Festivals   November

There are three Professional Rodeo Cowboys Association rodeos, a parade, a bluegrass concert, Western dances, barbecues, a chuckwagon breakfast, and chili and beef cook-offs. There's also a 10K run early Saturday morning.

Don't go off to a Colorado dude ranch to get a taste of the Old West—you can get it right here in California.

Calico Fine Arts Festival
Barstow   (619) 254-2122

First weekend in November (Friday-Sunday). 6,000. 12 years. $4 per car; camping $9. Calico Ghost Town. I-15, 10 miles north of Barstow, take Ghost Town Rd. exit.

The silver-mining ghost town of Calico becomes a showplace for Southwestern art when nearly 50 of the West's foremost artists gather to display and sell hundreds of oil, charcoal, watercolor and sculpture works along the historis Ghost Town Main Street. Several art auctions take place over the three days, and you'll hear country and bluegrass music.

This festival is also a chance to visit a real live ghost town and experience a little bit of life in the Old West. Camping is available for $9 per night, and restaurants and a confectionary can be found in town.

Carlsbad Village Faire
Carlsbad   (619) 729-9072

First Sunday in November. 80,000. 13 years. Free. Village of Carlsbad. I-5 to Elm off ramp—head straight for ocean, 5 blocks.

This one-day street fair features over 500 exhibitors of arts and crafts. Begun as an effort to revitalize the village of Carlsbad, this festival has grown into an event that meanders throughout 24 city blocks and attracts some 80,000 people. In addition to the arts and crafts, you'll find booths featuring Greek, Thai, Italian, Polish, Chinese, and Japanese foods, plus three stages of continuous live music, from country and rock to jazz.

For the kids, there's a petting zoo and pony, llama, and elephant rides, plus lots of games and a beach nearby. It's a fun-filled day in this beautiful beach city just north of San Diego.

California Festivals   November

Pilgrim Festival
Claremont   (714) 621-9581

Second Friday and Saturday in November. 15,000. 43 years. Free. Pilgrim Place. From San Bernardino Hwy 10 take Indian Hill Blvd. exit north to Harrison Rd. in Claremont. Turn west and drive two blocks to Pilgrim Place.

The site for the Pilgrim Festival is a retirement community for some 325 residents, most of whom have served as missionaries, ministers, teachers, seminarians, etc. from all over the U.S. and abroad. For two days, all residents dress as Pilgrims and decorate the 33-acre community with all of the trappings of our Pilgrim forefathers.

The highlight of the festival is a staging of The Pilgrim Story with over 50 cast members, which recreates the journey of the Pilgrims from Scrooby England in July of 1606 to the Mayflower voyage of 1620 and the settlement of the Plymouth Plantation.

Visitors can ride a scale replica of the Mayflower called "the Mayflower on Wheels," visit the nearby Petterson Museum, or stroll through the Bazaar, filled with fresh-baked goods and sweets, international food booths and a variety of crafts, such as ceramics, pottery, sculpture, copper enamel, corncob dolls, holiday decorations, Plymouth rocks, Pilgrim gems, knitting, crocheting, linens, needlework, Norwegian Rosemaling, stainedglass, weaving, Wendellglass & stained glass and wood crafts.

Most of the crowd likes to sit down for the Turkey Casserole Buffet luncheon, where for $6 you can feast on turkey, carrots, noodles, cranberry and a piece of homemade pie.

For the kids there's the Massasoit Superchief Ride, a free puppet show, a "glue-in," and a host of such treats as cotton candy, sno-cones, popcorn and lemonade.

Sonora Christmas Festival
Sonora   (209) 533-3473

Thanksgiving weekend (Friday-Sunday). 20,000. 17 years. $4 adults, $1 children, 5 and under free. Motherlode Fairgrounds. From Hwy 120 go to Hwy 108 and take the downtown Sonora exit (Hwy 49).

Why should you go to a drab mall to do your Christmas shopping this year when you can go to the Sonora Christmas Festival? Your spirits will be lifted by fine entertainment, top quality crafts, festive food and, of course, Santa and his merry elves.

California Festivals — November

You'll see many unusual crafts at this festival including wreaths and folk decorations made from cornhusks, fantasy toys for children, bamboo flutes, vases, sushi-ware, original poetry and calligraphy on paper castings.

Once you are ready to drop from shopping you can settle down to lively entertainment - - including hot Caribbean rhythms on vibes, Celtic folk dancing and accordian combo yodeling and crooning while you enjoy drinks of the season such as hot and cold cider, hot buttered rum and mulled wine.

Santa's little helpers await you in Sonora (Photo by Robert Westgate)

California Festivals   December

Christmas on the Prado
San Diego   (619) 232-0512

First Friday and Saturday evenings in December. 150,000. 14 years. Free. Balboa Park. From I-5 or Hwy. 163, take Park Blvd. exit. Turn left onto Park, then left on either Presidents Way or Space Theater Way.

Christmas on the Prado in San Diego is Balboa Park's present to the community. There is no charge for admission to most of these museums, and you'll find holiday entertainment and international foods throughout the park. A visitor to the Museum of Man can sip Swedish gloog (a spicy, hot wine drink) and eat international pastries while viewing displays, and a candlelight Santa Lucia procession is held outside the museum each night. That's just one of the 27 institutions participating in the holiday event, so it's best to arrive at 5 p.m., when the museums open their doors. Otherwise, four hours just isn't enough time to enjoy all the activities.

The evening event is a perfect start to the holiday season. The park is decorated with wreaths and lights, and chestnuts roast on the barbecue outside the San Diego Art Institute Gallery. Centro Cultural de la Raza serves Nicaraguan coffee and Mexican and Latin American pastries. Other food on the Prado includes croissants, turkey sandwiches, western and German hot dogs, hot cider, and gingerbread cookies.

A world of celebration can be found at the House of

The singing Christmas tree is always a highlight of San Diego's Christmas on the Prado. (Photo Courtesy of Christmas on the Prado)

233

Pacific Relations, nine cottages representing 27 countries. There are also folk dancing exhibitions and musical performances by community groups at the Organ Pavilion

There's much more to see and sample during Christmas at the Prado. The holiday season can be hectic, but don't let that keep you away. Between the community groups and the museum gift shops, there are many reasonably priced gift ideas. You'll find handcrafted tree ornaments at the Museum of San Diego History. The Museum of Photographic Arts gift shop has some great find.

Christmas Walk
Corona del Mar   (714) 673-4050

First Sunday in December. 8,000. 14 years. Free. Corona del Mar. I-405 to McArthur exit. Right on McArthur to Pacific Highway.

The Christmas Walk is a holiday street fair, with the shops along this stretch of the Pacific Coast Highway opening their doors and offering free cookies, cider, finger sandwiches, and other goodies. You may not see snow, but you will see dancers, mimes, carolers, a puppet show, a music mobile, a zoomobile, and, of course, Santa Claus. Local merchants donate approximately 85 prizes for a drawing, and all festival attendees can participate in the drawing for a small donation.

Currier and Ives Christmas Open House
Sutter Creek   (209) 267-5987

First Friday evening in December. 5,000. 16 years. Free. Throughout downtown. I-80 from Sacramento to Hwy. 16 to Hwy. 49. Sutter Creek is 8 miles from Hwy. 16 and 42 miles from Sacramento.

Imagine a picturesque village nestled in a valley, Main Street bordered with two-story structures dating from the 1870s, and tiny white lights covering balconies, buildings, and fences from Tucker Hill on the north end of town to the classic 1862 Greek Revival church on the south. Up and down the streets of this historic Gold Rush town, fresh-cut cedar boughs decked with bright red bows adorn buildings, balcony balustrades, and shop fronts. Store windows are filled with fragrant greens and trees, candy canes, carousel horses, and sparkling ornaments. Costumed merchants

California Festivals   December

offer hot beverages and home-baked cakes and cookies to shoppers and revelers. Music fills the air, from choirs singing "Jingle Bells" and "Hark the Herald Angels Sing" to brass ensembles and country and bluegrass bands. You'll also see Santa Claus, Dickens street urchins, and special plays for the kids. Several food booths offer hot-buttered rum, hot mulled wine and cider, stews, and chili.

Isn't this what you'd expect from a festival named after a pair of famous holiday artists?

Frontier Christmas
Oroville   (916) 538-2219

Second Saturday in December. 1,500. 12 years. Free. Lake Oroville Visitor Center. From Hwy. 70 take Hwy. 162 east out of Oroville for 7 miles; turn left onto Kelly Ridge Rd. and travel 2 1/2 miles to the end.

This festival's name says it all: it's a Gold Rush Christmas celebration in the old mining town of Bidwell Bar, with all the trimmings—and a few modern touches. You'll see historic characters in costume, Victorian marriage ceremonies, and Victorian decorations, plus have a chance to rub elbows with Santa Claus, Smokey the Bear, and Woodsy Owl. Munch on Christmas sweets and sip coffee and punch while you check out the pioneer crafts, gift items, and souvenir photos for sale.

You'll be entertained by a children's choir, Swiss bell ringers, and the Bidwell Bar Band as you wander from activity to activity, and you can test your vocal chords during the Christmas sing-along or your luck at cards during the Gold Rush card game, faro.

This festival is a small, homey gathering, just right to get you into the spirit of Christmas.

Mendocino Christmas Festival
Mendocino   (707) 964-3153

First three weeks of December. 2,000. 2 years. Mostly free. Village of Mendocino. From Hwy 101 take Hwy 128 west to Hwy 1.

The closest thing to a New England Christmas celebration you'll find this side of the Mississippi is in Mendocino. This three-week festival is sure to put you in the Christmas spirit. Events include the "Lights On" celebration, stage productions, "The Elves and the Shoemaker", Little River Inn a Christmas Gala, candle-light tours of the bed and breakfast's of Little River and Mendocino, Christmas Tea, horse-drawn carriage rides and much

235

more Christmas fun. Make your lodging reservations early; the town fills up fast.

Mission Christmas Faire
Oceanside   (619) 721-1101

First weekend in December (Saturday and Sunday). 12 years. 30,000. Free. Mission San Luis Rey. I-5 to Mission Ave. Exit to the Mission.

California's largest mission, Mission San Luis Rey, is the setting for two days of arts and crafts, bringing crafters from all over the southwest. Glass blowers, leather crafters, doll makers, and many other artisans perform their crafts on site. Holiday shoppers are always delighted with their finds.

Other things to be found at this festival include a children's area with booths, clowns, face painting, a petting zoo, rides, games, and Santa Claus; strolling clowns and musicians; a band playing Christmas carols; and food booths serving ethnic foods, wine, and beer.

Motherlode Scots Scottish Fair and Christmas Walk (Festival of Lights)
Volcano   (209) 223-1510

Early December. 400. 7 years. Free. Armory Hall. From Stockton, Hwy. 88 to Pine Grove. From Sacramento, Hwy. 16 to Hwy. 49 south to Jackson to Hwy. 88 to Pine Grove. Follow signs to Volcano.

If you're looking for a little foreign flavor this Christmas, you may want to travel to Volcano, a Gold Rush town in a deep, wooded valley in the Mother Lode country east of Sacramento. This community's Festival of Lights is a celebration both of Christmas and the glories of being Scottish, with Scottish clans gathering to help decorate the small town and carry on many Scottish traditions, old and new.

One of the festival's highlights is the evening Christmas Walk, featuring pipe bands, Scottish marching groups, banners, and flags. It begins at 5 p.m., just as the town's Christmas lights come on, and travels all over this small community's streets.

Before the parade, you can wander the Scottish Fair and feast on such traditional foods as meat pies, stew, shortbread, and scones smothered with jam (a highlight in itself); cut the day's chill with some hot spiced punch or wine; discover many Scottish arts and crafts; and be treated to some fine Highland music, including, of course, bagpipes. And like any good Scottish celebration, there's lots of dancing, both Highland and country.

With many of the clans displaying their tartans, maybe you'll finally get a chance to answer that age-old question: is there anything under those kilts?

Nation's Christmas Tree Festival
Sanger   (209) 875-4575

Second weekend in December. 1,800. 65 years. Free. Tree lighting and parade—downtown Sanger; trek to the tree—King's Canyon National Park. Hwy. 99 to Jensen. East at Jensen, then 12 miles to Sanger. Take the bus caravan to Kings Canyon National Park.

With a little girl's words—"What a wonderful Christmas tree it would be"—efforts to have the General Grant tree in Kings Canyon National Park designated the Nation's Christmas Tree began in 1924, with members of the Sanger Chamber of Commerce holding a Christmas program at the base of the tree. Two years later, President Calvin Coolidge made it official, and since 1926 people have been traveling to Sanger the second weekend of each December to join in the trek to the tree and participate in the Christmas services held there.

The people of Sanger take their town's title—The Nation's Christmas Tree City—pretty seriously, with many natives going back each year to take part in this festival. The festival features the lighting of the downtown Christmas tree; a parade, with a special Toyland segment for the kids; Christmas carols; and, of course, a visit from Santa Claus.

Parade of Lights
Oxnard   (805) 985-4852

Second Saturday in December. 25,000. 26 years. Free. Oxnard. Ventura Freeway (Hwy. 101) to Victoria Ave. South to Channel Islands Blvd.

For a nautical twist on the holiday spirit, travel to Ventura County's Channel Islands Harbor this December for the harbor's annual Parade of Lights. This celebration includes the evening light parade, followed by an awards ceremony.

This traditional event is held at the beautiful Channel Islands Harbor in Oxnard.

California Festivals   December

Santa Lucia Festival of Lights
Kingsburg   (209) 897-2925

Saturday nearest December 13. 5,000. Free. Downtown Kingsburg. About 20 miles south of Fresno on Hwy 99. 20 miles north of Visalia.

Every culture has its own special Christmas traditions, and this festival celebrates a unique Swedish custom in which the oldest daughter of each household, wearing a crown of lighted candles, serves hot coffee and sweet rolls to her family in bed.

This one-day event combines this custom with more Americanized Christmas celebrations, such as a children's parade, lighted Christmas trees, window decorations, booths along the street featuring seasonal arts and crafts, and, of course, Santa Claus—this time making his entrance on an antique fire engine. Also offered is a combination of Swedish and American foods, plus special treats for the kids.

Spirit of Christmas Crafts Faire and Celebration
Santa Rosa   (707) 575-9355

First and second weekends of December (Friday-Sunday). 25,000. 14 years. $2.50. Sonoma County Fairgrounds. One mile east of Hwy. 101 (north of San Francisco) on Hwy. 12 in Santa Rosa.

Sometimes the true spirit of Christmas gets lost in the rush to find the perfect present for that special someone. Though the emphasis is on crafts and gifts (over 250 artists and craftspeople display their work), this festival recaptures some of that old-time Christmas charm with holiday decorations, a variety of costumed characters, continuous quality entertainment (such as Jesse Colin Young), and a booth decorating contest that inspires the arts and crafts vendors to carry out the holiday theme.

In addition to the musicians, dancers, magicians, jugglers, and clowns, several of Santa's helpers are on hand to entertain you, including Rudolph the Red-Nosed Reindeer, Frosty the Snowman, the Tin Soldier, the Snow Queen, and of course a bevy of elves. An international variety of natural foods are served, and a 100-prize raffle highlights this three-day event.

California Festivals   December

Weihnachtsmarkt
Carmel   (408) 624-8886

First Sunday in December. 600. 12 years. Free. The Barnyard, Hwy. 1 and Carmel Valley Rd. Hwy. 1 to Carmel Valley Rd. Look for the windmill.

The story of Santa Claus begins with the legendary life of a Spanish bishop, Nicholas of Myra. Many variations of St. Nicholas have traveled through time and around the world, as have many Christmas customs and traditions. One such tradition is the Weihnachtsmarkt, the German Hallowed Eve Market that celebrates the Feast Day of St. Nicholas.

For the past several years, the merchants in a unique shopping center at the mouth of the Carmel Valley have been recreating the Weihnachtsmarkt, with tables of food (offering cider, Polish sausages, sandwiches, popcorn, hot pretzels, and more) and Christmas trees set up around the center's gardens, plus lots of Christmas cheer. You can spend the afternoon browsing from shop to shop, dine at one of the many restaurants, or just wander the gardens and enjoy the many jugglers, musicians (playing lutes, flugle horns, etc.), clowns, and carolers. Other entertainment includes storytellers and vaudeville-type shows.

With evening comes St. Nicholas himself, making a grand entrance on a white horse, then "magically" lighting the Christmas tree around which everyone has gathered while awaiting his arrival. As a children's choir sings, St. Nick sits on his throne greeting the children and giving each a special treat.

St. Nicholas arrives to celebrate St. Nicholas Day, at The Barnyard in Carmel. (Photo courtesy of The Barnyard)

California Festivals

California Festival Regions

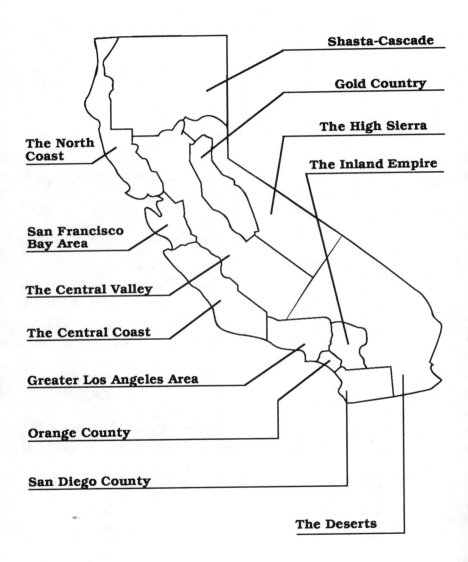

California Festivals

Festivals by Region

Central Coast Festivals

Festival / **City**

Adobe Tour — Monterey
Apple Festival — Templeton
California Avocado Festival — Carpinteria
California Festival of Beers — San Luis Obispo
California Rodeo Salinas — Salinas
California Strawberry Festival — Oxnard
Carmel Bach Festival — Carmel
Ceres Wesyern Art Show & Sale — Ceres
Clam Festival — Pismo Beach
Colony Days Celebration — Atascadero
Danish Days — Solvang
Dixieland Monterey — Monterey
Fall Fun Fest — Seaside
Fiesta Italiana — Santa Barbara
Goleta Valley Days — Goleta
Great Monterey Squid Festival — Monterey
Greenfield Broccoli Festival — Greenfield
Harvest Festival — Carmel
I Madonnari Italian St. Painting Festival — Santa Barbara
La Fiesta de San Luis Obispo — San Luis Obispo
Lompoc Valley Festival — Lompoc
May Festival — Fillmore
Monterey Jazz Festival — Monterey
Morro Bay Harbor Festival — Morro Bay
Mozart Festival — San Luis Obispo

California Festivals

Central Coast Festivals Continued

Festival	City
North Monterey County Strawberry Festival	Castroville
Ojai Music Festival	Ojai
Old Spanish Days Fiesta	Santa Barbara
San Luis Obispo Mardi Gras	San Luis Obispo
Santa Barbara Arts Festival	Santa Barbara
Santa Barbara International Film Festival	Santa Barbara
Santa Rosalia Festival	Monterey
Semana Nautica	Santa Barbara
Strawberry Festival	Arroyo Grande
Weihnachtsmarkt	Carmel

California Festivals

Central Valley Festivals

Festival	City
Almond Blossom Festival	Ripon
Anderson Marsh Blackberry Festival	Lower Lake
Arvin Wildflower Festival	Arvin
Atwater Fall Festival	Atwater
Balloons Over the Valley Hot Air Balloon Festival	Modesto
Bidwell Bar Day	Oroville
Bok Kai Festival	Marysville
Cajun Crawfish Festival	Fairfield
California Dry Bean Festival	Tracy
California Prune Festival	Yuba City
Camellia Festival	Sacramento
Cherry Festival	Linden
Cinco de Mayo Kermesse	Lamont
Coalinga Horned Toad Derby	Coalinga
Cotton Harvest Festival	Buttonwillow
Davis Street Faire	Davis
Delicato Charity Grape Stomp	Manteca
Dinuba Raisin Festival	Dinuba
Dixon Lambtown Festival	Dixon
Exeter Fall Festival	Exeter
Festival of Cultures	Merced
Field and Fair Day	Lodi
Gold Nugget Days	Paradise
Grape Bowl Festival	Sanger
Greek Food Festival	Modesto
Harvest Craft Faire	Rocklin
Hilmar Dairy Festival	Hilmar
Hughson Fruit & Nut Festival	Hughson
Isleton Crawdad Festival	Isleton

243

California Festivals

Central Valley Festivals Continued

Festival	City
Jackass Mail Run	Porterville
Jazzaffair	Three Rivers
Jazz on the Waterfront	Stockton
Johnny Appleseed Day	Paradise
July 4th Celebration	Lemoore
July 4th Independence Celebration	Modesto
Kingsburg Swedish Festival	Kingsburg
Konocti Winery Harvest Festival	Kelseyville
Lamb Derby Festival	Willows
Lodi Grape Festival & National Wine Show	Lodi
Nation's Christmas Tree Festival	Sanger
Newman Fall Festival	Newman
Nut Tree Pumpkin Festival & Scarecrow Contest	Vacaville
Patterson Apricot Fiesta	Patterson
Pear Fair	Courtland
Pumpkin Festival	Manteca
Raisin Festival	Selma
Red Suspenders Days	Red Bluff
Reedley Fiesta	Reedley
Renaissance of Kings Cultural Arts Faire	Hanford
Riverbank's Cheese and Wine Exposition	Riverbank
Rocklin Jubilee	Rocklin
Sacramento Dixieland Jubilee	Sacramento
Salsa Tasting & Music Festival	Fresno
Santa Lucia Festival of Lights	Kingsburg
Shafter Potato 'n Cotton Festival	Shafter
Sierra Showcase of Wine	Plymouth
Springville Apple Festival	Springville
Stockton Asparagus Festival	Stockton
Swedish Crayfish Festival	Kingsburg
Tehachapi Mountain Festival	Tehachapi
Vacaville Fiesta Days	Vacaville
Vacaville Onion Festival	Vacaville
Wasco Festival of Roses	Wasco
Waterford Western Heritage Day	Waterford
Whiskey Flat Days	Kernville
Whole Earth Days	Davis

California Festivals

Desert Festivals

Festival / **City**

Festival	City
Brawley Cattle Call	Brawley
Calico Days	Barstow
Calico Fine Arts Festival	Barstow
Calico Hullabaloo	Barstow
Calico Spring Festival	Barstow
Desert Festival	Borrego Springs
Fall Festival	Desert Hot Springs
Festival of the Springs	Desert Hot Springs
Grubstake Days	Yucca Valley
Holtville Annual Carrot Festival	Holtville
Imperial Sweet Onion Festival	Imperial
La Quinta Arts Festival	La Quinta
Pioneer Days	Twenty Nine Palms
Riverside County's National Date Festival	Indio
Sixteenth of September Fiesta	Calexico
Twenty Mule Team Days	Boron

California Festivals

Gold Country Festivals

Festival	City
Annual Italian Benevolent Society Picnic and Parade	Sutter Creek
Auburn Craft & Christmas Marketplace	Soulsbyville
Brownsville Mountain Fair	Brownsville
Columbia Diggin's	Columbia
Coulterville Coyote Howling	Coulterville
Currier and Ives Christmas Open House	Sutter Creek
Frontier Christmas	Oroville
Great Sutter Creek Duck Race	Sutter Creek
Gunfighters' Rendevous	Coulterville
Jumping Frog Jubilee	Angels Camp
Mother Lode Dixieland Jazz Benefit	Jackson
Motherlode Scots Festival of Lights	Amador County
Secession Day	Rough & Ready
Sonora Christmas Festival	Sonora
Spring Wine Festival	Gilroy
Tuolumne County Wild West Film Fair	Sonora
Zucchini Festival	Angele Camp

California Festivals

High Sierra Festivals

Festival	City
Cherries Jubilee	Placerville
Chocolate Lovers Fantasy Faire	S. Lake Tahoe
Denver Dan's Apple Bake Off	Camino
Feather River Railroad Days	Eastern Plumas
Fourth of July	Bridgeport
Fourth of July	Exeter
Great Potato Harvest Festival	Somerset
Hangtown Dixieland Jazz Jubilee	Placerville
Lake Tahoe Kokanne Salmon Festival	S. Lake Tahoe
Lake Tahoe Starlight Jazz Festival	S. Lake Tahoe
Mariposa County Storytelling Festival	Mariposa
Mule Days Celebration	Bishop
Music at Sand Harbor	North Tahoe
North Lake Tahoe Chocolate Festival	Tahoe City
Shakespeare at Sand Harbor	North Tahoe
Snowfest Winter Carnival	Tahoe City

California Festivals

Inland Empire Festivals

Festival	City
Apple Fest	Yucaipa
Big Bear Lake Oktoberfest	Big Bear Lake
Cherry Festival	Beaumont
Frontier Days	Lake Elsinore Valley
Huck Finn Jubilee	Victorville
Old Miner's Days	Big Bear Lake
Ontario Worldfest	Ontario
Rancho California Balloon & Wine Festival	Temecula
San Dimas Festival of Western Art	San Dimas
Stagecoach Days	Banning

California Festivals

Los Angeles Area Festivals

Festival	City
California Wine Exposition	Redondo Beach
Cinco de Mayo Fiesta and Art Fair	El Monte
East West Orchid Show	Los Angeles
Fall Festival of Wines	Gardena Valley
Fiesta de las Artes	Hermosa Beach
Fiesta La Ballona	Culver City
Fishermen's Fiesta	San Pedro
Friendship Festival	Torrance
Frontier Days	Canyon Country
Grape Harvest Festival	Rancho Cucamonga
La Habra Corn Festival	La Habra
Lilac Festival	Palmdale
Los Angeles Classic Jazz Festival	Los Angeles
Maritime Days	Oxnard
Monrovia Days	Monrovia
Nisei Week Japanese Festival	Los Angeles
Oktoberfest	Montrose
Pan American Festival	Lakewood
Parade of Lights	Oxnard
Pilgrim Festival	Claremont
Pioneer Days	Artesia
San Fernando Fiesta	San Fernando
Scandinavian Festival	Thousand Oaks
Sierra Madre Art Fair	Sierra Madre
Sunset Junction Street Fair	Los Angeles
Temple City Camellia Festival	Temple City
Village Venture Street Faire	Claremont
Western Daze	San Dimas

California Festivals

North Coast Festivals

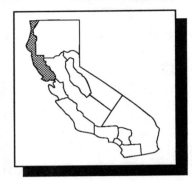

Festival **City**

Annie & Mary Day Fair — Blue Lake
Apple Blossom Festival — Sebastopol
Arcata's Fourth of July Celebration — Arcata
Banana Slug Derby — Orick
Bigfoot Daze — Willow Creek
Bodega Bay Fisherman's Festival — Bodega Bay
Butter and Eggs Day Parade — Petaluma
Calistoga Beer & Sausage Fest — Calistoga
Cloverdale Grape Festival — Cloverdale
Cotati Indian Festival — Cotati
Dolbeer Steam Donkey Days — Eureka
Easter in July Lily Festival — Crescent City
Fort Bragg Whaler Beer Fest — Fort Bragg
Fort Ross VFD Summer Music Festival — Fort Ross
Fourth of July Celebration — Crescent City
Gasquet Raft Races — Crescent City
Gravenstein Apple Fair — Sebastopol
Health & Harmony Music and Arts Festival — Santa Rosa
Hometown Festival — Greater Ukiah
Humboldt Folklife Festival — Ukiah
Jazz on the Lake — Garberville
Klamath Salmon Festival — Klamath
Lakeport Revival on Clear Lake — Lakeport
Living History Days — Petaluma
Mendocino Christmas Festival — Menocino
Mendocino Music Festival — Mendocino
Mendocino Whale Festival — Mendocino
Rhododendron Festival — Eureka
Novato Art and Wine Festival — Novato
Old Adobe Fiesta — Petaluma

California Festivals

North Coast Festivals Continued

Festival	City
Peach Festival and Annual Rickshaw Race	Willow Creek
Petaluma River Festival	Petaluma
Reggae on the River	Garberville
Renaissance Pleasure Faire	Novato
Round Valley Blackberry Festival	Covelo
Russian River Jazz Festival	Russian River
Russian River Wine Festival	Healdsburg
Scandinavian Midsummer Festival	Ferndale
Seafood Festival	Crescent City
Somethin's Brewing: A Fine Beer Tasting	Santa Rosa
Sonora Summer Arts Festival	Sonora
Sonoma Valley Salute to the Arts	Sonoma
Spirit of Christmas Crafts Faire & Celebration	Santa Rosa
Summer Arts Festivals	Garberville
Valley of the Moon Vintage Festival	Sonoma
Westhaven Wild Blackberry Festival	Trinidad
Whaleboat Regatta Wine and Cheese Exposition	Vallejo
Wildwood Days	Rio Dell
Windsor Laff-Off	Windsor
Winefest	Healdsburg
Wine & Food Renaissance	Lakeport
WINESONG!	Fort Bragg
World Championship Crab Races	Crescent City

California Festivals

Orange County Festivals

Festival	City
Christmas Walk	Corona Del Mar
For Our Children Food & Wine Festival	Redondo Beach
Heritage Festival	San Juan Capistrano
Long Beach Lesbian and GAy Pride Celebration	Long Beach
Newport Salute to the Arts	Newport Beach
Orange County Fiesta	Fountain Valley
Sawdust Festival	Laguna Beach
Silverado Days	Buena Park
Strawberry Festival	Garden Grove
Winterfest	Laguna Beach

California Festivals

San Francisco Bay Area Festivals

Festival	**City**
A la carte, a la Park	San Francisco
African Cultural Festival	Oakland
Art & Wine Festival	Walnut Creek
Beach Street Revival	Santa Cruz
Berryessa Art & Wine Festival	San Jose
Brussels Sprout Harvest Festival	Santa Cruz
Campbell Highland Games	Campbell
Cajun & Zydeco Festival	San Rafael
Capitola Art and Wine Festival	Capitola
Capitola National Begonia Festival	Capitola
Carnaval San Francisco	San Francisco
Castroville Artichoke Festival	Castroville
Cherry Blossom Festival	San Francisco
Clam Chowder Cook-Off and Chowder Chase	Santa Cruz
Columbus Day Celebration	San Francisco
Concord Fall Fest	Concord
Dickens Christmas Fair	San Francisco
East Palo Alto Juneteenth Festival	East Palo Alto
Eastfield Ming Quong Strawberry Festival	Campbell
Egyptian Festival	Hayward
Fall Festival	Castro Valley
Festival at the Lake	Oakland
Festival of Greece	Oakland
Fiestas Patrias Celebration	San Jose
Fourth of July Festival	Martinez
Gilroy Garlic Festival	Gilroy
Gilroy Hispanic Cultural Festival	Gilroy
Gladiola Festival	Union City
Great Halloween and Pumpkin Festival	San Francisco
Half Moon Bay Art & Pumpkin Festival	Half Moon Bay

California Festivals

San Francisco Bay Area Festivals Continued

Festival	City
Hayward Art & Wine Festival	Hayward
Hayward Zucchini Festival	Hayward
International Beer and Food Festival	San Francisco
International Calamari Festival	Santa Cruz
International Percussion Explosion	Oakland
Italian American Cultural Festival	San Jose
Jazz And All That on Fillmore	San Francisco
Juneteenth	Berkeley
KQED Wine and Food Festival	San Francisco
Millbrae Art & Wine Festival	Millbrae
Morgan Hill Mushroom Mardi Gras	Morgan Hill
Mountain View Art and Wine Festival	Mountain View
Newark Days Celebration	Newark
New York Landing Seafood Festival	Pittsburg
North Beach Fair	San Francisco
Oakland Chinatown Street Festival	Oakland
Old-Fashioned Ice Cream Social & Tasting	San Francisco
Pacific Coast Collegiate Jazz Festival	Berkeley
Pacific Coast Fog Fest	Pacifica
Pacific States Craft Fair	San Francisco
Palo Alto Celebrates the Arts	Palo Alto
Park Street Art and Wine Faire	Alameda
Prunefestival Wine & Arts	Campbell
Renaissance Pleasure Faire	Novato
San Anselmo Art and Wine Festival	San Anselmo
San Francisco Examiner Bay to Breakers—Footstock	San Francisco
San Francisco International Film Festival	San Francisco
Santa Clara Art & Wine Festival	Santa Clara
Santa Cruz Spring Fair	Santa Cruz
Saratoga Blossom Festival	Saratoga
Sausalito Art Festival	Sausalito
Spring Wine Festival	Gilroy
Sunnyvale Art and Wine Festival	Sunnyvale
Tapestry in Talent	San Jose
Taste of San Mateo	San Mateo
Tet Vietnamese New Year Festival	San Jose
Union Street Spring Festival Arts and Crafts Fair	San Francisco
Walnut Festival	Walnut Creek

California Festivals

San Diego County Festivals

Festival	City
Carlsbad Village Faire	Carlsbad
Christmas on the Prado	San Diego
Cinco de Mayo	Borrego Springs
Cinco de Mayo	San Diego
Encinitas Flower Festival	Encinitas
Escondido Harvest Festival	Escondido
Fiesta del Sol	Solana Beach
Greek Festival	Cardiff
Harbor Days	Oceanside
Julian Fall Apple Harvest Festival	Julian
La Jolla Festival of the Arts and Food Faire	La Jolla
La Mesa Oktoberfest	La Mesa
Lakeside Chili Cook-Off	Lakeside
Lemon Grove Old TIme Days	Lemon Grove
Linda Vista Multicultural Fair	Linda Vista
Mission Christmas Fair	Oceanside
Pacific Beach Block Party	San Diego
Poway Days	Poway
San Diego St. Patrick's Day Annual Parade	San Diego
San Marcos Chili Cook-Off	San Marcos
Sandcastle Days	Imperial Beach
Serbian Festival	San Diego
Western Days	Alpine
Ye Olde English Faire	San Marcos

California Festivals

Shasta-Cascade Festivals

Festival	City
Alpenfest	Mount Shasta
Big Time Indian Days	Pine Grove
Festival —Red Bluff	Red Bluff
Railroad Days	Dunsmuir
Shasta Dixieland Jazz Festival	Redding
Weaverville Fourth of July	Weaverville
Weed Carnivale	Weed

California Festivals

Festivals by Theme

Agriculture Festivals

Apple Blossom Festival
Apple Fest
Apple Festival
Brawley Cattle Call
California Avocado Festival
California Prune Festival
Camellia Festival
Capitola National Begonia Festival
Cherries Jubilee
Cherry Festival—Beaumont
Cloverdale Grape Festival
Cotton Harvest Festival
Denver Dan's Apple Bake Off
Dinuba Raisin Festival
Dixon Lambtown Festival
Easter in July Lily Festival
East West Orchid Show
Encinitas Flower Festival
Escondido Harvest Festival
Gladiola Festival
Grape Bowl Festival
Grape Harvest Festival
Gravenstein Apple Fair
Half Moon Bay Art & Pumpkin Festival
Harvest Festival
Hilmar Dairy Festival
Holtville Annual Carrot Festival
Hughson Friut & Nut Festival
Johnny Appleseed Day
Julian Fall Apple Harvest Festival
La Habra Annual Corn Festival
Lilac Festival
North Coast "Bloomin' Best" Rhododendron Festival
Patterson Apricot Fiesta
Pear Fair
Pumpkin Fair
Raisin Festival
Sacramento Camellia Festival
Shafter Potato 'n Cotton Festival
Springville Apple Festival
Strawberry Festival
Wasco Festival of Roses
Westhaven Blackberry Festival

California Festivals

Arts & Crafts Festivals

Atwater Fall Festival
Auburn Craft & ChristmasMarketplace
Berryessa Art & Wine Festival
Currier and Ives Christmas Open House
Calico Fine Arts Festival
Ceres Western Art Show & Sale
Dickens Christmas Fair
Fiesta de las Artes
Half Moon Bay Art & Pumpkin Festival
Harvest Craft Faire
Hayward Art & Wine Festival
La Jolla Festival of the Arts & Food Faire
La Quinta Arts Festival
Mission Christmas Fair
Mountain View Art and Wine Festival
Novato Art and Wine Festival
Pacific States Craft Fair
Palo Alto Celebrate the Arts
Park Street Art and Wine Faire
Prunefestival Wine & Arts
Santa Barbara Arts Festival
Sausalito Art Festival
Sawdust Festival
Sierra Madre Art Fair
Sonoma Summer Atrs Festival
Sonoma Valley Salute to the Arts
Summer Arts Festivals
Sunnyvale Art and Wine Festival
Union Street Spring Festival Arts and Crafts Fair
Weihnachtsmarkt

Community Festivals

Almond Blossom Festival
Alpenfest
Annual Italian Benevolent Society Picnic and Parade
Apple Fest
Arcata's Fourth of July Celebration
Art & wine Festival
Arvin Wildflower Festival
Bigfoot Daze
Brownsville Mountain Fair
Butter and Eggs Day Parade
California Dry Bean Festival
Capitola National Begonia Festival
Carlsbad Village Faire
Christmas on the Prado
Christmas Walk

California Festivals

Cloverdale Citrus Fair
Coalinga Horned Toad Derby
Concord Fall Fest
Cotton Harvest Festival
Davis Street Faire
Desert Festival
Dinuba Raisin Festival
Encinitas Flower Festival
Exeter Fall Festival
Fair Oaks Fiesta
Fall Festival
Fall Festival—Desert Hot Springs
Festival —Red Bluff
Festival of the Springs
Field and Fair Day
Fiesta del Sol
Fiesta La Ballona
Fort Ross VFD Summer Music Festival
Fourth of July
Fourth of July—Exeter
Fourth of July Celebration
Fourth of July Festival
Friendship Festival
Goleta Valley Days
Great Halloween and Pumpkin Festival
Harvest Festival
Hometown Festival
Huntington Beach Sea Festival
International Bazaar and Bed Races
Johnny Appleseed Day
July 4th Celebration
July 4th Independence Celebration
Klamath Salmon Festival
La Habra Annual Corn Festival
Lakeport revival on Clear Lake
Lamb Derby Festival
Lemon Grove Old TIme Days
Lompoc Valley Festival
Long Beach Lesbian and Gay Pride Celebration
May Festival
Mendocino Christmas Festival
Morro Bay Harbor Festival
Newark Days Celebration
Newman Fall Festival
North Coast "Bloomin' Best" Rhododendron Festival
Orange County Fiesta Days
Pacific Beach Block Party
Pacific Coast Fog Fest
Patterson Apricot Fiesta
Peach Festival and Annual Rickshaw Race
Rancho Chico Days
Red Suspenders Days

California Festivals

Reedley Fiesta
Rialto Days
San Diego St. Patrick's Day Annual Parade
San Francisco Examiner Bay to Breakers - Footstock
Sandcastle Days
Santa Cruz Spring Fair
Saratoga Blossom Festival
Shafter Potato 'n Cotton Festival
Shasta Damboree
Snowfest Winter Carnival
Sonora Christnmas Festival
Strawberry Festival
Sunset Junction Street Fair
Temple City Camellia Festival
Village Venture Street Faire
Vacaville Fiesta Days
Vacaville Onion Festival
Vallejo Waterfront Festival
Walnut Festival
Wasco Festival of Roses
Weaverville Fourth of July
Weed Carnivale
Westminster Labor Day Festival
Wildwood Days
Windsor Laff-Off
whole Earth Festival
World Championship Crab Races

Ethnic Festivals

African Cultural Festival
Big Bear Lake Oktoberfest
Big Time Indian Days
Bok Kai Festival
Campbell Highland Games
Carnaval San Francisco
Cherry Blossom Festival
Chinese New Year Food and Cultural Faire
Cinco de Mayo
Cinco de Mayo Fiesta and Art Fair
Cinco de Mayo Kermesse
Cinco de Mayo— San Diego
Columbus Day Celebration
Cotati Indian Festival
Danish Days
East Palo Alto Juneteenth Festival
Egyptian Festival
Festa Italiana
Festival at the Lake
Festival of Greece

California Festivals

Festival of Cultures
Fiestas Patrias Celebrations
Gilroy Hispanic Cultural Festival
Greek Festival-Cardiff
Greek Food Festival
I Madonnari Italian St. Painting Festival
Italian American Cultural Festival
Juneteenth
Kingsburg Swedish Festival
La Fiesta de San Luis Obispo
La Mesa Oktoberfest
Linda Vista Multicultural Fair
Motherlode Scots Festival of Lights
Nisei Week Japanese Festival
North Beach Fair
Oakland Chinatown Street Festival
Oktoberfest
Old Spanish Days Fiesta
Ontario Worldfest
Pan American Festival
San Fernando Fiesta
Santa Lucia Festival of Lights
Scandinavian Festival
Scandinavian Mid-Summer Festival
Scottish & Irish Festival & Games
Serbian Festival
Sixteenth of September Fiesta
Sonora Celtic Celebration
Tapestry In Talent
Tet Vietnamese New Year Festival
Ye Olde English Faire

Film & Theatre Festivals

Robin Hood Days
San Francisco International Film Festival
Santa Barbara International Film Festival
Shakespeare at Sand Harbor
Tuolumne County Wild West Film Fair

Food & Drink Festivals

A la carte, a la park
Apple Blossom Festival
Brussels Sprout Harvest Festival
Cajun Crawfish Festival
Cajun & Zydeco Festival
California Festival of Beers
California Prune Festival

California Festivals

California Strawberry Festival
California Wine Exposition
Calistoga Beer & Sausage Fest
Castroville Artichoke Festival
Cherry Festival
Cherry Festival-Beaumont
Chocolate Lovers Fantasy Faire
Clam Chowder Cook-Off and Chowder Chase
Clam Festival
Cloverdale Grape Festival
Delicato Charity Grape Stomp
Eastfield Ming Quong Strawberry Festival
Fall Festival of Wines
For Our Children Food & Wine Festival
Gilroy Garlic Festival
Gravenstein Apple Fair
Great Monterey Squid Festival
Great potato Harvest Festival
Greenfield Broccoli Festival
Hayward Zucchini Festival
Imperial Sweet Onion Festival
International Beer and Food Festival
International Calamari Festival
Isleton Crawdad Festival
Jumbleberry Jubilee
KQED Wine and Food Festival
Konocti Winery Harvest Festival
La Habra Corn Festival
Lakeside Chili Cook-Off
Lake Tahoe Kokanne Salmon Festival
Lodi Grape Festival & National Wine Show
Millbrae Art & Wine Festival
Morgan Hill Mushroom Mardi Gras
New York Landing Seafood Festival
North Lake Tahoe Chocolate Festival
Old-Fashioned Ice Cream Social & Tasting
Riverbank's Cheese and Wine Exposition
Riverside County's National Date Festival
Round Valley Blackberry Festival
Russian River Wine Festival
Salinas Valley Produce Festival
San Anselmo Art and Wine Festival
San Marcos Chili Cook-Off
Santa Clara Art & Wine Festival
Seafood Festival
Sierra Showcase of Wine
Somethin's Brewing: A Fine Beer Tasting
Spring Wine Festival
Stockton Asparagus Festival
Swedish Crayfish Festival
Taste of San Mateo
Valley of the Moon Vintage Festival

California Festivals

Whaleboat Regatta Wine and Cheese Exposition
Wild Game Barbeque
WINESONG!
Zucchini Festival

Historical Festivals

Adobe Tour
Anderson Marsh Blackberry Festival
Beach Street Revival
Colony Days Celebration
Exeter Fall Festival
Feather River Railroad Days
Great Lake Tahoe Sternwheeler Race & Festival
Huck Finn Jubilee
Living History Days
Mariposa County Storytelling Festival
Old Adobe Fiesta
Pilgrim Festival
Pioneer Days
Railroad Days
Renaissance of Kings Cultural Arts Faire
Renaissance Pleasure Faire
Weihnachtsmarkt
Western Days
Ye Olde English Fair

Hot Air Balloon Festivals

Balloons Over the Valley Hot Air Balloon Festival
Rancho California Balloon & Wine Festival

Marine/Aquatic Festivals

Bodega Bay Fisherman's Festival
Fishermen's Fiesta
Fort Bragg Whaler Beer Fest
Gasquet Raft Races
Great Sutter Creek Duck Race
Harbor Days
Mendocino Whale Festival
Petaluma River Festival
Santa Rosalia Festival
Whaleboat Regatta Wine and Cheese Exposition

California Festivals

Music Festivals

Calico Spring Festival
Carmel Bach Festival
Dixieland Monterey
Golden West Bluegrass Festival
Health and Harmony Music and Arts Festival
Hangtown Dixieland Jazz Jubilee
Jazz And All That Art On Fillmore
Jazz on the Lake
Jazz on the Waterfront
Jazzaffair
Lake Tahoe Starlight Jazz Festival
Los Angeles Classic Jazz Festival
Mendocino Music Festival
Monterey Jazz Festival
Mother Lode Dixieland Jazz Benefit
Mozart Festival
Music at Sand Harbor
Ojai Music Festival
Pacific Coast Collegiate Jazz Festival
Raisin Dixie Festival
Reggae on the River
Russian River Jazz Festival
Sacramento Dixieland Jubilee
Salsa Tasting & Music Festival
San Luis Obispo Mardi Gras
Shasta Dixieland Jazz Festival

Western Festivals

Bidwell Bar Day
Calico Days
Calico Hullabaloo
California Rodeo Salinas
Columbia Diggin's
Conejo Valley Days
Coulterville Coyte Howling
Dolbeer Steam Donkey Days
Frontier Christmas
Frontier Days
Frontier Days—Lake Elsinore Valley
Gold Nugget Days
Grubstake Days
Gunfighters' Rendevous
Jackass Mail Run
Jumping Frog Jubilee
Mule Days Celebration
Old Miner's Days
Pioneer Days

California Festivals

Secession Day
Silverado Days
Stagecoach Days
Tehachapi Moutain Festival
Twenty Mule Team Days
Waterford Western Heritage Day
Western Daze
Whiskey Flat Days

1991

JANUARY
S	M	T	W	T	F	S
		1	2	3	4	5
6	7	8	9	10	11	12
13	14	15	16	17	18	19
20	21	22	23	24	25	26
27	28	29	30	31		

FEBRUARY
S	M	T	W	T	F	S
					1	2
3	4	5	6	7	8	9
10	11	12	13	14	15	16
17	18	19	20	21	22	23
24	25	26	27	28		

MARCH
S	M	T	W	T	F	S
					1	2
3	4	5	6	7	8	9
10	11	12	13	14	15	16
17	18	19	20	21	22	23
24	25	26	27	28	29	30
31						

APRIL
S	M	T	W	T	F	S
	1	2	3	4	5	6
7	8	9	10	11	12	13
14	15	16	17	18	19	20
21	22	23	24	25	26	27
28	29	30				

MAY
S	M	T	W	T	F	S
			1	2	3	4
5	6	7	8	9	10	11
12	13	14	15	16	17	18
19	20	21	22	23	24	25
26	27	28	29	30	31	

JUNE
S	M	T	W	T	F	S
						1
2	3	4	5	6	7	8
9	10	11	12	13	14	15
16	17	18	19	20	21	22
23	24	25	26	27	28	29
30						

Important Dates

JANUARY
1 New Year's Day
21 Martin Luther King Jr. Day

FEBRUARY
12 Lincoln's Birthday
13 Ash Wednesday
14 Valentine's Day
18 Washington's Birthday Obsvd.
22 Washington's Birthday

MARCH
17 St. Patrick's Day
24 Palm Sunday
29 Good Friday
30 Passover
31 Easter Sunday

MAY
12 Mother's Day
18 Armed Forces Day
27 Memorial Day - Obsvd.
30 Memorial Day

JUNE
14 Flag Day
16 Father's Day

JULY
4 Independence Day

SEPTEMBER
2 Labor Day
9 Rosh Hashanah
18 Yom Kippur

OCTOBER
11 Columbus Day
12 Columbus Day
24 United Nations Day
31 Halloween

NOVEMBER
5 Election Day
11 Veterans Day
28 Thanksgiving Day

DECEMBER
2 Hanukkah
25 Christmas Day

JULY
S	M	T	W	T	F	S
	1	2	3	4	5	6
7	8	9	10	11	12	13
14	15	16	17	18	19	20
21	22	23	24	25	26	27
28	29	30	31			

AUGUST
S	M	T	W	T	F	S
				1	2	3
4	5	6	7	8	9	10
11	12	13	14	15	16	17
18	19	20	21	22	23	24
25	26	27	28	29	30	31

SEPTEMBER
S	M	T	W	T	F	S
1	2	3	4	5	6	7
8	9	10	11	12	13	14
15	16	17	18	19	20	21
22	23	24	25	26	27	28
29	30					

OCTOBER
S	M	T	W	T	F	S
		1	2	3	4	5
6	7	8	9	10	11	12
13	14	15	16	17	18	19
20	21	22	23	24	25	26
27	28	29	30	31		

NOVEMBER
S	M	T	W	T	F	S
					1	2
3	4	5	6	7	8	9
10	11	12	13	14	15	16
17	18	19	20	21	22	23
24	25	26	27	28	29	30

DECEMBER
S	M	T	W	T	F	S
1	2	3	4	5	6	7
8	9	10	11	12	13	14
15	16	17	18	19	20	21
22	23	24	25	26	27	28
29	30	31				

1992

JANUARY
S	M	T	W	T	F	S
			1	2	3	4
5	6	7	8	9	10	11
12	13	14	15	16	17	18
19	20	21	22	23	24	25
26	27	28	29	30	31	

FEBRUARY
S	M	T	W	T	F	S
						1
2	3	4	5	6	7	8
9	10	11	12	13	14	15
16	17	18	19	20	21	22
23	24	25	26	27	28	29

MARCH
S	M	T	W	T	F	S
1	2	3	4	5	6	7
8	9	10	11	12	13	14
15	16	17	18	19	20	21
22	23	24	25	26	27	28
29	30	31				

APRIL
S	M	T	W	T	F	S
			1	2	3	4
5	6	7	8	9	10	11
12	13	14	15	16	17	18
19	20	21	22	23	24	25
26	27	28	29	30		

MAY
S	M	T	W	T	F	S
					1	2
3	4	5	6	7	8	9
10	11	12	13	14	15	16
17	18	19	20	21	22	23
24	25	26	27	28	29	30
31						

JUNE
S	M	T	W	T	F	S
	1	2	3	4	5	6
7	8	9	10	11	12	13
14	15	16	17	18	19	20
21	22	23	24	25	26	27
28	29	30				

JULY
S	M	T	W	T	F	S
			1	2	3	4
5	6	7	8	9	10	11
12	13	14	15	16	17	18
19	20	21	22	23	24	25
26	27	28	29	30	31	

AUGUST
S	M	T	W	T	F	S
						1
2	3	4	5	6	7	8
9	10	11	12	13	14	15
16	17	18	19	20	21	22
23	24	25	26	27	28	29
30	31					

SEPTEMBER
S	M	T	W	T	F	S
		1	2	3	4	5
6	7	8	9	10	11	12
13	14	15	16	17	18	19
20	21	22	23	24	25	26
27	28	29	30			

OCTOBER
S	M	T	W	T	F	S
				1	2	3
4	5	6	7	8	9	10
11	12	13	14	15	16	17
18	19	20	21	22	23	24
25	26	27	28	29	30	31

NOVEMBER
S	M	T	W	T	F	S
1	2	3	4	5	6	7
8	9	10	11	12	13	14
15	16	17	18	19	20	21
22	23	24	25	26	27	28
29	30					

DECEMBER
S	M	T	W	T	F	S
		1	2	3	4	5
6	7	8	9	10	11	12
13	14	15	16	17	18	19
20	21	22	23	24	25	26
27	28	29	30	31		

Important Dates

JANUARY
- 1 New Year's Day
- 20 Martin Luther King Jr. Day

FEBRUARY
- 12 Lincoln's Birthday
- 14 Valentine's Day
- 17 Washington's Birthday-Obsvd.
- 22 Washington's Birthday

MARCH
- 4 Ash Wednesday
- 17 St. Patrick's Day

APRIL
- 12 Palm Sunday
- 17 Good Friday
- 18 Passover
- 19 Easter Sunday

MAY
- 10 Mother's Day
- 16 Armed Forces Day
- 25 Memorial Day - Obsvd.
- 30 Memorial Day

JUNE
- 14 Flag Day
- 21 Father's Day

JULY
- 4 Independence Day

SEPTEMBER
- 7 Labor Day
- 28 Rosh Hashanah

OCTOBER
- 7 Yom Kippur
- 12 Columbus Day
- 24 United Nations Day
- 31 Halloween

NOVEMBER
- 3 Election Day
- 11 Veterans Day
- 26 Thanksgiving Day

DECEMBER
- 20 Hanukkah
- 25 Christmas Day

1993

JANUARY
S	M	T	W	T	F	S
					1	2
3	4	5	6	7	8	9
10	11	12	13	14	15	16
17	18	19	20	21	22	23
24	25	26	27	28	29	30
31						

FEBRUARY
S	M	T	W	T	F	S
	1	2	3	4	5	6
7	8	9	10	11	12	13
14	15	16	17	18	19	20
21	22	23	24	25	26	27
28						

MARCH
S	M	T	W	T	F	S
	1	2	3	4	5	6
7	8	9	10	11	12	13
14	15	16	17	18	19	20
21	22	23	24	25	26	27
28	29	30	31			

APRIL
S	M	T	W	T	F	S
				1	2	3
4	5	6	7	8	9	10
11	12	13	14	15	16	17
18	19	20	21	22	23	24
25	26	27	28	29	30	

MAY
S	M	T	W	T	F	S
						1
2	3	4	5	6	7	8
9	10	11	12	13	14	15
16	17	18	19	20	21	22
23	24	25	26	27	28	29
30	31					

JUNE
S	M	T	W	T	F	S
		1	2	3	4	5
6	7	8	9	10	11	12
13	14	15	16	17	18	19
20	21	22	23	24	25	26
27	28	29	30			

Important Dates

JANUARY
1 New Year's Day
18 Martin Luther King Jr. Day

FEBRUARY
12 Lincoln's Birthday
14 Valentine's Day
15 Washington's Birthday Obsvd.
22 Washington's Birthday
24 Ash Wednesday

MARCH
17 St. Patrick's Day

APRIL
4 Palm Sunday
6 Passover
9 Good Friday
11 Easter Sunday

MAY
9 Mother's Day
15 Armed Forces Day
30 Memorial Day
31 Memorial Day-Obsvd.

JUNE
14 Flag Day
20 Father's Day

JULY
4 Independence Day

SEPTEMBER
6 Labor Day
16 Rosh Hashanah
25 Yom Kippur

OCTOBER
11 Columbus Day
24 United Nations Day
31 Halloween

NOVEMBER
2 Election Day
11 Veterans Day
25 Thanksgiving Day

DECEMBER
9 Hanukkah
25 Christmas Day

JULY
S	M	T	W	T	F	S
				1	2	3
4	5	6	7	8	9	10
11	12	13	14	15	16	17
18	19	20	21	22	23	24
25	26	27	28	29	30	31

AUGUST
S	M	T	W	T	F	S
1	2	3	4	5	6	7
8	9	10	11	12	13	14
15	16	17	18	19	20	21
22	23	24	25	26	27	28
29	30	31				

SEPTEMBER
S	M	T	W	T	F	S
			1	2	3	4
5	6	7	8	9	10	11
12	13	14	15	16	17	18
19	20	21	22	23	24	25
26	27	28	29	30		

OCTOBER
S	M	T	W	T	F	S
					1	2
3	4	5	6	7	8	9
10	11	12	13	14	15	16
17	18	19	20	21	22	23
24	25	26	27	28	29	30
31						

NOVEMBER
S	M	T	W	T	F	S
	1	2	3	4	5	6
7	8	9	10	11	12	13
14	15	16	17	18	19	20
21	22	23	24	25	26	27
28	29	30				

DECEMBER
S	M	T	W	T	F	S
			1	2	3	4
5	6	7	8	9	10	11
12	13	14	15	16	17	18
19	20	21	22	23	24	25
26	27	28	29	30	31	

About the Authors

This is the first book written by the husband and wife team of Carl and Katie Landau, but publishing is not entirely unfamiliar territory for Carl. In 1984 he co-founded and published a popular computer magazine for software developers called *Computer Language*. In 1987 he sold the magazine and since has become, in his own words, "something of a goof-off." He enjoys playing rotisserie baseball. Carl's team the Cellar Dwellers are the only team to finish in the money every year in the history of Spec's Rotisserie Baseball League.

Katie is a sixth generation Californian. Her family proudly boasts that they are distant relatives of President Andrew Johnson—the first president to almost be impeached.

The couple resides in San Francisco with their daughter Sophie and cat Alti. Incidentally, Alti's favorite festival was the Great Monterey Squid Festival, while Sophie preferred Lake Tahoe's Chocolate Lovers Fantasy Faire.

California Festivals is also the first book endeavor for Kathy Kincade, who began working with Carl in 1985 and has worked closely with him on many projects since. She recently relocated from San Francisco to Portsmouth, NH to naively pursue a career in writing. She has just completed her first novel, *Dancing on the Highway*.

California Festivals

Did we leave your favorite festival out?

If you know about a festival we should include in our next edition, please let us know.

Festival Name: _____

City: _____

Organizer's Name: _____

Phone Number: (_____) _____

Festival Name: _____

City: _____

Organizer's Name: _____

Phone Number: (_____) _____

Your Name: _____

Phone Number: (_____) _____

Send your suggestions to:

>   **Landau Communications**
>   **1032 Irving Street, Suite 604**
>   **San Francisco, CA   94122**

Tour Festivals Throughout the USA.

Landau Communications has just completed a series of festival books from the best regions of the country. Enjoy the fun and excitement of festivals wherever you travel.

Order a book today! Please write in the quantity of books you want to order:

Quantity   **Cost**

____ California Festivals ($11.95) .... $ _____
      ISBN: 0-929881-13-3

____ Festivals of New England ($9.95) .... $ _____
      ISBN: 0-929881-28-1

____ Festivals of the Pacific Northwest ($9.95) .... $ _____
      ISBN: 0-929881-26-5

____ Festivals of the Southwest ($9.95) .... $ _____
      ISBN: 0-929881-27-3

____ ***Sub Total*** .... $ _____

California residents add 8 1/4% sales tax .... $ _____

Shipping ($1.65 book rate for first book and .50¢ for each additional book. Or $3.25 per book sent air mail and $1.25 for each additional book). .... $ _____

Total (I've enclosed a check) .... $ _____

Make check payable to Landau Communications

Name: _____

Address: _____

City, State, Zip: _____

_____

Phone: (_____) _____

Send to: **Landau Communications**
                1032 Irving Street, Suite 604B
                San Francisco, CA   94122

Or call (415) 564-5689: have your VISA or Master Card number ready.